My Life with Benjamin Franklin

My Life with Benjamin Franklin

Claude-Anne Lopez

YALE UNIVERSITY PRESS

NEW HAVEN & LONDON

Published with the assistance of the Annie Burr Lewis Fund.

Part of Chapter 17 is reprinted with the permission of Macmillan Library
Reference USA, a division of Ahsuog, Inc., from *Macmillan Encyclopedia of
World Slavery,* edited by Paul Finkleman and Joseph C. Miller, copyright © 1998
Simon & Schuster Macmillan.

Designed by James J. Johnson and set in Fairfield Medium type by
Keystone Typesetting, Inc.
Printed in the United States of America by
R. R. Donnelley & Sons, Harrisonburg, Virginia.

Library of Congress Cataloging-in-Publication Data
Lopez, Claude Anne.
  My life with Benjamin Franklin / Claude-Anne Lopez.
    p.   cm.
  Includes bibliographical references and index.
  ISBN 0-300-08192-8 (alk. paper)
    1. Franklin, Benjamin, 1706–1790—Anecdotes.   2. Statesmen—United
States—Biography—Anecdotes.   3. Scientists—United States—Biography—
Anecdotes.   4. Printers—United States—Biography—Anecdotes.   5. Lopez,
Claude Anne—Anecdotes.   I. Title.
E302.6.F8 L815 2000
973.3'092—dc21   99-046231
[B]   CIP

A catalog record for this book is available from the British Library.

10   9   8   7   6   5   4   3   2   1

To my Franklin family,
Barbara Oberg,
Jonathan Dull,
Ellen Cohn,
Karen Duval,
Kate Ohno,
and
to the
Friends of Franklin
all over the
country

Contents

A Chronology of Franklin's Life and Curiosity

BOSTON (January 1706–September 1723)

1706 January 17 born in Boston, on Milk Street, the tenth son and fifteenth child of Josiah Franklin, a soap and candle maker.

1718 Apprenticed to his brother James to learn the printer's trade. Peddles on the streets a ballad of his own composition.

1722 Under the pseudonym Silence Dogood, publishes fourteen essays in his brother's *New England Courant*.

1723 February 11 his name appears as publisher of *New England Courant*. James is in jail from February 12 to May 7. In September quarrels with James and runs off to Philadelphia.

PHILADELPHIA (October 1723–November 1724)

1723 Finds employment as a journeyman. Impresses the governor of Pennsylvania, who sends him to London to buy printing equipment.

LONDON (December 1724–July 1726)

1725 Discovers on arrival in London that the governor has made no provision for him. Stranded there, he soon finds work as a printer. Writes and prints *A Dissertation on Liberty and Necessity*, which he will later regret and destroy.

1726   Makes notes on ocean currents and temperature on voyage
        home.

PHILADELPHIA (October 1726–June 1757)

1727   Founds the Junto, a self-improvement club.

1729   Experiments with color and heat absorption.

1730   Birth of illegitimate son William. Marries Deborah Read.
        Made official printer for Pennsylvania. Starts publication of
        the *Pennsylvania Gazette*.

1731   Becomes a Freemason. Helps establish the Library Company.

1732   Birth of Francis Folger Franklin. First appearance of *Poor
        Richard's Almanack*. Reports observations on aurora
        borealis.

1736   Francis dies of smallpox. Establishment of the Union Fire
        Company.

1739   Designs the Pennsylvania Fireplace (Franklin stove). Does
        not patent it.

1742   Discusses behavior of comets.

1743   Birth of Sarah Franklin. Founds the American Philosophical
        Society. Observes eclipse of the moon and motions of storms.

1745   First experiments with electricity on electrical tube sent
        from London by Peter Collinson.

1747   Letters to Peter Collinson on theory of electricity.

1748   Retires from business at forty-two. Acquires the first of sev-
        eral slaves he will own. Elected alderman.

1750   Proposes experiment to prove the identity of lightning and
        electricity.

1751   *Experiments and Observations on Electricity* published in
        London. There will be four later, augmented editions. Open-
        ing of the Academy of Philadelphia. Becomes a member of
        the Philadelphia Assembly.

1752   Conducts kite experiment. *Experiments and Observations*
        translated and published in Paris. Installs lightning rod on
        his house. Invents flexible catheter.

1753   Honorary degree from Harvard, then Yale. Appointed joint deputy postmaster general of North America. Publication of treaties with the Indians.

1754   Proposes the Albany Plan of Union to counteract French and Indian raids. Plan rejected.

1755   Writes *Observations Concerning the Increase of Mankind.* Organizes defense in French and Indian War. Cornerstone of Pennsylvania Hospital laid.

1756   Elected Fellow of the Royal Society (London).

1757   In February appointed Pennsylvania Assembly agent in England to make Penn family lands taxable.

FIRST MISSION TO ENGLAND
(July 1757–August 1762)

1757   Writes *The Way to Wealth* on board ship. William attends law school in London.

1758   Performs experiments on evaporation at Cambridge University. Father and son visit ancestral homes, collect genealogical data.

1759   Made honorary doctor of laws by the University of St. Andrews (Scotland).

1760   William has a child (William Temple) by an unknown woman.

1761   Travels to Belgium and Holland. Attends coronation of George III.

1762   Invents glass armonica. William appointed royal governor of New Jersey; marries Elizabeth Downes in London.

INTERLUDE IN PHILADELPHIA
(November 1762–November 1764)

1763   Travels through New England on post office business. Starts building a house.

1764   Elected speaker of Pennsylvania assembly but defeated for reelection. Appointed agent to London. Returns to Mrs. Stevenson's house on Craven Street.

SECOND MISSION TO ENGLAND
(December 1764–March 1775)

1765   The Stamp Act controversy. Deborah defends their house against possible mob attack.

1766   Explains to House of Commons the American opposition to Stamp Act. It is repealed. Travels to Holland and Germany with Dr. John Pringle.

1767   Visits Paris with Dr. Pringle, presented to Louis XV in Versailles. Sally marries Richard Bache against her father's wishes.

1768   Devises phonetic alphabet and publishes first map of the Gulf Stream.

1769   Joins with others to form the Ohio Company with a view of re-selling land to potential settlers. Deborah suffers a serious stroke. Sally gives birth to Benjamin Franklin ("Benny") Bache.

1770   Appointed agent to London by the assemblies of Pennsylvania, Georgia, New Jersey, and Massachusetts.

1771   Visits Ireland and Scotland with a friend. Makes peace (more or less) with his son-in-law, Richard Bache, who is visiting his family in England.

1772   Elected foreign member of the Académie Royale des Sciences. Transmits to Thomas Cushing, speaker of the Massachusetts Assembly, letters from Governor Hutchinson advising repression of the rebellious elements in the colony.

1773   British government probes the mystery of the Hutchinson letters. Franklin takes responsibility for having sent them to Boston. Won't reveal who gave them to him. Conducts experiments on the calming effects of oil on water.

1774   News of Boston Tea Party reaches London in January. Offers to pay for losses. Denounced as a thief by the solicitor general. Dismissed from post office job. Death of Deborah on December 19.

1775   Embarks for Philadelphia with grandson Temple, henceforth given the Franklin name. They arrive on May 5. Chosen as

Pennsylvania delegate to the Second Continental Congress. Designs paper money, confers with General Washington in Cambridge, breaks with his son William. Elected postmaster general of the colonies.

1776   Turns seventy. Appointed commissioner to Canada to negotiate an alliance. Leads a delegation to Montreal but fails. Signs Declaration of Independence. Elected one of three commissioners to France. Governor William Franklin is arrested and taken to Connecticut.

MISSION TO FRANCE (December 1776–July 1785)

1776   Embarks with two grandsons, William Temple Franklin ("Temple") and Benny Bache, on October 27. Lands in Brittany on December 3. Proceeds to Paris.

1777   Settles in Passy, a pleasant village not far from Paris. Temple becomes his secretary; Benny goes to a local school. France secretly lends 2 million livres to the American Congress but won't consider an alliance. Britain accuses France of harboring American privateers. Elected to the Société Royale de Médecine. News of Saratoga victory reaching Paris in December changes the political atmosphere.

1778   Treaty of Amity and Commerce signed with France on February 6. France goes to war with Britain on June 17. He is made sole minister plenipotentiary but will not hear about it until February 1779. Inducted into the Lodge of the Nine Sisters shortly after Voltaire. John Adams replaces Silas Deane as commissioner.

1779   Spain declares war on England. Another loan of 3 million livres from France. Benjamin Vaughan publishes in London the first edition of Franklin's *Political, Miscellaneous, and Philosophical Pieces*. Installs a printing press in Passy. Benny sent to school in Geneva. Adams sails back to America.

1780   Adams comes back to Paris, quarrels with Vergennes, goes off to Holland. A 4 million livres loan from France.

1781   Peace Commission appointed by Congress. October 19: victory at Yorktown.

1782   Peace negotiations carried on mostly by John Jay; Franklin is
        ill. "Preliminary Articles of Peace" signed on November 30.
        Vergennes protests that France has not been consulted but
        grants a new loan of 6 million livres.

1783   The Treaty of Paris, marking the end of the American Revo-
        lution, is signed on September 3. Signs Treaty of Amity and
        Commerce with Sweden. Helps the Papal Nuncio organize
        the Roman Catholic Church in America. Benny returns
        from Geneva. The balloons.

1784   On royal commission to investigate Mesmer's "animal mag-
        netism." Is opposed to the creation of the Society of the Cin-
        cinnati (too aristocratic). Peace Treaty with England is
        ratified in May.

1785   Leaves Paris on July 12. Stops briefly on the Isle of Wight to
        have a last, unsuccessful interview with his son William,
        from whom he buys the New Jersey farm in which Temple
        will reside. Reaches Philadelphia on September 14, having
        written *Maritime Observations* during the crossing. Imme-
        diately elected president of the executive council (that is,
        governor) of Pennsylvania.

BACK IN PHILADELPHIA
(September 1785–April 1790)

1786   Builds an addition to his house with a large room for meet-
        ings and a library for four thousand books.

1787   Elected delegate from Pennsylvania to the Constitutional
        Convention, where he is the oldest delegate. Becomes presi-
        dent of the Pennsylvania Society for the Abolition of Slavery.

1788   Disinherits William. Ends his career in public service.

1789   Sends to Congress a remonstrance (the first ever) against
        slavery; Congress puts the responsibility on the states.
        Learns of Bastille Day. Takes increasing doses of laudanum
        for his pain.

1790   Dies of pleurisy, on April 17. More than twenty thousand peo-
        ple pay him homage in Philadelphia. The French National As-
        sembly goes into mourning. The American Senate does not.

Introduction:
Benjamin Franklin Enters
My Life

RANKLIN, you have been my passport to America. To be sure, I held interesting jobs during the war years—in the Office of War Information, as staff member of the Belgian delegation to the first United Nations Conference in San Francisco—but I hardly ever met what we French-speaking émigrés referred to as "des vrais Américains," that enviable species born and bred in this country.

When at the end of the war I married Robert Lopez, an Italian-born medievalist, and moved to New Haven, where Yale had offered him a teaching position, I found myself plunged into the midst of "real Americans," but still not in a meaningful way. A faculty wife, in those days, was supposed to provide elegant entertainment for her husband's colleagues, to help her husband prepare the index of his latest book—or to do it herself if she was exceptionally gifted—and above all to keep clear of any personal goal. Anti-nepotism reigned supreme, the prevalent dogma being that the university would collapse if both spouses were connected to it. Until you entered my life, Franklin, I was becoming resigned to a non-career of typing dissertations about rats in mazes or transcribing tapes pertaining to those unfortunates who had undergone a lobotomy.

But all that changed in the mid-1950s, when President Truman decided that every document associated with the foundation of the Republic should be made available to the American public in a clear and intelligible way. The work was distributed among several universities and historical societies. Yale was entrusted with the publication of your papers, Franklin, because one of its alumni, William Mason, spent his considerable fortune in gathering every available book and pamphlet relevant to your life and times. He bequeathed his priceless collection to his alma mater on the condition that it remain intact and at Yale.

Then came my stroke of luck. The first editor of your papers, Professor Leonard Labaree, had been chairman of my husband's department, and he remembered that my native language was French. After some testing, he offered me the position of transcriber from French—not translator, since it had been decided, in an elitist fashion that some people now regret, that the texts in French, unlike those in Latin, German, or Italian, would be published in the original.

I am often asked what it was that drew me to you. The only answer I can give is that it was the prospect of part-time work that could be done at home while keeping an eye on our two little boys. I knew practically nothing about you, and that little did not enchant me. As a schoolgirl in Brussels, I had been taught something about a battle being lost because a nail was missing from a horseshoe, and that a penny saved was a penny earned. This seemed irrelevant to my generation, and I must admit that your words of wisdom left me cold. But I had no choice: it was your papers or nothing.

I was warned at the outset that the edition would be proceeding chronologically, so that French would not make a serious appearance in your papers until your Paris mission, late in your life. It would take about ten years for the scholarly staff to catch up with my work. Those ten years turned out to be twenty-seven, but much happened in the meantime: I discovered a powerful link between us.

It happened by chance. I encountered a letter of yours commenting ironically about the way the French tend to overstate their feelings:

> You must know that the Desire of pleasing by a perpetual use of Compliments in this polite Nation, has so us'd up all the common Expressions of Approbation, that they are become flat and insipid, and to use them almost implies Censure. Hence Musick, that formerly might be sufficiently praised when it was call'd *bonne,* to go a little farther they called it *excellente,* then *superbe, magnifique, exquise, celeste,* all which being their turns worn out, there remains only *divine;* and when that is grown as insignificant as its Predecessors, I think they must return to common Speech and common Sense.[1]

What you said about the French was exactly the opposite of my opinion of New England society: ever so polite, yes, but hopelessly unemotional. You were a famous man in his seventies while I was an unknown young woman, we were an ocean and almost two centuries apart, but we had undergone the same culture shock. Now, finally, I could relate to the transplanted side of you, one I had never seen stressed in any book. Now you were a fellow human being and no longer an icon.

Your personal life, I dreamed, could become my turf. It would give me the courage to start studying you—maybe even to write about you?—from a woman's point of view; more precisely, from a French woman's point of view. The result of this daydreaming was my first book, *Mon Cher Papa: Franklin and the Ladies of Paris* (New Haven, 1966), which evoked a number of encouraging reviews.

Consequently, I was sent on a lecture tour, and I understood from the public's questions that there was real interest in your family life, a topic nobody had tackled so far. My friend Eugenia Herbert and I decided to describe you from that angle. What kind of father were you? Husband? Brother? *The Private Franklin: The Man and His Family* was rejected by several publishers, one of which asserted that your relatives belonged, at best, to the footnotes of history. But it found its readership among people more interested in human relations and the problems of everyday life than in a more academic approach. It won several prizes and was a selection, in 1976, of the Literary Guild. The publishing finger is not always on the public pulse.

And now . . . The literature on every aspect of your multifarious life has grown awesome in its bulk, its depth of scholarship, its range of interpretation. With my out-of-fashion attachment to the text, the fact, the vignette, do I still fit in anywhere? I love stories. Those I love best are woven from scraps of information found here and there and brought together, like a quilt, into a pattern. I have been lucky enough to spend most of my adult life sitting among almost thirty thousand documents pertaining to you. Some of them are dull and dry, of course, but one's hope never dies that the next letter, oyster-like, will contain a pearl, something hidden up to now and suddenly glittering with promise.

One of those episodes happened many years ago. I was happy about finishing the transcription of a boring letter sent to you by your Paris banker on November 29, 1783. I turned it over, and there, on the fourth page, were a few lines in your own hand. They had no connection with the banker's message

and were truly cryptic. First came a week's worth of conse-
cutive dates beginning with Monday, September 23, but without any indication of year or event. After that, the following
six entries:

Bay Tuesd—1 Oct.
Amboy-Wedny—Water
Pines-Thurd—3 Amb
Brown's Friday—4
River D-Sat—5
Philad-Sund—6

After several wrong guesses, I suddenly remembered that a
Dr. Brown had been mentioned somewhere in your *Autobiography.* I looked him up in the index . . . and everything fell into
place. For some reason, there you were, sixty years after the
fact, jotting down the itinerary of your adolescent escape from
Boston to Philadelphia! That your tremulous flight had taken
place in 1723 was well known, but the exact dates of your journey and arrival in Philadelphia had remained a mystery. The
perpetual calendar on my desk confirmed that there really was
a Sunday, October 6, in 1723. With incredible joy, I reread the
account of the big, the seminal adventure of your life—your
dash to freedom.

You arrived in New York *1 Oct.,* after three days at sea, to
discover that the only printer in town could not give you employment. He advised you to push on to Philadelphia, one
hundred miles away. You found passage on a boat but while
crossing the New York *Bay* met with a squall that drove you to
Long Island, where the wild weather made it impossible to go
ashore. On October 2, having been pelted by the rain all night
on that leaky boat, you made sail for *Amboy.* "Very feverish,"
as you said, you drank a large quantity of *Water* and felt better the next morning. The following day, you proceeded on
foot through the region known as the New Jersey *Pines.* On

day four, wet, miserable, and fearful of being identified as the guilty runaway that you were, you spent the night at an inn kept by "one *Dr. Brown*" about ten miles from Burlington. This Brown, a well-traveled doctor, befriended you and you kept up the acquaintance for life. The *River D* on Saturday the 5th alluded to your boarding a boat on the Delaware, rowing with your fellow passengers, and reaching Philadelphia on Sunday, October 6.

What a pearl! A pearl that would allow Philadelphia to celebrate your arrival in the balmy first days of October rather than have scholars and admirers from all over the country fight the perils of ice and snow to evoke . . . what? Your birthday on January 17 in faraway Boston. October 6 was the day you were truly reborn, the dawn of your glorious life.

My euphoria was complete when I found a letter from your son-in-law advising you in 1783 that the British had plundered the trunk in which the manuscript of your *Memoirs* had been stored. That explains why you were trying in 1783 to reconstruct the salient moments of your past, just as your French friends were urging you to do.

The real world soon crushed my pearl. As I was waiting at a red light on my way home, a teenager lifted from the basket of my bicycle the pocketbook that, in my excitement, I had not secured properly. The last I saw of him, he was swinging it above his head and jumping over a hedge, to his friends' applause.

Still, the little discovery, sent to the *Philadelphia Inquirer,* was picked up by newspapers around the country. An editorial suggested that Philadelphia mark October 6 as a festive occasion, and the then mayor of the city wrote me that he was directing his commissioner of parades and special events to look into the matter. Eighteen years later, the commissioner must still be mulling it over. Sorry, Franklin.

But there have been other discoveries along the way. In the

following eighteen essays—some previously published, some not—I have tried to reveal little-known episodes of your life as well as unexplored nooks and crannies of your personality.

Through you, Franklin, I have met so many interesting people. My colleagues, first of all, to whom I dedicate this collection in which you are sometimes the inscrutable center, and sometimes a peripheral character who gives the episode its historical interest. Through you I have met "real Americans" all over the country and feel that I finally belong. Surrounded by the Friends of Franklin, I have traveled to Paris, Chicago, Boston, and many other places where your name is the key to cordial hospitality. I have talked about you on television and imagined how comfortable you would feel in our electronic world where you would surely have innovative ideas for software. And let me tell you, by the way, that the latest scientific program on lightning admitted that the causes of that terrifyingly beautiful phenomenon are not better known than in your day.

The portrait that I have painted of you may not be altogether flattering—you would not want that, would you?—but I hope that it conveys your humor, your resiliency, your courage, your faith in a better future, and, above all, your scintillating intelligence.

Thanks, Franklin.

And thank you to the people who have helped me along the way. To the Florence Gould Foundation for helping to send Ellen Cohn and myself to France; to Professor Ed Morgan, whose advice was, as always, spirited and wise; to Max Hall, my good friend, senior editor emeritus at Harvard University Press, who trimmed my style of its Gallic effusiveness; to Cathy Briganti, whose ease in the world of modern technology enchants me (still a manual typewriter user); to Julie Carlson, a subtle and supportive copy editor; and to Yale University Press. My very first book was published by Yale, and this one closes the cycle. My thanks also go to Richard Ryerson, editor of the Adams Papers, and Roy Goodman, curator of printed materials at the American Philosophical Society.

Finally, however strange it may sound, thank you, William Temple Franklin, errant grandson of the great man and reluctant editor of the gigantic mass of papers you inherited.[2] If one considers that the successive teams who have been working on them since the mid-fifties, with all modern conveniences, will only conclude the work in 2006—just in time for Franklin's tercentenary—one can forgive you for having been, let us say, dilatory. (Twenty-seven years just to get going!) Still, Temple, you should be our patron saint. If you had done a perfect job, we would not be enjoying those everchanging tasks we have so much fun grumbling about.

PART I

Some Facets of Franklin's Personality

1

Franklin, Hitler, Mussolini, and the Internet

I ENDED my Introduction by thanking Franklin for having given me an interesting life. This seems like the right time to prove my gratitude by coming to the defense of his reputation, which has recently been sullied on the Internet, where he has been represented as a rabid anti-Semite.

As I was wondering how to proceed, I received a request from Sandro Gerbi, a freelance journalist in Milan who is a lifelong friend of our family. He needed a quotation from a book that I would surely find at the Yale Library. The book in question, Morris Kominsky's *The Hoaxers* (Boston, 1970) was indeed easy to locate, and the passage that Sandro desired (pages 135–37), had to do with Franklin and an anti-Semitic speech that he had supposedly delivered. Sandro informed me further that he was writing a piece on the Fascist era and had collected a number of clippings from the German and Italian press dealing with Franklin and the Jews. Would he mind, I asked, if I looked into the question from the American side? Not at all, he replied.

My search led me to a fascinating book by Nian-Sheng Huang, *Benjamin Franklin in Thought and Culture, 1790–1990*

(Philadelphia, American Philosophical Society, 1994) and from there to old files of the *New York Times* and the exploration of territory that was new to me. The result of my research, published in the January 27, 1997, issue of the *New Republic*, has been of some use, I hope, in answering the many queries sent in by people who wonder whether they should believe this tale of narrow-mindedness and hatred. Here is a somewhat fuller version of that article.

On February 3, 1934, there appeared in *Liberation*, a weekly journal published in Asheville, North Carolina, the text of a speech Franklin was alleged to have delivered at "the Constitutional Convention of 1789"—a date that should arouse one's suspicion, since it was in 1787, not 1789, that the Constitutional Convention was held. This speech was discovered, we are told, in a hitherto unknown diary kept by Charles Cotesworth Pinckney, South Carolina's delegate to that convention, a diary titled "Chit-Chat around the Table during Intermissions." The authorship of the text has not been definitely ascertained, but it is surely modern and most likely the brainchild of William Dudley Pelley, the head of an American Nazi movement.

Born in Lynn, Massachusetts, in 1890, the son of a Protestant minister, Pelley worked for a stretch as a scriptwriter in Hollywood until sometime in the 1920s, when he "experienced death" for seven minutes. During this period, he claimed to have made contact with an oracle. Shortly after Hitler's rise to power in 1933, Pelley's oracle instructed him to organize the Silver Shirts Legion, a secret group whose membership was recruited mostly in the South, the Pacific Northwest, and California. At its peak, it numbered somewhere between fifteen thousand and fifty thousand adherents. Known as "the Chief"—he obviously thought of himself as the American

Hitler—Pelley was a prolific writer and an ardent propagandist whose mouthpiece *Liberation* sold at least a million copies in its heyday, 1934–39.

The "Prophecy" has appeared in somewhat different versions over the years. One of them stresses that Jews are Asiatics. The version I offer here is the one originally published by Pelley and the most frequently reproduced.

There is a great danger for the United States of America. This great danger is the Jew. Gentlemen, in every land the Jews have settled, they have depressed the moral level and lowered the degree of commercial honesty. They have remained a-part and un-assimilated; oppressed, they attempt to strangle the nation financially, as in the case of Portugal and Spain.

For more than seventeen hundred years they have lamented their sorrowful fate—namely, that they have been driven out of their home land; but, gentlemen, if the civilized world today should give them back Palestine and their property, they would immediately find pressing reason for not returning there. Why? . . . Because they are vampires and vampires cannot live on other vampires—they cannot live among themselves. They must live among Christians and others who do not belong to their race.

If they are not expelled from the United States by the Constitution within less than one hundred years, they will stream into this country in such numbers that they will rule and destroy us and change our form of Government for which we Americans shed our blood and sacrificed our life, property and personal freedom. If the Jews are not excluded within two hundred years, our children will be working in the fields to feed Jews while they remain in counting houses, gleefully rubbing their hands.

I warn you, gentlemen, if you do not exclude the Jews forever, your children and your children's children will curse you in their graves. Their ideas are not those of Americans, even when they lived among us for ten generations. The leopard cannot change his spots. The Jews are a danger to this land and if they are allowed to enter, they will imperil our institutions. They should be excluded by the Constitution.

The original of this copy is in the Franklin Institute, Philadelphia.[1]

The Hoax Is Up and Running

Had this fake prophecy been immediately denounced, it might have been stopped in its tracks. But mainstream historians did not read publications like *Liberation,* and the forgery's appearance provoked no American reaction, leaving it free to jump the Atlantic.

By August 1934, it was reproduced in *Der Weltdienst,* a bulletin of international propaganda published in German, French, and English in Erfurt (Germany). Within a few days it was picked up by *Der Volksbund,* the organ of the Swiss Nazi movement, and by September it had acquired the resonance that only Julius Streicher, Hitler's anti-Semite par excellence, could give it in *Der Stürmer.* In a special edition devoted exclusively to Jews *(Das Jüdische Volk),* Streicher included the piece attributed to Franklin prominently in a list of anti-Semitic quotations from famous people ranging from Tacitus, Erasmus, Luther, and Goethe to Voltaire and Gibbon. The passage from Franklin's "Prophecy" had the dubious honor of being the only one underlined.

Back in the United States, a certain Robert Edward Edmondson used his financial newsletter on September 25, 1934, to distribute the so-called prophecy to a large number of investment banks, businessmen, and other subscribers. This brought the hoax to the attention of Charles Beard, who decided to look into this surprising text with the care of a professional historian and political scientist of great repute. But his investigation was to take half a year, during which time the fabrication spread even further. The "Prophecy"'s consecration among anti-Semitic diatribes was its appearance in the thirty-eighth edition of Theodor Fritsch's bible of Nazism, *Handbuch der Judenfrage* (Leipzig, 1934). Simultaneously, the Right Cause Publishing Company, operating in Chicago, brought out a ten-cent pamphlet by one Victor de Kayville in which Franklin is mentioned in a long list of people who had warned the country against the Jews.

A Brief Overview of Anti-Semitism in the United States

The 1930s proved a fertile time for anti-Semitism in the United States, but it had not always been so. In the early days of colonial America, anti-Semitism was less rabid than in Europe for several reasons: the perception of Catholicism as the main rival of the dominant Protestant faith; the influence of the Enlightenment's emphasis on reason and individual rights; the need for settlers; agricultural abundance; and especially the role of Jews in Puritan thought. The Puritans viewed them as the descendants of the Hebrews of the Old Testament. It was believed that when the Jews finally saw the light and embraced Jesus, the millennium would begin. "By the end of the seventeenth century, the approximately two hundred and fifty Jews in America enjoyed de facto and, for the most part, de jure economic and religious liberty."[2]

During the eighteenth century Jews were accepted even more widely. Parallels were often drawn by the clergy between the revolutionary happenings in America and the events of the Old Testament. When the Continental Congress was considering designs for the new nation's seal in 1776, "Franklin proposed that the seal represent Moses dividing the Red Sea . . .

and Jefferson suggested that it portray the children of Israel in the wilderness."[3]

Hebrew was taught at Harvard and Yale. At the time that young Benjamin Franklin was secretly preparing to flee from Boston, much talk in Cambridge was centered on the conversion to Christianity of a learned Jew, Judah Monis. Such conversions were regarded as suspicious, probably motivated by material goals—in this case Monis's hope for a Harvard professorship, which he never received, although he became a tutor.[4]

The Pennsylvania Academy admitted Jewish students as of 1757. High society started opening its doors to wealthy Jews, as did the Revolutionary army (up to the rank of colonel) and several Masonic lodges. Some anti-Semitic episodes—vandalization of cemeteries, attacks in the press or from the pulpit—did occur in the young country, but on the whole a climate of tolerance prevailed for about a century after the Revolution.

The turning point came around 1880. The number of Jewish immigrants, mostly from Germany, had grown from 15,000 to 300,000 in only forty years. Hotels began turning away Jews, as did country clubs, the higher degrees of Masonic lodges, and some educational institutions. The situation grew worse during the early years of the twentieth century, when millions of impoverished Eastern Jews, clinging tenaciously to what were viewed as outlandish habits, arrived in America. After the Russian Revolution in 1917, when the seeds of racial hatred for its own sake had been sown, the Jews, especially New York Jews, were accused of helping the Bolsheviks. A systematic campaign against "the international Jewish conspiracy" was launched in May 1920 by Henry Ford in the *Dearborn Independent*; several of his themes were subsequently used by Pelley. Those attacks lasted until the summer of 1927, when Ford suddenly desisted after a reluctant apology.

More than 120 Fascist organizations sprang up during the 1930s and '40s. The Protestant fundamentalists who had spearheaded anti-Semitic literature were joined by the charismatic Catholic priest Father Charles Coughlin of Detroit, whose radio programs attracted millions of followers.

The new wave of evangelical anti-Semitism provoked a response. In 1906, the American Jewish Committee was founded, and six years later, the Anti-Defamation League was established to combat the threat. Non-Jews, too, figure in the struggle, among them Clarence Darrow, Evangeline Booth, and the presidents of some prestigious universities, notably Brown and Stanford.

A First, Isolated American Reaction

By March 1935, Charles Beard was ready to assert that Franklin's "Prophecy" was no more than a barefaced forgery. He had searched for Pinckney's diary in all the probable places—at the National Archives, the Library of Congress, the Franklin Institute, and in numerous other historical repositories—without finding any trace of it. He had written to Edmondson, asking him for the source of Franklin's "Prophecy." Edmondson answered that a copy of it had emanated from Mr. Madison Grant, of New York City. Beard wrote to Grant on October 20, 1934, asking him where the original document could be found.

Madison Grant, according to his obituary in the *New York Times* (May 31, 1937), was an independently wealthy man who had devoted his life to zoology, environmental causes, and the building of the Bronx River Parkway. Equally enthusiastic about the cause of eugenics, the so-called improvement of the human race by careful breeding, he served on the Eugenics International Committee. This committee reflected the growth of agitation in favor of the conservation of the Nordic type. In 1915, on the eve of the United States' entry into World War I, Grant published a deeply bigoted book, *The Passing of the Great Race,* in which he denounced the Jews as Public Enemy No. 1. About the Polish Jews, he writes: "These immigrants borrow the language of the original Americans, adopt their dress, steal their names, and begin to take their women. . . . New York is in the process of becoming a *cloaca gentium.*"[5] Logically enough, Madison Grant pushed for the passage of anti-immigration laws, notably the Johnson Restrictive Act of 1924. In other words, he was a man more interested in saving endangered animals than distraught humans.

Grant's answer to Beard was circumspect. Some years ago, he said, he had received what purported to be a copy of Franklin's remarks before the convention in Philadelphia, but he had no information whatsoever as to the authenticity of the paper.

Well aware of the difficulty of proving a negative, Charles Beard ascertained from the librarian of Congress that Pinckney had almost certainly *not* kept a diary of the convention proceedings and that no evidence exists that Franklin ever made such a speech. A stylistic analysis shows that the phraseology of the "Prophecy" is not that of the eighteenth century, and that it contains anachronisms such as the Jews' longing for their "homeland"—which was not a term employed at the time, and not a Jewish concern in Franklin's day, when Palestine was still under Turkish domination. "Homeland" came in use when the Balfour Declaration was issued in Great Britain in 1917. The forgery was not even a good one.

Furthermore, the "Prophecy" is totally at odds with Franklin's well-known principles of tolerance, especially in religious concerns. The archives of the Congregation Mikveh Israel in Philadelphia contain a subscription paper dated April 30, 1788, according to which Franklin, along with forty-four other cit-

izens of all faiths, contributed toward relieving the debt incurred by the congregation in building a synagogue. The appeal may well have been written by Franklin himself: he had
been such a vigorous fund-raiser over the years that a distressed Hebrew Society would very likely have tried first to
enlist his help. Even though the Hebrews, commonly called
Israelites, worship Almighty God in a different manner, says
the preamble, "the enlightened citizens of Philadelphia" will
surely want to assist them. Indeed, many prominent Philadelphia names appear on that subscription list: Rittenhouse,
Ingersoll, Rush, Muhlenberg, Biddle, Cowperthwait, Benezet,
and so on. The three most generous donors—Franklin was one
of them—gave five pounds each.

Two Problems with Charles Beard's Refutation

Beard's counterargument is not without holes, however.
The first problem concerns Beard's assertion that never in his
life had Franklin expressed anti-Semitic views. In truth, we
know of two instances of anti-Semitic language by Franklin.
Both were related to his frustration with a man who, Jewish or
not, had behaved in an irritating manner.

The offending gentleman was an Amsterdam merchant
and banker, Jean de Neufville, who back in 1779 had promised
to raise a loan in the Netherlands for the American cause after
a similar attempt by another banker had failed. If Franklin kept
negotiating with this Neufville, a "self-interested vain pro-
moter" whose original demands had been extravagant, it was
out of his embarrassment to be forever milking the French
Treasury. The promised loan never materialized. Two years
later, when another unpleasant matter was embroiling John
Adams, then in Holland, with Neufville, Franklin saw fit to
warn his colleague: "I believe him to be as much a Jew as any in

Jerusalem."[6] One month later, commenting on the document that he had sent Adams to back up his charges, Franklin elaborated sarcastically: "By this time I fancy your Excellency is satisfied that I was wrong in supposing J. de Neufville as much a Jew as any in Jerusalem, since Jacob was not content with any percents, but took the whole of his Brother Esau's Birthright; and his posterity did the same by the Canaanites, and cut their throats in the bargain, which in my conscience I do not think Mr. J. de Neufville has the least inclination to do by us, while he can get anything by our being alive." Only recently have we learned—or are we still learning?—to exclude racial slurs from our vocabulary; in the 1700s no consciousness had been raised in that respect.

The second problem with Beard's refutation was that he published it in the *Jewish Frontier,* which made it unlikely that it would reach the general reading public.

Enter Fiorello La Guardia

And there the matter rested for two years until, on March 3, 1937, New York's colorful mayor La Guardia gave a speech at a luncheon of the women's division of the American Jewish Congress. He suggested displaying that "brown-shirted fanatic who is menacing the peace of the world" in a chamber of horrors at the upcoming New York World's Fair.

The German embassy, of course, reacted with indignation, and the following day Secretary of State Cordell Hull expressed regret over "the use of language by any American citizen calculated to offend a friendly power." Questioned by the press, the feisty and impenitent La Guardia stood by his original statement and added some. At this point, everybody jumped into the fray: the mayor's allies and his political enemies, German-American organizations, and a number of concerned citizens whose views were reported in the columns of the *New York Times*. But nothing could equal the pitch of fury reached by the German press: threats of boycotting the World's Fair unless La Guardia were removed, slurs on the mayor's partial Jewish ancestry, a photograph showing his resemblance to a gorilla, the accusation of his being an *Obergangster*, and so on.

And Franklin in all this? His vitriolic "Prophecy" was trotted out once more, warmly praised, and declared in Germany to represent the views of a venerable elder statesman on the brink of death. Under the headline "Franklin was right," *Der Angriff*, pretending that it had just received the document from a reader, published a translation of it on March 9, 1937. *Die Deutsche Allgemeine Zeitung* did the same thing on the same day, stating, "The Jews will devour America."

During the following weeks of that agitated month of March, two very different developments occurred: Mussolini's press took up the cudgel, and the American intelligentsia woke up to the seriousness of the situation.

II Duce Follows der Führer

Mussolini had concluded his alliance with Hitler in 1936. By early 1937, he felt that it was time to drag his basically tolerant countrymen into a closer alignment with their formidable partner to the north. The La Guardia fracas provided the perfect pretext for opening an anti-Semitic campaign.

On March 20, the chairman of the Banca d'Italia sent Mussolini a letter quoting the *Deutsche Allgemeine Zeitung* to the effect that the Jews would devour America. This was enough to set the ball rolling. In 1938, the minister of popular culture, Dino Alfieri, cabled the Italian embassy in Washington to obtain more background on the now intriguing Franklin allegation. The embassy's answer has not been found, but Milano's

Corriere della Sera eventually ran an article entitled "Benjamin Franklin's Terrible Anathema against the Jews." Rome's *Popolo d'Italia* went even further, with comments that the United States was indeed in a dreadful mess precisely because the Jews had been allowed to take over. The moral: Italians, beware!

The German propaganda machine, in a bold piece of escalation, now elevated Franklin to the rank of president of the United States. It was with that title that he was referred to by Rudolf Hess, deputy leader of the Reich, in two addresses to the workmen of the freshly conquered Sudetenland in what was then Czechoslovakia (November 30 and December 2, 1938).

Neither dictator cared whether their propaganda was true. Mussolini proclaimed that "the regime needs myths, not history," and Hitler asserted in *Mein Kampf* that "a lie is believed because of the unconditional and insolent inflexibility with which it is propagated." The more brazen the lie, the better it will work. But in the United States, the search for truth in the matter of Franklin's "Prophecy" was finally resumed in earnest.

American Scholars Speak Up

On March 10, 1937, three years and five weeks after the birth of the canard, the *New York Times* gave full play to the imposture and published Beard's refutation of 1935. By November 1938, the International Benjamin Franklin Society had published a fifteen-page pamphlet entitled *Benjamin Franklin Vindicated: An Exposure of the Franklin "Prophecy" by American Scholars.* The authors reaffirmed the mythical nature of Pinckney's diary, exposed the grossness of the forgery, and deplored the way a lie can gain credence as it spreads. Only one of them, however, J. Henry Smythe Jr., saw fit to remark that "this libel of the Jewish race is unjust both to Jews and to the nature and fame of Franklin." The others concentrated only on defending Franklin.[7]

That very year, 1938, an opening salvo was launched in what would be a bitter, protracted struggle between William Dudley Pelley and the North Carolina authorities. The Silver Shirts' financial enterprises were in violation of the state's security laws, and Pelley, who had received a suspended sentence in 1935, was charged with parole violation. More dangerously, his pro-Nazi propaganda caused him to be embroiled with the Martin Dies Committee on Un-American Activities.

The printing equipment of *Liberation* was sold in 1940, and Pelley moved to Indiana, where he published inflammatory anti-war articles in the *Galilean*. They caused him to be arrested in 1942 under the Espionage Act of 1917, the first instance of the legislation's use in a major prosecution after Pearl Harbor. Found guilty on eleven counts by a jury composed of farmers and small tradesmen of southern Indiana, Pelley was sentenced to fifteen years in jail. He was released from the federal penitentiary in Terre Haute after eight years, in 1950, and died in 1965.

One would imagine that the discredited old chestnut died along with its author, but no, it is giving signs these days of sprouting anew. At the annual convention of the Muslim Arab Youth Association held in Kansas City in December 1990, one of the speakers, Rajib Najib, paraphrased Franklin's "Prophecy" once again, the only novelty being that the Jews' "counting houses" became "palaces."[8] A controversy sparked by Salah Jafar (who quotes the entire spurious text) has been taking place on the Internet's bulletin boards, where several people are refuting his statements. The question has also been discussed in home pages on the World Wide Web.

Poor Franklin. Nobody loved a good hoax more than he did. He published his first at sixteen, his last less than one month before he died, and many in between. But with the exception of his anti-British propaganda during the Revolution, those hoaxes had benevolent purposes. The persona he adopted in adolescence, that of the outspoken middle-aged widow Silence Dogood, pleaded in favor of education for girls, tolerance, freedom of speech, and other worthy causes in a series of fourteen essays that Benjamin slipped before dawn under the door of his brother's printing shop.

And who can forget Franklin's most charming literary creation, Polly Baker, the spunky lass who not only bore many children out of wedlock but spoke up in a Connecticut court in defense of all seduced girls? So vivid was she that many years later people still thought of her as a real person.[9]

At the end of his life, Franklin called on his sense of humor one last time to produce the speech supposedly delivered by Sidi Mehemet Ibrahim to the divan of Algiers in defense of the traditional custom of enslaving the Christians captured by Barbary pirates.[10]

Now, through an ironic twist of fate, Franklin's own posthumous reputation is being muddied by a hoax. *Poor Richard* used to say that truth stands on two legs, whereas a lie stands only on one. These days the only legs a lie needs are virtual ones.

2

The Only Founding Father in a Sports Hall of Fame

I T HAS long been my dream to present on educational television some of Franklin's scientific accomplishments in a manner that would interest adolescents—to show students the thrill of discoveries achieved in an atmosphere of warm international comradeship, as they were in the eighteenth century, rather than in the secrecy imposed today by the competition for prizes or grants.

In order to create a framework for Franklin's scientific inquiries and those of his colleagues, I proposed to divide them into broad categories such as water, fire, air, and earth, with Franklin, as narrator, conversing with his contemporaries. The account of his discoveries would then lead to imaginary meetings with today's scientists, from whom he would learn where his less sophisticated experiments might have led him.

The program on water, for instance, would allow the viewers to follow Franklin's dogged pursuit of the Gulf Stream, carried out in connection with the whaling captains of Nantucket. Doesn't the Gulf Stream warrant a leisurely study instead of the three or four seconds it receives in Franklin's televised biographies? Another field to investigate would be his intensive study of the calming effect of oil on water, still experimental in his day but later elaborated into the theory of surface tension. Or the discovery of oxygen by his friend Joseph Priestley, the dissenting clergyman and celebrated chemist, also the originator of carbonated water, the source of our soft drinks.

Alas, when I described my project to television producers, they were enthusiastic about both the idea and the format but pessimistic about the possibilities for funding it. That is why I am offering here a part of what would have been that first episode—water; or Franklin's lifelong love affair with the sea.

In 1726, when the young Franklin had booked his passage back to Philadelphia from London, prepared to start over and make his fortune in trade, he received an offer that nearly kept him in England. Sir William Wyndham sent for him to ask that he teach the nobleman's two sons to swim before they set out on their tour of the Continent: "He proposed to gratify me handsomely if I would teach them," Franklin later recalled. "From this Incident I thought it likely, that if I were to remain in England and open a Swimming School, I might get a good Deal of Money. And it struck me so strongly, that had the Overture been sooner made me, probably I should not so soon have returned to America."[1]

Franklin was an accomplished and enthusiastic swimmer at a time when few people entered water voluntarily. In the seventeenth and eighteenth centuries, swimming was a subject at once empirical and theoretical—a combination dear to the Enlightenment. Franklin's own start as a swimmer embraces the two extremes, showing how intellectual this man's interest in practical matters could be and how much these contrasts were a part of the advanced thought of the time. Growing up only steps away from Boston Bay, a poor boy who rarely could afford toys, Benjamin spent many happy hours in the water. "I . . . learnt early to swim well, and to manage Boats, and when in a Boat or a Canoe with other Boys I was commonly allow'd to govern, especially in any case of Difficulty."[2] This may sound like the natural course of events for a child with more vigor than money, who by dint of falling in and paddling would learn to swim, much as animals do. But Benjamin in fact borrowed a treatise called *The Art of swimming . . . with advice for bathing,* abundantly illustrated "by proper figures" from which he practiced every stroke. He even went beyond the manual, inventing some strokes of his own "aiming at the graceful and easy, as well as the useful." In his passionate search for knowledge, the boy unexpectedly found himself in the spiritual company of two major figures of the early Enlightenment.

The author of the treatise, Melchisedec de Thévenot (1620–92), had traveled extensively throughout Europe and published accounts of others' explorations. He also held gatherings at his home that eventually gave rise to the Académie Royale des Sciences. Thévenot had been a friend of John Locke when the political philosopher lived in Paris, and Locke, too, had written about swimming. The practical skill was introduced and recommended in the grand manner, by means of theory and classical allusion:

'Tis supposed that every Parent would be glad to have their Children skill'd in *Swimming,* if it might be learnt in a Place chosen for its Safety, and under the Eye of a careful Person. . . . 'Tis that saves many a Man's Life; and the Romans thought it so necessary that they ranked it with Letters; and it was the common Phrase to mark one ill educated, and good for nothing, that he had neither learnt to read nor to swim; *Nec Literas didicit nec Natare.* But besides gaining a Skill which may serve him at Need, the Advantages to Health by often Bathing in cold Water during the Heat of the Summer, are so many, that I think nothing need be said to encourage it.[3]

Yet however much Benjamin learned from his reading, he also experimented on his own. He was inventive in the water. Playing with his kite one day, he reached the edge of a pond about one mile wide. Thinking it would be fun to continue playing with the kite while in the water, he waded into the pond, lay on his back, and let himself be dragged, pulling down the kite only occasionally when it dragged him too fast. He also fabricated paddles for his hands and feet in order to move more quickly in the water and use less energy.[4]

By his late teens, when he was living in London and working in a printing shop, Franklin was accomplished enough to put on an impromptu display in the Thames. Through an "ingenious" friend whom he had taught to swim in two sessions, he was invited to accompany some gentlemen from the country who were going to Chelsea by water. "In our Return, at the Request of the Company . . . I stript and leapt into the River, and swam from near Chelsea to Blackfryars [about three and a half miles], performing on the way many Feats of Activity both upon and under Water, that surpriz'd and pleas'd those to whom they were Novelties."[5] The event was remarkable enough to be talked about beyond Franklin's own circle of acquaintance, and a few months later Sir William Wyndham made his tempting offer.

Although Franklin remained a printer, he continued to advocate swimming lessons in his educational proposals. When, in 1749, he took the first steps toward creating an academy for the youth of Pennsylvania and wrote a series of proposals—modestly termed "hints"—to be circulated among future trustees and donors, he invoked a number of authorities, including John Locke and John Milton, who recommended daily vigorous exercise to toughen the bodies and minds of boys. To this day, some institutions of higher learning require entering students to prove that they can swim.

Even after helping launch the academy, Franklin was not through with his swimming propaganda. He understood that the biggest danger for the novice is panic, and he wrote a long, soothing letter to an apprehensive friend. A river ran through this friend's garden, and Franklin's purpose was to convince him that he could trust the water to support him, especially after he had mastered the technique of lying flat on his back. As a first step, Franklin wanted his disciple to enter the water confidently up to his breast, then turn around toward shore and throw an egg ahead of him. When the egg had settled on the bottom it would have to be retrieved, and the act of plunging after it would show the beginner how hard it is to lower one's body down through the water, since the water pushes you to float.[6] Franklin eventually published this letter, and it has been reprinted many times as a treatise on swimming.[7] Even so, it was not detailed enough to satisfy the first French translator of his works, Dr. Jacques Barbeu-Dubourg.

Never having learned to swim, Dubourg, good French intellectual that he was, proceeded to gather all possible information on the *theory* of swimming, and upon consulting Diderot's *Encyclopédie,* discovered to his shock that there was not much to be found there. To fill the gap, he asked Franklin a daunting series of questions, divided into three sections and filling ten printed pages.[8] The first section deals in relentless detail with the comparative weight of water and of the various parts of the human body. The second advocates a thorough study of the behavior of aquatic animals and deep-sea divers, such as pearl fishers, and sketches the outlines of such a study. Part two continues with inquiries about the best ways of keeping the crucial parts of the body (nose, mouth) out of the water and how to prevent a dreadful variety of accidents. (One wonders how any reader, at this point, would dare venture even a toe in a shallow pond.) The third section, somewhat less apprehensive, deals with the pleasures of swimming and asks: At what age should young men learn? Would it be absurd to teach the art of swimming to persons of the other sex? When is it healthy to bathe, and when is it dangerous? Should one swim before or after meals? What is the ideal water temperature? Would it be possible to eat or drink while in the water? What should one wear? What should a non-swimmer do if he falls into the water? How does one know if a drowned person is really dead? What did the writers of antiquity have to say on the topic? and many other queries that young Benjamin surely never pondered when he jumped into Boston Bay with his boyhood friends.

Franklin, who was still living in London at the time, answered half-heartedly, pleading lack of time. He referred Dubourg to an article published in the American Philosophical Society's *Transactions,* the gist of which was that fat people with small bones float the best.[9] His advice to the long-distance swimmer was to turn occasionally on his back and to vary his propulsion methods. As to a leg cramp, one should give the affected limb a sudden and violent shake, which can be done in the air if one is swimming on one's back. Jumping into very cold water when one is very hot can be dangerous. Most of his reply, however, was a hymn in praise of swimming. "It is the healthiest and most pleasant of all exercises. . . . After swimming an hour or two in the evening, one sleeps coolly all night even during the summer's worst heats. . . . Maybe this is due to the pores being so thoroughly cleansed that they allow a more abundant perspiration which in turn is refreshing."

And finally he recommends his childhood experience of letting himself be pulled by a kite as a relaxing and exquisite way of speeding through the water. "A man could cross from Calais to Dover with that system," he muses, "but a boat is probably preferable."

Franklin's last swimming disciple was to be his grandson Benny Bache, who had returned from his four years at boarding school in Geneva and was in Paris for that heady summer of 1783, when the first lighter-than-air balloons were going up, soon to be followed by the first manned ones. At the age of almost eighty, relates a friend, Franklin "would teach one of his grandsons how to swim by swimming himself across the Seine, at Passy, early in the morning."[10] As Benny noted in his diary: "My grandfather is not like other old people."[11]

When the International Swimming Hall of Fame was created in Fort Lauderdale, Florida, in the mid-1960s, Benjamin Franklin—whose bust rests on the grand table in the center of the boardroom—became its icon. Reproductions of his portraits appear among the famous swimmers of this century, next to photographs of Tedford Cann, the first American to win the Congressional Medal of Honor in World War I and a splendid swimmer.[12]

3

Three Women, Three Styles

IN EUROPE, Franklin has always been considered an extraordinary figure—in science, diplomacy, writing talent, humor, and philanthropy. The bicentennial of his death was celebrated in France in 1990 in a variety of ways, including with sumptuous brochures underwritten by corporations—one of which was, appropriately, France-Electricité.

The popular image of Franklin in his own country is—regrettably—quite different. While a great symposium ("Reappraising Franklin") was orchestrated in Philadelphia on the bicentennial by Professor Leo Lemay, the local papers filled their pages with salacious tales about the supposedly inexhaustible sexual drive of the man being remembered, as if there was nothing else to write about.

While lecturing around the country, I have been asked repeatedly how many affairs Franklin had, how many illegitimate children, and so forth. My answer is always the same: I don't know and I don't care. Our function as documentary editors is not to speculate idly over what might have happened but to rely on letters, diaries, and memoirs; and there are no letters, diaries, or memoirs that ever mention a specific liaison after

Franklin's marriage to Deborah Read. Even if there were affairs, as there may well have been during those fifteen years that he lived an ocean away from his wife, of what interest are they if they left no trace?

What is true, and captivating, is that Franklin had vibrant relationships with a number of women—American, English, and French; young and old—and that world literature has been enriched by the range of emotions and the language these feelings evoked from both himself and his correspondents.

The secret of his powerful bonds with so many different women resides, I believe, in the fact that he considered each one not merely as an object of conquest but as a unique personality well worth listening to. His writing style varies considerably from woman to woman.

Here follow three samples of Franklin's style, in letters to one American young woman and two English ones. He goes from sensuous to sensible when addressing Catharine Ray, from intellectual to quasi-reverential with Polly Stevenson, from grandfatherly to tender when dealing with Georgiana Shipley. Three love stories? Yes, three facets of love, all of them warm and highly personal while remaining—at least in my opinion—purely platonic.[1]

The episode involving Catharine Ray took place during an interlude as potentially erotic as one can imagine. It started in Boston, during the Christmas week of 1754, while Franklin was paying a visit to his brother John, whose stepson was married to Catharine's sister. Franklin, a man approaching fifty who, having given up his profitable profession in publishing and printing, was now basking in his scientific triumphs—the stove that bore his name, the nature of lightning—and a girl in her early twenties, euphoric on one of her rare trips away from her aging parents, vivacious, romantic, glorying in her obvious

effect on that celebrated man. Catharine chatted away and
Franklin listened. He really listened. She made sugar plums
and he claimed that they were the best he had ever tasted. He
"guessed her thoughts" and she called him a "conjurer."[2]

On December 30, they set out together for Newport, Rhode
Island. When they reached an icy hill, their horses, improperly
shod by a dishonest smith, kept falling on their noses and
knees, "no more able to stand than if they had been shod on
skates." Yet both travelers would remember with delight, for
years to come, how they had talked away the hours "on a winter
journey, a wrong road and a soaking shower." In middle age,
she would assert that a great part of her life's happiness was
due to the lessons he had given her on that journey. What those
lessons were will remain forever their secret.[3]

A few more days in Newport, a few in nearby Westerly to
visit another sister of hers, and then she had to rush home to
windswept Block Island, to the bedside of a sick parent. Franklin watched her sail away. "I thought too much was hazarded,
when I saw you put off to Sea in that very little Skiff, tossed by
every Wave. . . . I stood on the Shore, and looked after you, till
I could no longer distinguish you, even with my Glass." He
could not bring himself to leave. After an absence of almost six
months, he lingered in New England. "I almost forgot I had a
Home," he wrote, "till I was more than half-way towards it."

He had barely reached Philadelphia when her first letter
arrived. The northeast wind, he declared, was the gayest wind
since it brought him her kisses, as promised, her kisses all
mixed with snowflakes, "pure as your Virgin Innocence, white
as your lively Bosom, and—as cold."

A romance? Yes, but a romance in the Franklin manner,
hovering between the risqué and the avuncular, taking a bold
step forward and an ironic step backward, implying that he
is tempted as a man but respectful as a friend. Such a rela-

tionship was flattering for the woman who could not but feel the depth of his emotion, yet knew that it would not lead to what was, in those days, a catastrophe. And with Franklin's many reminders that he could easily be mistaken for her father, Catharine must have felt young, always.

That first letter to her was typical. One moment of folly: "I almost forgot I had a Home." But it did not last. "Then, like an old man who, having buried all he loved in this world, begins to think of heaven, I began to think of and wish for home. . . . My diligence and speed increased with my impatience. I drove on violently and made such long stretches that a very few days brought me to my own house and to the arms of my good old wife and children where I remain, thanks to God, at present well and happy." Saved! Reason prevailed.

When the situation was threatening to become too passionate, Franklin managed to put it back in perspective in such a way that his correspondent could have no doubt about his desire, spiritual and carnal, for her, yet no delusion about his being totally carried away. And what can be more unimpeachable in appearance yet more sobering in effect than a pleasant, casual mention of one's dear mate? There never was to be a letter to "Katy," even a flirtatious one, without some reference to Deborah.

> The Cheeses, particularly one of them, were excellent. All our Friends have tasted it, and all agree that it exceeds any English Cheese they ever tasted. Mrs. Franklin was very proud that a young Lady should have so much Regard for her old Husband, as to send him such a Present. We talk of you every Time it comes to Table. She is sure you are a sensible Girl, and a notable Housewife, and talks of bequeathing me to you as a Legacy, but I ought to wish you a better, and hope she will live these hundred years; for we are grown old together, and if she has any faults I am so used to 'em that I don't perceive 'em. . . . Indeed I begin to think she has none, as I think of you. And

since she is willing I should love you as much as you are willing to be lov'd by me, let us join in wishing the old Lady a long Life and a happy.[4]

Catharine felt no such compunction and remembered Deborah only in polite postscripts. She wrote breathlessly, effusively: "Absence rather increases than lessens my affections. . . . Love me one thousandth part so well as I do you."[5] She poured out her soul, then feared she had been indiscreet, and shed many tears when he did not answer promptly. He reassured her but hinted that because even the most innocent expressions of friendship between persons of different sexes are liable to be misinterpreted, he would be cautious, "and therefore though you say more, I say less than I think."[6]

Soon she was consulting him about affairs of the heart and sending—supposedly for translation—the love message that a young Spaniard had written her, with the incongruous result that among Franklin's political tracts and philosophical pamphlets there appears an English rendering, in his hand, of the ardent lines once penned by Don Laureano Donado de el Castillo to his "dear Heart." Franklin took it all in good spirit, encouraging her to tell him more about her "pretty mischief," but refusing to help her choose among suitors, though he made it clear that he favored any worthy Englishman over the Spaniard.

Finally, he advised her to lead a good Christian life, get married, and surround herself like his grapevine with "clusters of plump, juicy, blushing, pretty little rogues like their Mama."[7] Which is just what Catharine eventually did. The next time they met, she was Mrs. William Greene, wife of the future governor of Rhode Island, to whom she had already borne the first two of their six children.

Franklin and Catharine remained friends for life. Even

though they did not recapture the magic of that first encounter, the spark never went out of their letters, and neither did their gratitude toward fate, which had given them that much and no more—the warmth of the embers without the devastation of the flame. To Catharine Ray Greene the world is indebted for some of Franklin's most poetic letters.

Three years later, he was off on his first political mission to England, a mission that was supposed to last six months but took five years. Accompanied by his son William, who was to study law in London, he settled near the Strand in the Craven Street house of Margaret Stevenson, an obliging and warm-hearted widow.[8] After an interlude of eighteen months back in Philadelphia, during which he started building a home for Deborah and himself, he returned to London and spent almost ten more years under Mrs. Stevenson's roof. They were considered a couple by their mutual friends, who generally invited them together. In the eyes of those friends, there is no doubt that Mrs. Stevenson was in love with her lodger and that after Deborah's death in 1774, she hoped he would marry her. Joseph Priestley reported to Franklin, by then back in Philadelphia: "Mrs. Stephenson is much as usual. She can talk about nothing but you." And shortly after Franklin reached Paris, a certain Emma Thompson, whom he must have known well in London, referred to "your good friend Stevenson who I think would have risqued all tarring and feathering to have paid you a visit in Philadelphia."[9]

But years later, when Franklin invited Mrs. Stevenson to join him in Paris, again it was as manager of his household. By then the lady was too ill to travel, and she died the following year.

The person who really captured Franklin's attention in England was young Mary ("Polly"), the Stevenson daughter, who was eighteen when he arrived. Highly intelligent, eager to learn, serious, even a bit strait-laced, Polly was the ideal student, the perfect answer to Franklin's urge to teach. Since she was dispatched to live outside London with an elderly aunt from whom she was expected to inherit a tidy fortune (or was it because of the growing closeness between landlady and tenant on Craven Street?), a large number of letters between Franklin and Polly have survived. Their agenda was nothing less than the study of all moral and natural philosophy. Polly asked questions, Franklin answered in careful detail, she in turn discussed his answers. The topics they tackled included barometers, insects, rising tides in rivers, why water becomes warmer after being pumped (if, in fact, it does), waterspouts, bubbles in a teacup, the distillation of seawater, fire, electrical storms, his phonetic spelling system, why rain is not salty, why wet clothes do not provoke a cold, and more.

His tone with Polly was anything but flirtatious; it was affectionate and at times verged on reverential.

After writing six Folio Pages of Philosophy to a young Girl, is it necessary to finish such a Letter with a Compliment? . . . Does it not say that she has a Mind thirsty after Knowledge, and capable of receiving it; and that the most agreeable Things one can write to her are those that tend to the Improvement of her Understanding? It does indeed say all this, but then it is still no Compliment; it is no more than plain honest Truth which is *not* the Character of a Compliment. So if I would finish my Letter in the Mode, I should yet add something that means nothing, and is *merely* civil and polite. But being naturally awkward at every Circumstance of Ceremony, I shall not attempt it. I had rather conclude abruptly with what pleases me more than any Compliment can please you, that I am allow'd to subscribe myself Your affectionate Friend.

To which she replied, in a style that Jane Austen would not have disavowed: "Such a Letter is indeed the highest Compliment. . . . The warmth of your affection makes you see Merit in me that I do not possess. It would be too great Vanity to think I deserve the Encomiums you give me, and it would be Ingratitude to doubt your Sincerity. Continue, my indulgent Friend, your favourable opinion of me, and I will endeavour to be what you imagine me."[10]

His dream was to see Polly marry his son and "become his own in the tender Relation of a Child," and Polly, it seems, was attracted to William, but William decided to marry Elizabeth Downes, the daughter of a Barbados planter. Franklin's disappointment was so keen that he left England less than one month before the wedding. The date of his departure for Philadelphia is traditionally attributed to the fact that his political mission was over, but considering that he had been away from home for five full years on his first mission, it is surprising, even astonishing, that he did not postpone his return for a few more weeks.

The farewell message Franklin sent from a "wretched inn" in Portsmouth on August 11, 1762, is the one letter in his life in which he admits to being overwhelmed by sadness. The "bad paper" that he found at the inn was adequate, he felt, to tell his Polly that he was afflicted at the thought of never seeing her again, but would it tell *how* afflicted he was? No, it could not. And he ends, "Adieu, my dearest Child: I will call you so; Why would I not call you so, since I love you with all the Tenderness, all the Fondness of a Father? Adieu. May the God of all Goodness shower down his choicest Blessings upon you, and make you infinitely Happier than that Event could have made you."[11]

Franklin and Polly did meet again, some two years later, when he embarked on his second mission to London, but their relationship, while still very cordial, lost some of its élan. Polly, in her thirties, fell in love with the gifted young Dr. William Hewson, and Franklin gave her away in marriage. No more science was discussed; her letters were all about babies and toddlers. She must have really taken to heart the advice Franklin had once given her: "The Knowledge of Nature may be ornamental, and it may be useful, but if to attain an Eminence in that, we neglect the Knowledge and Practice of essential Duties, we deserve Reprehension. For there is no Rank in Natural Knowledge of equal Dignity and Importance with that of being a good Parent, a good Child, a good Husband, or Wife, a good Neighbour or Friend, a good Subject or Citizen, that is, in short, a good Christian."[12]

Polly's happiness did not last long. Shortly before the birth of their third child, Dr. Hewson died of septicemia contracted while performing an autopsy, and Franklin's attitude toward the widow became a warmly protective stance. To comfort her, he daydreamed of marrying his own little grandson Benny—whom he had not yet seen and would not meet for years to come—with her last child, Eliza, and of dancing with Polly at the wedding.

On the twenty-fifth anniversary of their friendship, he celebrated their abiding closeness. "It is to all our Honours," he wrote, "that in all that time we never had among us the smallest Misunderstanding. Our Friendship has been all clear Sunshine, without any the least Cloud in its Hemisphere."[13]

Polly joined Franklin in Paris with her three children during the winter of 1784–85. Her visit was immensely pleasurable for him, as the pain of a kidney stone kept him homebound. Polly did not fail to express her British contempt for the dissolute French, among whom she included the beloved grandson Temple, who was well on his way, she felt, to becoming a playboy.

Finally, in 1786, the four Hewsons followed Franklin to Philadelphia—never to go home again. Anxious for his religious orthodoxy, Polly was at her friend's bedside when he died.

She survived him by only five years and was buried in Bristol, Pennsylvania.

Catharine Ray was in her early twenties when she met Franklin, and Polly Stevenson was eighteen. Georgiana Shipley, another recipient of intensely personal letters, was at the cusp between child and woman, that brief and fragile moment in a girl's mid-teens. Named after her cousin the duchess of Devonshire, Georgiana was the fourth of the five daughters of Jonathan Shipley, bishop of St. Asaph, a man whose views grew more liberal as he grew older and who became, along with his whole family, a close friend of Franklin and champion of the American cause.[14] It was in 1771 at the Shipley summer house, Twyford, near Winchester, that Franklin wrote the first and sprightliest installment of his *Memoirs*, spurred on by the enthusiastic reception given to nightly readings of his work in progress.

Some months later, Georgiana, in great distress, informed Franklin of the death of Mungo, the pet squirrel he had imported for her from America. His letter of condolence is a model of the way an adult should comfort a child. It is grandfatherly in tone—he was well in his sixties at the time—but without a hint of condescension. First, he joins her in lamenting the unfortunate end of poor Mungo, who had escaped from his cage and been killed by a dog. A little praise for the deceased: "He had had a good Education, had travell'd far, and seen much of the World." Whereupon he introduces her to the healing power of words and the magic of converting sorrow into art: "Let us give him an Elegy in the monumental Stile and Measure, which being neither Prose nor Verse, is perhaps the properest for Grief; since to use the common Language would look as if we were not affected, and to make Rhymes would seem Trifling in Sorrow."[15]

The twenty-two-line epitaph or elegy opens on a somber note—

> Alas! Poor *Mungo!*
> Happy wert thou, hadst thou known
>   Thy own Felicity!
> Remote from the fierce Bald-Eagle,
>   Tyrant of thy native Woods,
> Thou hadst nought to fear from his piercing Talons;
>   Nor from the murdering Gun
>   Of the thoughtless Sportsman

and ends on a cautionary one:

> Learn hence, ye who blindly wish more Liberty,
> Whether Subjects, Sons, Squirrels or Daughters,
> That apparent *Restraint* may be real *Protection*,
>   Yielding Peace, Plenty, and Security.[16]

Come to think of it, only four years after penning this prudent advice, Franklin cast off the Restraint that yielded Peace, Plenty, and Security, in order to sign the Declaration of Independence.

Debbie was soon asked to find a new American squirrel for Georgiana and given a chance to read the literary output pertaining to the episode. As usual, she promptly set to work and shipped "a verey fine one" after having had mishaps with two other squirrels who ran away even though they had been "bred up tame." Georgiana, who had a distinct preference for the American variety of squirrel, which she deemed more gentle and good-humored than the European, was delighted. She reported that "Beebee" was growing fat and enjoyed "as much liberty as even a North American can desire." Five years later she told Franklin, then in Paris, that Beebee was still alive and much caressed; even while old and blind, "he preserves his spirits and wonted activity."[17]

Georgiana herself grew into a beauty. Well versed in modern languages and the classics, she studied painting under Sir Joshua Reynolds, and was in all respects an accomplished young woman. She certainly knew how to flirt in writing. Admitting a touch of vanity, she says about her sisters and herself, "we have grown excessively conceited of having acquired your good opinion, for we prefer Dr. Franklin's commendation far before the finest things the smartest Macaroni [meaning dandy] could say of us."

Two years of silence ensued as Franklin, back in Philadelphia, assumed a leading role in the Revolution. Almost as soon as he reached Paris, he renewed contact with the Shipley family, and Georgiana's answer—written in secret because her father thought that corresponding in wartime was a dangerous thing—is an explosion of joy. She wonders whether her friend has read Edward Gibbon and Adam Smith, both recently published. She herself is studying Socrates because he reminds her of Dr. Franklin. She envies Temple for being so close to his grandfather. She describes an electrical machine. One can hardly be more effusive than Georgiana on that February 11, 1777.[18]

She requested a better picture of Franklin than the many prints and medals she had seen so far. In case a good painting of her friend has been made in Paris, could she have a miniature copy of it? It would make her "the happiest of beings, and next to that, a lock of your own dear grey hair."[19] In exchange she will send him a silhouette of her father and some of her more recent drawings. Franklin obliged, of course, first by sending her one of the small Sèvres medallions that he distributed among friends as souvenirs and, in early 1780, the hair lock as well as a snuff box adorned with an exquisite miniature on its lid.[20] She kissed both the hair and the picture a thousand times, she exclaims. Yes, she could imagine Franklin smiling at the excess of her happiness. Still, she has to tell him that the gift will not only make her happier but a better person because—she concludes in Latin—her character will be shaped by reflecting on his.

Three young women, three styles, three destinies. Catherine, the warm-hearted girl from Block Island, turned out to be the happiest of the three. She kept her exuberance through the hard days of the Revolution and took Franklin's sister, Jane Mecom, into her house when Jane had to flee from Boston. Even though Jane, quite old by then, did not have an easy temper and was quick to take offense (she was "miffy," said her brother), the two women became and remained close friends.

Polly turned despondent during the five years that separated Franklin's death from her own. She did not get along with the Baches, which is hardly surprising considering the resentment Sally must have felt toward this London "ex-rival" who occupied such a prominent place in her father's affection. Polly's son Thomas went to study medicine in Edinburgh and their correspondence, preserved in microfilm at the American Philosophical Society, resonates with the clash between the homesick mother, longing for England, and the youth who is enamored of America and pines to return there. The Hewsons remained in the New World and produced at least one doctor per generation.

And Georgiana, the star of her lively family? Her life, so full of promise, took an irreversible downward turn in 1784 when, in defiance of her family, she married the attractive but ineffectual Francis Hare. Strapped for money, the couple toyed with the idea of settling on a farm in Pennsylvania, and Franklin tried to help them with down-to-earth advice, but work was repugnant to the husband. They spent a vagabond life in modest European inns on the small pension granted them by the duchess of Devonshire. Georgiana died in Switzerland in 1810.

They had such different destinies, those three young women who never met one another, and yet they had one thing in common: their memories. Nobody put it better than Mme Brillon, Franklin's Parisian friend, long after his return to Philadelphia: "To have been, to still be, forever, the friend of this amiable sage who knew how to be a great man without pomp, a learned man without ostentation, a philosopher without austerity, a sensitive human being without weakness, yes, my good papa, your name will be engraved in the temple of memory but each of our hearts is, for you, a temple of affection."[21]

4
Grandfathers, Fathers, and Sons

WHEN Miss Jane Persis Burn-Murdoch died in Florence almost forty years ago, she left among the papers bequeathed to her nephews and nieces some old letters that had belonged to her father, long-time minister of the Church of Scotland at Nice. Among them was a bundle contained in a wrapper addressed to her father's own father, a man whose life spanned the first half of the nineteenth century.

Almost twenty years elapsed before the heirs opened the bundle, which turned out to contain ten mysterious and apparently unrelated letters dating back to 1782. One of them, addressed to "my dear young friend," was signed by Benjamin Franklin. Two others, sent to "dear Sam," and signed Jack and Jacky, had been written by an adolescent John Quincy Adams. These three alone were enough to make the discovery exciting.

The whole batch was offered to Yale and was eventually acquired for the Beinecke Rare Book and Manuscript Library. On examination it was found that all the letters had something to do with a young Bostonian, Samuel Cooper Johonnot, who had been for two years the schoolmate, in Geneva, of Franklin's grandson, Benjamin Franklin ("Benny") Bache. Since I have dealt at some length with this Sammy in a book devoted to Franklin's family, I was asked to look at the documents.[1] As I did so, I had the pleasant sensation of entering a room full of friends: here were the lofty Reverend Samuel Cooper, pastor of Boston's Brattle Street Church; Mrs. Dorcas Montgomery, who fluttered on the fringes of the philosophic group centered around the Doctor in Passy; Gabriel Johonnot, Sammy's muddling father; and the eminent Boston judge James Sullivan. And above all, here were the boys themselves: not only Sammy, but also the Adams boys, the Morris boys, Benny Bache, Robert Montgomery—all those children in exile who were expected to take full advantage of their European education, to make their parents proud and prepare themselves for the service of their country, to somehow manage, without complaint, to forge their manhood out of the very stuff of loneliness and homesickness.

As the new pieces fitted neatly into the larger mosaic of the Franklin Collection at Yale and the Adams Papers at the Massachusetts Historical Society in Boston, there emerged a story of love and misunderstanding between generations, very eighteenth century in flavor yet psychologically valid for all times. Here it is, such as I published it in the *Yale University Library Gazette* 53, no. 4 (April 1979): 177–95.

The story opens with a letter sent on November 12, 1779, by the Reverend Samuel Cooper, Franklin's closest friend and political associate in Boston.[2] Addressing himself to his fellow grandfather, then minister plenipotentiary in Paris, Cooper wrote: "My little Grandson Samuel Cooper Johonnot will have the Honour of presenting this to you. Mr. Adams kindly indulged him with a Portion of that Care which he gives to his own Sons who are nearly of his Age. He goes to France with a

View to acquire the Purity of the French Language. . . . I send him partly, as a dear Pledge of my own Esteem and Gratitude for a Nation to whom my Country is so much indebted, and of my sincere Inclination to act, even in the tenderest Cases, in the true Spirit of the Alliance."[3]

It was a tender case indeed. Sammy, the child of Judith Cooper, who had died when the boy was five, and of Gabriel Johonnot, a brave colonel in the early days of the Revolution but an unreliable, ne'er-do-well merchant after that, was Samuel Cooper's only grandson, the love and hope of his later years. Still, when Sammy reached eleven, it was time for him to be sent away.[4]

Sending boys to Europe for their education was becoming fairly standard practice among the American elite. Silas Deane had brought his young Jesse to Paris in 1776; Franklin, the following year, had taken along Benny Bache (seven), the eldest of his daughter's children; some years later, Robert Morris would send his two adolescent sons to France; and John Adams had already been accompanied by John Quincy on his previous trip to Paris in 1778 and was about to set sail again, this time with John Quincy (now twelve), his second son Charles (nine and a half), the Johonnot boy, the lawyer Francis Dana (the peace commission's secretary), John Thaxter (Adams's private secretary), and some manservants.

Marked "The Gift of SCJ to JQA—His Manuscript Book," the diary that Sammy kept on board (under the pseudonym George Beaufort) still lies among the papers of the Adams family.[5] Its young author starts out bravely enough with farewells to the family, Hancocks, and Trumbulls; descriptions of the Adams boys as "agreeable young gentlemen, very polite"; huzzas and gunboat salutes, but soon sobers down to terse notations of violent storms and widespread seasickness. Between one tempest and the next, young Sammy recovered suf-

ficiently to enjoy the sight of porpoises and gulls off New-
foundland, the excitement of a possible clash with a supposed
enemy ship (alas, it turned out to be American), and some
episodes of life at sea.

The Adams party touched land in Spain instead of France,
their French frigate *La Sensible* badly in need of repair. Rather
than wait for another ship, Adams decided to lead his little
band on the long journey overland. Heartened on their way by
the best chocolate they had ever tasted, they braved rough
roads, winter hardships, and awful accommodations. In his
own diary, John Adams recorded that "Sometimes the Gentlemen mount the servants' mules—sometimes the Children—
sometimes all walk."[6]

They reached Paris on February 9, 1780, and the boys were
promptly placed at Monsieur Péchigny's school in Passy, which
Benny had attended. One month later, after a euphoric Sunday
dinner with the young generation, Franklin reported to Boston
that Sammy appeared to be "a very pretty promising Lad." In
the high-flown tone he generally reserved for the Reverend
Samuel Cooper, Franklin added: "If God spares his Life, [he]
may make a very serviceable Man to his Country."[7]

When Adams left for Holland in July, taking his sons along,
Sammy remained in Franklin's sole care. While still showing
great proficiency in his learning, the "dear pledge," as his
grandfather called him, was becoming restless by the year's
end: "The Master and Mistress complain of his being turbulent
and factious, and having in him too much of the Insurgent. I
give him occasionally my best Advice and hope those little
Unpleasantnesses will by degrees wear off."[8]

Best advice, however, was of no greater use then than it is
now. Within a week, a note of perplexity creeps into Franklin's
style: Sammy now wants a room and a fireplace to himself—
at an extra cost of three hundred pounds a year! Should the

additional burden be placed on his father's or grandfather's shoulders without their expressed consent? Besides, the school in Paris is good but not necessarily the best. Two years earlier, "intending him for a Presbyterian and a Republican," Franklin had sent his own grandson Benny to the Geneva College, founded by Calvin in 1559. This choice had probably been inspired by a fellow diplomat, Philibert Cramer, who represented the Republic of Geneva in Paris. A charming, witty man, nicknamed "The Prince" by Voltaire, whose publisher he was, and in whose house he often acted in plays, Cramer had taken charge of the ten-year-old Benny. They had traveled together most pleasantly, but Benny had been crushed when, within days of their arrival, his new mentor had suddenly died. He was then entrusted to both Cramer's widow and M. Gabriel Galissard de Marignac, one of the regents (as the teachers were called) of the Geneva College. The "Compagnie des Pasteurs," a clerical group that reviewed the regents' performance every year, always gave M. de Marignac glowing reports. Benny boarded with him. Even the French nobility, Franklin now explained to Cooper, often chose Geneva for their sons, in the belief that there the education was better and morals of young men more vigilantly safeguarded than in Paris. He might visit his grandson in the spring and, if Cooper approved, take Sammy along.

Franklin never went to Geneva, but Sammy's father turned up in Passy in March 1781 with the intention of establishing commercial connections with France. He could not have chosen a worse moment. The French merchants who had so eagerly rushed supplies to the *insurgents* were now shocked by the discovery that they would be paid at best in frightfully depreciated currency, at worst not at all. Having volunteered these and other warnings to Johonnot *père* (who proved no more receptive to good advice than Johonnot *fils*), Franklin felt that he could not refuse him a letter of introduction to Jonathan Williams Jr., his Bostonian grandnephew who was then a merchant in Nantes. Poor Williams would live to lament the problems that the Johonnots, father and son, created for him.

M. Johonnot had brought Samuel Cooper's and his own consent to the dispatching of Sammy to Geneva. On his way to the new school in September, the boy had a very pleasant stay in Lyons, where he was warmly received by a friend of Franklin's friends, M. Guillaume Jaume. By mid-October, Sammy had communicated his safe arrival in Geneva.

If Franklin thought he had now taken care of all his educational responsibilities, he was mistaken. The very week that Sammy reached his new school, Robert Morris, the Revolution's financier, was thinking Franklin and Geneva. Worried that his two elder sons, Robert Jr. and Thomas, were not getting a good education in their own country—what with lucrative war employment luring teachers away—he determined to send them abroad. "Geneva," he wrote, "has the reputation of good schools . . . Doctor Franklin fixed my faith when he placed a favorite grandson there."[9]

Ironically, by the time the Morris boys arrived in France, John Adams was having second thoughts about the value of a European education. His younger son, Charles, often sick, had been sent home because, as his father put it, he had "too exquisite a sensibility for Europe." Writing to Abigail, Adams proclaimed: "Every child ought to be educated in his own country"; moreover, "education is better at Cambridge than in Europe."[10] He expressed regret that John Quincy was missing that chance. Barely fourteen, John Quincy had been dispatched to Russia in 1781 to serve as private secretary and French interpreter to Francis Dana, who had hoped—in vain—to be accredited as American minister to St. Petersburg. Adams, of course, must have been perfectly aware that only by learning French in France could John Quincy have enjoyed such an early start in the diplomatic career; in any case, after his return from Russia, he would still be young enough to go to Harvard.

How the restless Sammy, now cooped up in righteous Geneva, must have envied John Quincy, only a few months older than himself, his real job in the real world! On November 20, 1781, a few weeks after young Johonnot's arrival, M. de Marignac sent Franklin a worried appraisal of the new student's personality: an intelligent youngster, no doubt, who knew how to reason clearly and well, but did not always act accordingly; a bright fellow who had unfortunately adopted the mannerisms and boastful chatter of the undesirable people he had kept company with; a scatterbrain who had lost all his money on the way. Still, the boy had a sense of humor, and there was hope that good advice would improve his behavior.[11]

On that very day, however, a letter from Lyons revealed that Sammy had been quietly plotting with his former host, M. Jaume, to get himself sent back to France. At the boy's request, Jaume sent Franklin the prospectus of a military academy at Ecully, near Lyons, whose curriculum offered mathematics and philosophy, several varieties of physics, natural history, rhetoric, mythology, commerce, virtues (indeed, commerce and virtues side by side), Latin, Italian, English, heraldry and spelling, catechism and fencing, dancing and drawing, plus the free exercise of the Protestant religion—all for one hundred pounds a year, including hair powder and pomade. Quite a well-rounded education, with the extra advantage of being at the same school as Jaume's own son. Sammy's father seemed inclined to let the boy transfer. What did Franklin think?[12]

Franklin replied politely, asking for further details, but concluding that since Johonnot *père* had not given any specific new instructions after being shown the prospectus, he would rather leave Sammy in Geneva. Samuel Cooper, back in Boston, was "a zealous Protestant Minister," and there was reason to fear that educating his grandson among Catholics would give him pain.[13] The reverend's possible distress obviously carried much more weight with Franklin than Gabriel Johonnot's vague desire to please his son.

Sammy, who shared with his father a talent for writing the politest letters imaginable, giving profuse thanks for advice he had no intention of following, composed a meek and grateful New Year's message to placate Franklin, while renewing his secret efforts to get away. But when a second letter from the ever-obliging Jaume revealed that the plan was now to take Benny along to the Ecully Academy, Franklin sent Sammy, that would-be corrupter of his own hitherto placid grandson, a blast on the evil consequences of switching schools. Though addressed to "my dear young friend," the warning was more peremptory than the language a modern academic adviser would ever dream of using:

> I hope you will . . . not indulge any Fancies of Change. It is time for you to think of establishing a Character for manly Steadiness, which you will find of great Use to you in Life. The Proverb says wisely, *A rolling Stone gathers no Moss.* So in frequent changing of Schools, much time is lost, before the Scholar can be well acquainted with new Rules and get into the Use of them. And Loss of Time will to you be a Loss of Learning. If I had not a great Regard for you, I should not take the Trouble of advising you.[14]

Did Franklin stop a moment to reflect that he had done a lot of rolling in his own youth, from Boston to Philadelphia to London and back, before gathering any moss? Or that no amount of paternal counsel could have dissuaded him from breaking free at seventeen? No, he preferred to remember his own epic struggle to acquire the education that poverty had denied him and to marvel at the luck of those children who had it all offered to them.

One person was made happy by Sammy's enforced stay at the Geneva College: Benny Bache. For two lonely years, he had been the only American child at the school, isolated to the point of forgetting his native tongue. Nobody ever came from Paris to visit, nor was he ever taken away for vacation. Communication with his parents in Philadelphia, slow and precarious at best, was made more difficult still by his use of French, which they did not know at all and was a source of frustration for them. Like Gabriel Johonnot, though for other reasons, Richard and Sally Bache had yielded their parental authority to the grandfather. And Franklin, plunged in the business of his mission, could do little more than send affectionate messages replete with praise for industry and frugality, the prevailing motto of colonial America. Benny kept asking in vain for Willy, his younger brother, to be sent over to join him (his other siblings, born after his departure, were mythical figures to whom he sent stilted professions of love). A stoic little boy, determined not to disturb his illustrious grandfather's peace of mind, Benny was drifting into an emotional apathy that had the kindly, Russian-born Mme Wesselow-Cramer quite worried.[15]

But now, in the fall of 1781, not only did the wonderfully mischievous Johonnot arrive, but also a boy called Robert Montgomery, whom Benny joyfully described as "my oldest friend from Philadelphia"—a touching statement from one who had left Philadelphia at the ripe age of seven.[16] The unusual side of this new boy was that his destiny was not entrusted to a father or a grandfather but to his widowed mother, Dorcas Montgomery. A lady of ample means, she had appeared in Paris that summer and requested Franklin's advice on her son's education. He had directed her, of course, to M. de Marignac.[17]

M. de Marignac and Mrs. Cramer, between them, kept

Franklin well informed of Benny's welfare. When political trouble started brewing in Geneva in the spring of 1781, they both promptly assured him that foreigners were in no peril. To be on the safe side, M. de Marignac had rented a house in the country and took Benny there at night.[18] So Franklin had no qualms about directing Mrs. Montgomery and her son to Geneva. But as soon as the lady had finally settled down to her satisfaction and declared that Geneva was "undoubtedly a very proper place for education," the troubles did, indeed, gain in intensity—so much so that the man in charge of the Morris boys, Matthew Ridley, upon reaching Paris in December 1781, did not dare send them into that hot spot but chose to keep them in a French boarding school.[19] When Robert Morris, back in Philadelphia, learned of this, he was exasperated at the thought that he was wasting his money and the time and republican virtue of his "poor little fellows."[20] In Europe, the alarm was widespread. A friend living in Bordeaux inquired worriedly about Benny's safety because he had heard that some students had been killed.[21] For a while Franklin did consider taking Benny out of school and sending him to Cheam in England, one more proof that wars were less "total" than today.

On a much smaller scale, the Geneva problems were a preview of the French Revolution. Theoretically a democratic republic, the fatherland of Rousseau was in fact ruled by a two-tiered oligarchy of birth and wealth, the *représentants* and the *négatifs*, the latter so called because they had veto power over the *représentants*. Although Rousseau's works were officially banned, his ideas had made such headway among the *représentants* that they ordered the enfranchisement of the mass of the population. This provoked the vehement opposition of the *négatifs*, which in turn touched off open insurrection and fighting in the streets. The leaders of the aristocracy were deported, and in April 1782, a committee of safety with dictatorial powers took over the government of the city, to the distress of France, Piedmont, and the Republic of Bern, which had long exercised a joint protectorate over Geneva. Much as the three powers disliked and distrusted each other, they feared still more the spread of radical ideas. All three sent sizable contingents to reverse the revolution. After a short resistance, the insurgents surrendered, the city was occupied by foreign troops, and the old rulers were restored.

All this was capital fun for the boys. In spite of official reassurances, the school virtually stopped functioning during those tumultuous months. Under Sammy's influence, Benny, that withdrawn "good" boy whose greatest achievement had been to win a Latin prize, rapidly woke up to the joys of life and mischief. His hitherto dull and repetitive letters began to crackle with the words "je m'amuse." He, who hardly ever dared ask for anything, dares to hint that a raise in allowance for Sammy and himself would be most welcome. He wheedles some books out of his grandfather, though not the gold watch for which he yearned. The diary he started in the summer of 1782 bubbles with his and Sammy's enterprises: together they go spelunking and stumble upon a terrified fugitive—a freethinker, they surmise; take part in an anti-dog expedition in the course of which Benny's coat is torn; and decide to kill a cat— in the vague hope that it will be the guilty party who had snatched Benny's guinea pig, but ready to wreak vengeance on any cat (how appropriate that the theme of their assignment for the following day is repentance!). Together they witness nasty incidents between the inhabitants and the occupying forces, watch reviews and parades, observe an execution by firing squad, see a spectacular fire, marvel at the magician Pinetti and at a very dirty giant, help pick grapes, collect butterflies, have a close look at a famished wolf, experience their first dance (awful), their second (not so bad), and their third (almost fun).[22]

None of this, of course, is related to Franklin. He receives only the dullest, most repetitive, pious and perfunctory messages replete with good wishes, good intentions, and the mention of prizes to be received—mostly by Sammy, who is by far the better student. The Coopers, back in Boston, were less well treated. In the fourteen months that followed Sammy's arrival in Geneva, they heard from him only once (some letters, of course, may have miscarried), and what they received, to judge from their reaction, must have been a gloomy picture of both the situation in Geneva and their hero's plight. Samuel Cooper's answer to his grandson, written the day after Christmas 1782, is the first of the new Yale documents. Even when addressing one he loved so much, Cooper obviously found it difficult to step down from the pulpit; his letter, sprinkled with Latin quotations, reads rather like a sermon. "Much of our hopes," he concludes, "much of our comfort is wrapped up in you. Do us honour and make us happy."[23]

Still, one paragraph must have made Sammy's heart jump: it told him that his father was about to sail from Baltimore to France once again. To pick him up, perhaps, and take him home? Yes, to take him home, promised Mrs. Hixon, the sister of Sammy's late mother, who strangely enough addresses Sammy as "brother," not "nephew." Obviously alarmed by what she had heard in Boston, she questions him anxiously about his boils and his "air of malincholy." No rival of her father's in the art of homiletics, she offers only one lame consolation: "we all have our troubles and it is what we must expect in this life."[24]

A third letter in the Yale acquisition—an undated, tattered one by Johonnot *père*—shows, as usual, quite a gap between

what he proposes to do and what he actually does. It turns out
that he cannot possibly come to France. This is not his fault, of
course, but a consequence of the soon-to-be-declared peace.
Having brought back from France a large amount of goods, he
now finds himself unable to dispose of them. He hopes nevertheless that Sammy will keep up his spirits. In a separate
letter to Franklin, Johonnot specifies that he wants his son
taken out of school and dispatched to Boston as soon as possible. Knowing how little credit he enjoys (Jonathan Williams, to
whom he had left a power of attorney, was at his wits' end about
ways of pacifying his creditors and untangling his affairs),
Johonnot adds that Samuel Cooper is looking forward to the
boy's return "with no small anxiety."[25]

Indeed, though he never mentioned it to his grandson,
Cooper was seriously ill. He wrote to Franklin that in case his
son-in-law could not make good on his pledge to bear the expenses of Sammy's voyage, since he had "met with some embarrassment in his affairs," he would take care of them himself. With unusual, poignant urgency, he stressed how much
he was longing to embrace his grandson, adding that he had
seen to it that a Harvard A.B. degree would be conferred on
Sammy at the next commencement.[26] For a man with his Harvard connections, that should not have been too difficult to
arrange.

Long before these messages arrived, Franklin had sum-
moned both boys back to Paris, for he had been jolted out of his
complacency by an alarming letter from one Robert Pigott.
The leftist descendant of an ultra-conservative English family,
a rich, eccentric man who loved to bet, who campaigned for
vegetarianism and against hats, Pigott, expecting England's total ruin, had left his vast estates at the onset of the American
war and had settled near Geneva. His name appears several
times in Benny's diary, always as the host who graciously enter-

tained Sammy and himself in his sumptuous villa, the domaine de Penthes.[27] Benny had met the duke of Gloucester there, King George's own brother, and had been disappointed by the simplicity of his outfit and of his horse's accoutrements. A friend of Voltaire and a would-be friend of Franklin, whom he admired, Mr. Pigott had constituted himself the boys' protector. While stressing the vast difference in the two boys' temperaments, he compared them to two young plants who were sure to bear good fruit when transplanted to their native soil.[28]

In June 1783, out of the blue, Pigott warned Franklin that all was not well at M. de Marignac's. Benny, he said, had been prey for some time to a fever "to be attributed to his unhealthy dwelling, improper diet and ignorance on the part of his tutors. His apartment is in no respect better than that of a prisoner, it is so confined with walls, included in a little alley, and so crowded with other contemporaries who sleep in the same chamber that it would be almost a miracle that he should escape some pestilential disorder. . . . In regard to his learning, I wish it to be of such quality and degree as to answer your expectations . . . but every Telemachus has a need of a Mentor."[29] And so, shortly after the Morris boys had finally arrived in Geneva and been enrolled at the academy there, Benny and Sammy left the city, July 9, 1783, and reached Paris ten days later.

What a time to be in Paris, the summer of 1783! It was the season of the first balloons. In early June, the Montgolfier brothers had launched into the Lyons sky their paper-lined linen balloon, and the capital, with mounting frenzy, was clamoring for an encore in Paris, where such feats belonged. As the second ascent was being prepared, it was rumored that a rival physicist, Jacques Charles, was also preparing to defy gravity by using a different technique. Which one would succeed first? How? When?[30]

Is it any wonder that Sammy, finally free, resisted being rushed off to Boston by the earliest conveyance? In spite of Franklin's urging him to book a seat on the first diligence to the coast, he stayed in Paris until at least August 4. We know this because a note written that day to Benny by the philosopher Lebègue de Presle, giving him an appointment to visit the Royal Library, is among the documents included in the lot acquired by Yale. The boys, presumably, mixed up their papers at the moment of parting.[31] Sammy had certainly gone by August 10, for on that day Benny sent him a list of the objects he has left behind: a shirt, a handkerchief, a bottle of resin, a bottle of varnish. Benny has dreamed that Sammy is married: "Tell me if it is true." He also reports swimming across the Seine, shows off a little Latin, jokes in the manner of a fourteen-year-old writing to a fifteen-year-old, and announces in a postscript that John Quincy Adams is back in Paris.[32]

Sammy had tarried too long. In a terse letter from Nantes on August 13, Jonathan Williams announces that young Cooper had missed by two days the last New England–bound vessel of the year. The only chance to get him across the ocean without an enormous delay is to put him on board the ship sailing to Philadelphia, "and as his father is in Baltimore he may as well be there as anywhere else, though I believe it would be better for the lad in a moral view if he was fatherless." The price of the passage, unfortunately, is "extravagant" (six hundred livres tournois), but cheaper in the long run than keeping the boy in France.[33]

Writing to Franklin the following day, Sammy glosses over the dire consequences of his dawdling and disingenuously talks about sailing to Philadelphia on the *Comte d'Estaing*, "as there is no vessel here bound to the northward." In the meantime, he is busy perfecting his handwriting under the watchful eye of Mr. Williams. Never one to stint on kind words, he ends

with a flourish: "Penetrated with the highest sense of gratitude, I have the honour of subscribing myself with submission
and esteem your most humble servant."[34]

Franklin was not taken in. Infirm, racked by gout and kidney stones, wondering whether he would live long enough to
see his homeland and his other grandchildren again, he was
more in sympathy with the mental agony of his old friend in
Boston than with Sammy's taking his good time. Yet the tone
of his reply—the most moving among the newly discovered
documents—is gentle:

> If you had gone in the first Diligence after you came here, as I
> directed . . . you would have been in Nantes in time to go in
> that vessel which sail'd but two days before you got there . . .
> and might now have been far on your Voyage, and have saved
> your Father all the expense of your waiting for the Phila-
> delphia Ship, and of the journey from there to Boston, which
> your wilfulness must now cost him. You are yet too young to
> reject safely the Advice of your Friends. You should continue
> to comply with it till you are wiser, which I doubt not you will
> be in time. In hopes of which I am still your affectionate
> Friend.[35]

Sammy's answer was, of course, all contrition. He acknowl-
edged his fault with sorrow. "However 'twill be a lesson for me
and I have already profited of it." He had to keep his letter
short, for he was leaving for Saint-Nazaire, thence to sail soon,
and once again expressed his repentance.[36]

In the meantime, Sammy had been engaged in a facetious
correspondence with his long-time friend John Quincy Adams,
whose two letters to him, dated August 25 and 31, 1783, are
fascinating. They reveal a poetic, eager, almost tender John
Quincy, such a far cry from the tormented, dour man the sixth
president of the United States was to become. He was sixteen
at the time, had shown his mettle in Russia working at a man's

job, had known hardship and loneliness, had laid the basis for his future great work on weights and measures, and yet he writes as gushingly as a schoolboy with a crush: "Dear Sam! Ay, and I don't read another letter of your's if it don't begin *dear Jack,* . . . you have not sent me a copy of your Journal thro' the icy hills, I will take no such an excuse as that you have not time, why Lord bless me! not time to copy a few pages for your friend?"[37]

After a roundup of the whereabouts of their fellow passengers on the *Sensible,* not forgetting the manservants, he launches into one of the anti-European tirades that will be so characteristic of his later life:

> I am almost tired also of this part of the world, Europe is composed of
> > "Nations of slaves with Tyranny debased
> > Their Maker's Image more than half defaced."
> Ours is the only country where *man* conserves his dignity. *A propos,* by my next I will send you a copy of a pretty ode upon that subject.

He then begs Sammy to send him poetry, his own or someone else's, "for I am in love with Poetry altho' a poor hand at it myself. But hoyty toyty! You talk of your first letter from America; I hope I shall have some more before you leave Europe; you don't renounce me, I hope. Let your letters be of 3 pages or 12, the longer the better. But mercy upon us! It is 1 o'clock, I wish you *a hundred thousand* times good night, and remain toujours à vous. JACK"[38]

John Quincy's second letter contains two momentous pieces of news: the first balloon flight over Paris and the imminent signature of the peace treaty. But the boyish John Quincy, in love with poetry, starts off with poetry—and a display of his agility in French and English. He has had *une idée:* "It is to establish a kind of litterary [sic] correspondance [sic], and to send one another all the *Nouveautés* which fall under our Eye, which should deserve the attention of an *Amateur*. What do you say to my project? Either I don't know you, or you will find it *charmant*. I have already begun, and the first letter you receive from me, after your arrival in our dear country, will contain several pretty pieces of poetry, which I believe will be new to you. If you don't like my proposition (but I think you will) or if you are too lazy to keep up to it (I hope not) only write me so, and then all will be done and we will be *toujours bons amis*." On the approaching peace, John Quincy writes: "Well, the Definitive Treaty, according to all accounts is to be signed within a short time, and then I suppose I shall decamp from Paris: Lord knows where." Finally, the balloon. The brainchild of Charles, it had soared up from the Champ de Mars on August 23, its oiled silk gleaming in a downpour, kept in the air for a full forty-five minutes by the hydrogen it carried, sailing ten miles in the sky before landing in the village of Gonesse, whose terror-stricken inhabitants promptly destroyed it with pitchforks. In John Quincy's words:

You can't conceive how it has set the imaginations of the Parisians at work. They say, oh—voila qui est bien—mais—... à quoi cela peut-il être bon? Then, (french fashion) they answer themselves: peut-être qu'on pourra voyager dans l'air avec ça; oui, mais ce ne serait pas moi qui voudrait être le premier qui essayerait.—Non, ni moi non plus. Mais comment gouverner cela? Ça serait un peu difficile, ça. Cependant, on pourra trouver manière.—Ah—le tems fera voir— and then they say how drole it would be to see ships sailing thro' the air: cannonading, battles &c. &c. &c. but I believe I shall tire you by my *babil* altho' I have a hundred thousand [things?] to say to you yet. And so good night.
    Yours

	Jack	J.Q.A.
	jacky!	alias
		Jack.[39]

Point and counterpoint. The old men, longing for a last embrace, feel a dreadful hurry. The young ones are joking and taking their time.

It is tempting to stop the story at this point and to imagine the lovely cake that grandmother Cooper baked, as promised, for Sammy's return, or to picture the joy of the grandfather, who had exclaimed: "I shall receive you to my arms and to my care with the highest pleasure." But the truth is that the ship Sammy finally boarded in mid-September took a full three months to reach Baltimore.[40]

While Sammy was at sea, his grandfather's messages turned frantic. "I am anxious for my dear Boy and most ardently wish for his return." He had not heard from Sammy's father in months but knew that his affairs were in bad shape. In what was to be his last letter to Franklin, Samuel Cooper scrawled: "I never in all my life wrote a letter with half the difficulty of this . . ." Franklin tried to calm his fears: "All the Vessells that left Europe for America about the time he did, have had long Passages." He reported without comment that Sammy's father, indeed, had never sent the money for the young man's return.[41]

The last of the new documents is a letter from Judge James Sullivan, one of Boston's top citizens. Dated December 17, 1783, it urges Sammy to waste no time if he wishes to see his grandfather: "He is now in a bed of languishment from which he will recover if the tears and prayers of his numerous friends can restore him." Several gentlemen, apprised of the situation, would help Sammy on his way. This appeal was unfortunately mailed to Philadelphia, whereas Sammy was relaxing with his father in Baltimore. The endorsement in his hand tersely notes: "Never reached me."[42]

Had Sammy rushed to Boston, he would have made it. But he did not arrive until January 12, 1784—fourteen days after his grandfather's death. "I acknowledge the fault. It will not bear reflection: may the lesson prove as useful as 'tis severe." After this outburst of remorse (or was it pseudo-remorse?), he turned his thoughts rather contentedly to the future: "I expect to study 12 or 13 months, as a graduate, at Harvard College, then to enter Judge Sullivan's Office as a Candidate for the Bar. My honoured Grandpappa has left Me one third of his estate, the income of which will, it is expected, with Oeconomy, compleat my Education and at 21, set me out handsomely in the world."[43]

What, one wonders, happened to those various American boys so briefly and intimately glimpsed in their mid-teens as they were moved over the map, at once held on a tight leash and left to fend for themselves? Did they live to become the kind of adults that their adolescent personalities seemed to foretell?

Benny, the placid one, remained obedient long enough to become a printer according to his grandfather's wishes. But a few months after Franklin's death in 1790, he launched into the most radical journalism of his day and disproved the opinion of Mme Wesselow-Cramer, who had judged him too aloof.[44]

Robert Montgomery, his mother's darling, broke her heart by eloping at seventeen with Mr. Pigott's daughter. Believing her son to have been kidnapped by the Pigotts, Mrs. Montgomery, in the middle of the night, roused the authorities in Pisa where the "abduction" had taken place. In vain. Later, she called upon Jefferson, then minister in Paris, to arbitrate in money matters so that her son's capital at least would not be swallowed up in the venture. Jefferson obliged.[45]

As for John Quincy Adams, caught here in a juvenile, jovial mood, he had but three years to go before turning inward and becoming the stiff, solemn figure of his historical persona.

And Sammy himself, the unreliable one, the boy who had

managed to slip through the web of good advice woven by Benjamin Franklin and John Adams, by the Reverend Samuel Cooper and Monsieur de Marignac? He proceeded, straight as an arrow, to obtain his law degree, clerk for Judge Sullivan, and settle in Portland, Maine, as a lawyer. (His father remained true to form and was referred to by Franklin's sister as "that vagabond and bankrupt.")[46] In 1791, Sammy went off to British Guiana, became a vice counsel, and died there in 1806. How some of his papers landed in Scotland is still a mystery. His greatest contribution to history may well be that during his early days in Geneva he met an older boy about to run away and try his luck in the New World. Sammy asked his grandfather to help the immigrant and indeed Samuel Cooper did, finding him a job at Harvard to teach French. That adventurous young Genevan's name was Albert Gallatin.

PART II

Enigmas and Tricks

5

The Man Who Frightened Franklin

MY INVOLVEMENT with this bizarre episode proceeded backwards. Since my work entails almost exclusively transcribing and interpreting documents in French, my first inkling of a potential story came from the Truffé letter that appears toward the end of the essay. There was something so poignant about that letter that my curiosity was piqued, as it always is when I sense a human drama buried among the commercial, legal, diplomatic, or purely routine topics that constitute the bulk of the Franklin Papers. What kind of a husband would abandon a wife and baby in such a callous way—penniless, in a foreign country?

The only clue was his name: Allaire. I looked it up in every index I could think of, with the help of Martha Toll, a Yale student who worked with us as an intern and became as excited as I was during the search. Finally, we put together the case against Peter Allaire. (Martha is now a lawyer.)

I decided to tell the story in the way it had unfolded for me, step by step. Professional historian that he was, my husband advised me to begin at the beginning and stick to chronology. I rebelled at what I thought would be a flat presentation, but after a number of history periodicals rejected my paper, I wrote it sequentially, if only to show him that even that way my poor story did not stand a chance. It was immediately accepted by the *Pennsylvania Magazine of History and Biography* 106, no. 4 (October 1982). Guess who gloated.

The only significant difference between the following essay and my original text is the identification of the French Allaire, Julien-Pierre, which was sent to me by a Parisian friend.

Franklin professed to be casual about spies. Shortly after he had settled in Paris in the early days of 1777, a woman friend warned him that he was surrounded by them. He replied flippantly that since he was not planning to do anything reprehensible, he did not care. "If I was sure . . . that my Valet de Place was a Spy, as probably he is, I think I should not discharge him for that, if in other Respects I liked him."[1] Though the French police kept a close watch on Franklin, the threat to his mission did not come from them. It came from the Paris network of British intelligence—a network made up mostly of Americans.

Franklin went to his grave without knowing that Paul Wentworth, the wealthy and suave émigré from New Hampshire, ran that network; nor did he ever discover the identity of several Americans who worked for Wentworth, a few ship captains among them. Still worse, he never suspected that his secretary and confidant, the Massachusetts-born Edward Bancroft, an old friend of Wentworth (they had met in Suriname, Dutch Guiana), had been industriously betraying the American cause from the very start. Bancroft also double-crossed his English masters, but that did not make up for the losses in American lives caused by his treachery, not to mention captured cargoes and delays in sorely needed military supplies. None of these informers was unmasked until historians, one century later, gained access to the files of the Public Record Office in London.

Given all of this intrigue, it is strange that the only character who ever alarmed Franklin himself, a man named Peter Allaire, has not been seriously investigated. Julian Boyd, it is true, had his suspicions, but he was not in possession of most of the evidence presented below, pieced together from a number of individually cryptic but cumulatively impressive scraps of information. Actually, to say that Allaire "alarmed Franklin" is an understatement. The Doctor believed the man had tried to kill him and had Allaire promptly turned over to the police, who delivered him to the tender mercies of the Bastille.

Who was Peter Allaire? Born around 1740 to a French Protestant family that had established itself at the end of the seventeenth century in the Huguenot settlement of New Rochelle, near New York, he led an adventurous life in international commerce. He purveyed wheat and rice to the French troops in Guiana, sold cannon and cloth in Morocco, traded on the Barbary Coast, in Spain and Jamaica, and traveled to Russia more than once. Based in London since 1776, he shuttled freely and frequently between England and France, even after hostilities broke out. Such liberty of movement, unthinkable in wartime today, was common in the eighteenth century. And it supplied excellent opportunities for an enterprising man to smuggle information as well as merchandise in one direction—or in both.[2]

Possibly introduced by Bancroft, Allaire got in touch with Franklin quite early in 1777 and offered his services as an American agent in London. Even though Franklin was meeting large numbers of new people during his first spring in France, the merchant must have felt that he had made enough of an impact not to have to sign his subsequent message (August 26) more explicitly than "An American whom you have met in Paris." The handwriting is unmistakably Allaire's. He wrote about the likelihood of insurrection in Britain and the growing friction between Prime Minister North and Lord Germain, secretary of state for the colonies. His letter consisted more of wishful thinking than hard facts.[3]

By May 22, 1778, Allaire's role as a shuttling intelligence agent seemed established. Just landed in Calais, he sent Franklin some English newspapers and sketchy information about the movements of British ships. Boulogne, where he was headed next, was such a notorious hotbed of espionage that the French police allowed no unauthorized person to remain there longer than twenty-four hours.

A year later, in May 1779, Allaire made a proposal that combined patriotism and business: would Franklin be interested in purchasing a huge quantity of the late Dr. James's fever powder "so well known all over Europe," which he could offer at a very attractive discount, thanks to a deal with a disgruntled former employee of the inventor? The powder, he stressed, could "be of Infinite service to the fleets and Armies of America."[4] In fact, the whitish chemical patented by Dr. James in 1747—based on a mixture of phosphate of lime and oxide of antimony— was much appreciated: Samuel Johnson, James Boswell, and Horace Walpole extolled its virtues; Mme du Deffand used it; and the royal doctors prescribed it to George III.[5]

We now know (but Franklin did not) that Allaire's partner in this business was the Scot Samuel Swinton, and that Swinton, like Bancroft, was a double agent.[6] Allaire enclosed two ounces of the fever powder for Franklin's inspection, offering to ship it in bulk to Calais. But Franklin was not in the habit of buying anything not specifically requested by Congress, and his carefully kept accounts of purchases have no entry concerning the fever powder.

Seven months later (January 31, 1780), Allaire, back in
Paris, forwarded a copy of an important document that Franklin had not yet seen: William Eden's *Letters to Carlisle*, the
report of one of the English commissioners on their failed
diplomatic efforts to make peace with the American colonies.
He also sent a bottle of old Madeira, the Doctor's favorite wine.
This time he attracted Franklin's attention, but not in the
way he had hoped. On February 14, Allaire addressed a short
note to William Temple Franklin requesting a passport for
Brussels, where he proposed to go the following day. "Do you
choose to grant his request?" scribbled young Franklin at the
bottom of the note. The grandfather's answer: a terse, cap-
italized "NO." Temple's expansion of this monosyllable was
just as blunt: "My Grandfather to whom I have made known
your request of a passport for Brussels does not choose to
comply therewith."

The next episode is told in Allaire's own voice. Many years
after the fact, he wrote a memoir about the ordeal he under-
went, but he did not complete it. In 1907, the unfinished manuscript was found in a drawer by a Dr. Wood. Without understanding what all this was about, Dr. Wood published the
account.[7]

In what is obviously a self-serving version of the events,
Allaire recounted how, on the day after Franklin's curt refusal of
a passport, he was breakfasting in his room at the Hôtel de Saxe
when "at eleven o'clock in the morning, two gentlemen called
upon me and, after the usual compliments . . . told me they had
an order from the Government to seize and examine all my
papers." The search lasted two hours and yielded nothing. The
gentlemen then asked him politely to step into their coach.
Always treated with the utmost courtesy, he was shuttled all day
long from one police commissioner to the next, winding up in
the office of Jean-Charles Pierre Lenoir, the head of the Paris

police. Told at last that no damaging evidence had been found against him but that his papers, being in English, would have to be examined at leisure, he was driven back. Not to his lodgings, however. "The coach stopping, the officer called out loudly: 'Put down the bridge by order of His Majesty the King.' The truth then dawned upon my bewildered mind that I was to be confined in that horrible prison known as the Bastille."

The guards on duty were equally courteous, but Allaire found himself locked up, alone and terrified—still ignorant, he said, of the crimes he was charged with. Nothing happened for the next ten days, while he listened to the clanking of chains down the corridor. His requests for communicating with Franklin or anyone else on the outside were ignored. Finally he was led to a large room where he saw two prison officials and two men dressed in black like chemists.

> They then proceeded to produce the bottle of wine that I had sent Dr. Franklin and ordered the guard to open it. I asked to look at the seal, which they permitted, but keeping hold of the bottle, I called for a tumbler and when the bottle was uncorked I asked them to fill it, when I drank it off, saying that I did not believe that any man was bad enough to put poison in it. The chemists, not satisfied with this proof, put some into three glasses and were going to put something into one of them with their backs turned to me. I called out I would drink nothing after they had mixed it. The lieutenant-governor then directed the chemists to turn and make their proof before me. Accordingly, one of them dropped about twelve drops of some liquid from a small vial, which turned the Madeira white as milk. I asked them if they were convinced of the goodness of the wine? They answered yes and each drank a glass saying it was excellent. I then desired them to give my compliments to M. Lenoir and Dr. Franklin.

This was not the end of Allaire's captivity. He was shut up for another fifteen days in solitary confinement, without pen, ink, or book, and then was called for questioning once again, in full view "of the larger instruments of torture; the smaller ones I could see placed in closets." In the course of this interrogation, he was informed for the first time that the government suspected him of being a spy for the king of England. He hotly denied the charge, yet was told that the truth about him would be disclosed the following day at noon. Haunted all night by nightmares of the rack, ready to confess anything rather than to submit to torture, he was so weak by morning that he had to be carried to the council chamber. The commissioner was already there. "His manner toward me was changed from the day before, and the sternness of his face had relaxed. He asked me would I swear to the truth of my answers to his questions. I replied willingly. After a long pause, he said: 'As you are an American, you shall have some indulgence, as much as possible. I believe you are not guilty of the charges,' and ordered me shut up again."

So great was Allaire's relief that for a while he found his confinement almost easy to bear. Eventually allowed some books, he chose the plays of Racine and read all the parts aloud as if he were on stage. But despair set in once more. "Weeks and months passed without a single word from the outside world, and I commenced to believe that, like the *Man in the Iron Mask* . . . the world was lost to me."

He was not quite as lost as he feared. On May 15, a Frenchman who was also named Allaire, and who identified himself as "administrateur des domaines du Roi," wrote to Franklin, reminding him of a conversation that they had held previously.[8] On that occasion the French Allaire had pleaded the cause of his American relative, he recalled, and Franklin had replied that nothing could be done as long as Rochambeau's fleet had not sailed from Brest on its way to America. But now, argued the Frenchman, the fleet was on the high seas "well out of reach of our common enemies." Why could his namesake not be allowed to reside in some town other than Paris? Boulogne-sur-Mer, where he had friends, might be just the place. Franklin, he stressed, should not doubt Peter Allaire's loyalty to the American cause; of this the writer, himself a devotee of human liberties and an admirer of the New World, was absolutely sure. The appeal closed with a discreet reminder of the respectable friends that he shared with Franklin in the Parisian scientific community.[9]

The prisoner, meanwhile, unaware that help was on the way, was devising ways to kill time. His narrative breaks off abruptly at this point, and the Dr. Wood who discovered it in 1907 never knew the end of the story. Thanks to the carefully kept records of the Bastille, however, we do. Peter Allaire was let go on May 24, 1780, at 4 P.M., after promising never to reveal anything that he had learned during his incarceration.[10] These records confirm that Allaire had been incarcerated at the Bastille on February 15 through an order signed by its *gouverneur,* Antoine-Jean Amelot de Chaillou. Amelot was a good friend of Franklin, and they often dined together. If any proof were needed of Franklin's clout in French society, this is it, for—contrary to myth—it was far from easy to get someone incarcerated in the Bastille. Not surprisingly, the minutes of Allaire's interrogations say nothing about the unsuccessful test for poison, but they make clear that he was suspected of spying and that he was questioned at length about his business affairs and social encounters in France.

Far from being allowed to reside in Boulogne-sur-Mer, where his partner Swinton was living in grand style and cheerfully dispatching information to both Paris and London, Allaire was expelled from the kingdom via the north. Franklin, whatever his private suspicions, did not tarry after the plea of the French Allaire. Having an American languish in the Bastille *sous inculpation d'espionnage*, as the jail's record put it, did nothing for his country's image.

Two days after his release, Allaire sent the Doctor the following brief note, which can be interpreted as heavy sarcasm, cool control, or both: "I am very sensible of your civilities. I shall take the first opportunity to return them."[11]

Even though Franklin left no comment about this bizarre episode, more light is thrown on it by a careful examination of his papers. If one looks at the first two weeks of February 1780, those that elapsed between Allaire's gift of the suspicious Madeira and his arrest, one finds that whereas Franklin wrote several letters every day from February 1 to 9, he wrote none on February 10 and 11, presumably when he fell ill. He resumed writing on February 12. Moreover, his grand-nephew Jonathan Williams Jr. made a facetious remark some two years later, when he sent a half-pipe of particularly good Madeira to the Doctor: "I hope I shall not get into the Bastille. . . . You may try it out on any dog you please, and were I present, I should have no objection to its being offered to me."[12]

Still later, the story, told in a lighter vein and probably spread by Allaire himself, found its way into an anonymous *American Jest Book.* Some of the details are different. The single bottle, for instance, has become three dozen, but the imprisonment of the donor is there, and it is attributed to the suspicion "that he had been hired by the English Court to poison the doctor who had been taken ill after receiving the present."[13]

It might be hasty to dismiss the episode as just an instance of Franklin's suffering from unwarranted panic. The times were tense. Though poison was no longer the favorite weapon of political plotters, spies have not entirely discarded it even in our own day. That very summer of 1780, General Clinton, British commander-in-chief in America, fancied that he had been the target of attempted poisoning, precisely by arsenic-tainted

Madeira.[14] Madeira is, in fact, an ideal vehicle for concealing foreign substances because of its strong nutty flavor. Arsenic is a close relative of antimony, one of the basic ingredients of Dr. James's fever powder. Bancroft and Swinton, the two double agents whose connections with Allaire are documented, were respectively an expert on poisons and an occasional merchant of wine. Had they, or possibly Allaire, feared that Franklin had suspicions about them, they too might have panicked and turned to their last resort. Finally, Julian Boyd made a plausible case for the hypothesis that Bancroft had poisoned Silas Deane on his way home to America.[15]

Allaire and poison resurfaced in Franklin's life four years later, albeit in an oblique way. In March 1784, after the peace treaty had been signed and the Doctor was awaiting permission to go home, he received a long letter from a French merchant named Truffé (first name unknown). Unlike other merchants, this one was not trying to sell his wares or claim old credits. He was not planning to open an establishment in the New World with Franklin's help, nor pushing any kind of scheme for profit. He was simply trying to help a fellow human being, and his account reads like the opening chapter of a novel.[16]

On a bitterly cold day of January, in the bleak northern French city of Amiens, Truffé had encountered a homeless, friendless, and penniless young woman, listened to her story, and taken pity on her. She was an American, about twenty years old, with a baby in her arms—a beautiful woman, thought Truffé, well-bred, well-educated. Her name was Rebecca Allaire.

As she sat shivering in Truffé's hired carriage, she explained that her husband, Peter Allaire, had sailed for America the previous May, leaving her and the baby in a convent at Armentières with a six-month supply of funds. She had not heard from him since or received any further money. The nuns, having warned her repeatedly that foreigners were not kept unless their board was paid for in advance, had eventually turned her out. Off to Lille she had gone, then to Amiens, in futile search of an Englishwoman who owed her money. Overcharged everywhere, exploited and pushed around, she was at the end of her rope and considered death as the only way out for the child and herself.

Did she know anybody in Paris? asked her new acquaintance. Yes, her husband had a friend in the capital, a fellow American by the name of John Jay. So Truffé brought her to Paris, but Jay was unfortunately out of town. Mrs. Jay played with the baby but was very cool toward the young mother. (Being close friends of Franklin, the Jays might well have heard of the Madeira affair.) Then Truffé, who was anxious to go home after four months on the road, made a bargain for Rebecca with an innkeeper he knew and prepared to take his leave. But seeing his protégée plunged into new depths of despair and remembering how, in Amiens, she had threatened to kill the baby and herself, he asked her how she had planned to do it. She replied that she had arsenic in her possession—a strange commodity, he may have reflected, for a young mother living in a convent. He managed to be present at the opening of her trunk and seized the packet of white powder he saw in it.

On January 12, three days after meeting Rebecca Allaire, Truffé went home, hoping that somebody else would be touched by her plight; but less than two months later, she wrote him that, once more, she was absolutely out of cash and determined to throw the baby and herself into the Seine. Then the good merchant decided that the best course was to explain the situation to Benjamin Franklin, who was not only America's minister plenipotentiary but also the benevolent "papa" to whom all classes of people in distress turned for guidance and comfort.

Whatever his feelings toward the irresponsible husband, Franklin did extend a helping hand to the wife and child. He must have done it through John Jay. For Jay, who had taken no interest in Rebecca so far, now wrote to his brother in New York: "Mrs. Allaire, the wife of Mr. Peter Allaire of New York will be the bearer of this. I found her here in a distressed situation. I have lent her thirty guineas and given her a credit . . . for her passage money and subsistence. Mention this *only* to her husband who I flatter myself will readily reimburse this money."[17] After all, Jay was, like Allaire, a member of a well-known Huguenot family; Rebecca was not for drowning, nor was her little daughter, Cilicia, who grew up and married a Mr. Wood. The genealogy in *La France Protestante* supplies no information on whether or not this Wood was related to George Wood, the publisher of Allaire's account of his incarceration in the Bastille.

Obviously Franklin had no decisive evidence against Allaire. In 1907, however, Frederic Turner published secret reports sent by an American intelligence agent to the English foreign office between 1787 and 1791, long after peace between England and America had been concluded. Turner misread Allaire's initials "P. A." as "R. D.," but Julian Boyd later corrected the reading, identified the sender, and called him a spy.[18] Allaire, in his reports of 1791, stressed the instability of the American government. He urged England to wrest Florida from Spain and hold it "for Ever in spite of Congress and all the world." He also asked the British secretary of war, Sir George Young, to continue the annual salary he had been receiving.

For selling American information to England in peacetime, Allaire was paid two hundred pounds a year. This is exactly the salary that Bancroft had received for selling information to England in time of war. The two men were birds of a feather. Franklin, who never suspected Bancroft, was not mistaken in mistrusting Allaire.

6

Franklin and the Unfortunate Divine

FRANKLIN is not at the center of the two next enigmas. But in both cases, I became so fascinated by the mystery involved and the personality of the main character in them that I tried to learn as much as I could about the events and Franklin's role. To be sure, the rise and fall of the Reverend Dodd has been described more than once, but previous historians were unaware of a relevant document in our treasure trove at Yale, and they did not know that in his hour of crisis, just before the act that would doom him, he had turned to Franklin for help.

The essay I wrote under the title "Benjamin Franklin and William Dodd: A New Look at an Old Cause Célèbre" was published in *Proceedings of the American Philosophical Society* 129, no. 3 (1985): 264–67. Here it is, with only minor stylistic changes.

The public hanging of the Reverend William Dodd in 1777 split popular opinion in England and abroad almost as deeply as the Dreyfus affair would split French and foreign opinion at the beginning of the twentieth century. One of the many petitions to spare Dodd's life, thirty-seven yards long, bore twenty-three thousand signatures, the largest number that had ever been gathered in England. Another was drawn up by the very jury that found him guilty. Dr. Samuel Johnson, who rose to his defense, was certainly no less famous than the champion of Captain Alfred Dreyfus, Emile Zola. What makes the Dodd affair comparable to the Dreyfus affair is the passion and duration of the emotional reaction against what was felt to be a miscarriage of justice. Captain Dreyfus was unquestionably not guilty of treason, however, whereas Dodd had unquestionably committed a forgery.[1] Reminiscing about the case some three months after the parson's death, Johnson is reported by Boswell to have said: "Dr. Dodd's pious friends were trying to console him by saying he was going to leave a wretched world. 'No, no,' said he, 'it has been very agreeable to me.' Dr. Johnson declared that he respected Dodd for thus telling the truth; for, in point of fact, he had for several years lived a life of great voluptuousness."[2]

The hitherto little noticed letter from Dodd to Benjamin Franklin will throw some light on the case, as well as on a distinguished female figure in American education and on an acquaintance of Dodd's who was, let us say, shadowy.

First, a brief account of Dodd's meteoric rise and unexpected downfall. The fate of that seductive, charismatic preacher reminds one of Greek tragedies: he did much good, but his hubris ultimately doomed him. A dynamic philanthropist, Dodd fought smallpox, redeemed prostitutes, helped people who had been jailed for debts, and crusaded against the excessive use of capital punishment. His sermons uplifted the souls of rich and poor, his drive was unflagging, his erudition impressive, his eloquence unequaled in the London of his day. But he was also a vain man, obsessed with mundane goals, forever in pursuit of money or patronage, a womanizer, and a spendthrift with no clear perception of professional behavior.

None of these flaws, however, was conspicuous in his early years. To be sure, he was impulsive. Soon after graduation, he married Mary Perkins, a penniless, low-born, sixteen-year-old actress, who was, rumor had it, the discarded mistress of the earl of Sandwich. Mary may not have been a great credit to her husband, especially after she took to drink, but she proved a devoted wife, loyal to the bitter end. The Reverend Dodd also had his unconventional streak. Consider, for example, his long hikes, always taken along the southern coast of England, in Sussex and Kent, long before the pleasures of beaches had been generally discovered. He walked from inn to inn, occasionally stopping to sketch.

Still, these peculiarities did not interfere with his startling success as a preacher. Most of Dodd's sermons were published hot off the pulpit, especially the ones he delivered at Magdalen House, where rescued child prostitutes—nine to fifteen years old—were sheltered. Horace Walpole has described the scene: modestly clad girls singing so beautifully, "their flat straw hats with a blue ribbon pulled quite over their faces . . . while the young clergyman, one Dodd . . . apostrophized the lost sheep who sobbed and cried for their souls."[3] The sermon was in what Walpole called the French style, so charged with emotion and oratory as to bring Catholicism to mind—a style that antagonized the haters of popery but held a powerful appeal for many otherwise reserved Anglo-Saxons. A single sermon at Magdalen House would often wrench from the fashionable assembly the amazing sum of thirteen hundred pounds. By the age of thirty-five, the indefatigable parson was lecturer at three churches, a frequent preacher at St. Paul's, chaplain-in-ordinary to the king, editor of the *Christian Magazine*—which he wrote practically by himself—and the compiler of a voluminous *Commentary on the Bible.*

Dodd's frivolous side, however, grew apace and was not lost on some contemporaries: he was seen at all the expensive spots in and near London—even at masquerades given by Giacomo Casanova's lady friend—he entertained fashionable women to tea, bought fancy books, published verse at his own expense, purchased a coach, and dressed in silks. A diamond ring and an elegantly waved handkerchief were the pastor's trademarks, along with his good looks, musical voice, fiery manner in church, and easy congeniality in society.

Dodd's expenses mounted, and he ran into debt. Hard-pressed, Dr. Dodd (he had acquired that title at Oxford) assumed still another function: tutor to the children of the nobility. Best known among his pupils was Philip Stanhope, a protégé of the earl of Chesterfield, not the illegitimate son for whose dubious benefit the earl had written the celebrated letters of advice, but the son's namesake, a distant relative. So enthusiastic was the earl about his protégé's tutor that he dubbed him "the best and most eloquent preacher in England, and perhaps the most learned clergyman."[4]

Over the years, however, Dodd's critics sharpened their attacks. The nickname "macaroni parson" began to stick. There were widespread hints of extravagance and of kept women, a devastating profile of the dandy cleric in *Town and Country Magazine,* and finally a dreadful setback. Dodd was accused of having tried to bribe his way into the fattest parish of London, St. George's. He did his best to shift the blame to his wife but was struck off the list of the king's chaplains and ridiculed in the press.

Dodd fled the country. In February 1774, he headed for Geneva, where Philip Stanhope, now himself the earl of Chesterfield, was residing as part of the obligatory grand tour. The former pupil gave his troubled tutor a warm welcome, some money, and the promise of a good parish in England. Buoyed, Dodd took off for Paris, where a stupefied Englishman recognized him out of clerical garb betting at the races and carousing with disreputable companions.

Back in London, it was to be all downhill, and fast—the loss of his position at the Magdalen, the sale of the chapel he had built at his own expense and named Charlotte after the queen, the threat of seeing his furniture sold on the street if his bills were not promptly paid. All this happened while he was still striving to keep up appearances, even taking a quick trip to Paris in the summer of 1776 to arrange for a *de luxe* reprinting of his works, including the first anthology of Shakespeare quotations to suit all purposes (Dodd's idea).

And then, the almost unbelievable act. On February 1, 1777, the Reverend Dodd committed a forgery. It was in the form of a bond for 8,400 pounds, with the counterfeit signature of the young earl of Chesterfield, to be cashed in great secrecy by Dodd, who was supposedly acting as go-between. The ruse worked: Dodd was handed the money, at an exorbitant rate of interest. But within two days, because of a mere technicality (the accident of an ink blot), the earl himself was shown the bond. He disavowed it immediately, and the game was up.

Dodd confessed right away and just as quickly returned almost the entire sum, but Chesterfield decided to prosecute anyway and the wheels of justice started grinding. For the following five months, nothing would stop them. There was no precedent for the hanging of an Anglican minister. The reverend was a first-time offender, abjectly repentant. Not only his faithful core of admirers but even many of his adversaries pleaded for a measure of mercy. Dr. Johnson, who took up the cudgels with all the passion in him in favor of a man he had never met and surely would not have liked, saw to it that a last-minute appeal for a stay of execution was delivered by hand. To no avail. It had not been transmitted, he was told, to the proper authority. Always regarded as an especially heinous crime in England, forgery had been made a capital offense in 1634, without benefit of clergy (that is, even clergy were not exempted from capital punishment). That punishment was hardly worse than the series of mutilations and tortures, followed by life imprisonment, that had been meted out before.

On June 1, 1777, amid a huge concourse of people, silent, with their heads bared—Horace Walpole was there, and Charles James Fox, and the abbé Raynal, and one of the sons of Johann Sebastian Bach—the Reverend William Dodd, age forty-nine, was hanged.

Why did royal justice, defying the mounting revulsion against excessive punishment (Cesare Beccaria's memorable *Dei delitti e delle pene* had appeared thirteen years earlier), rush through the execution of a man who, for a century thereafter, would be generally perceived as "the unfortunate divine" in America as elsewhere? The question has never been answered. Neither has another question, just as puzzling: Why would a man of Dodd's intelligence and stature panic so? Let us have a look at his frantic plea to Franklin.

Buried among the thousands of letters Franklin received, Dodd's desperate appeal, brief as it is, is astonishingly rich in revelations. The pastor's scrawled message bears a striking date: January 29, 1777—three days before the fatal forgery. Thirteen lines in all, fraught with cryptic references, the only extant proof that Dodd and Franklin knew each other, it presents a double challenge since two different topics are dealt with in its single paragraph.

The first sentence has to do with a woman. It reads:

Sir

I make no Apology for troubling you with a request I have heretofore made, of conveying the enclosed letter, if possible, to a worthy young Woman, who in an unfortunate Hour went to America; and to whose fortune and situation there I am a stranger.[5]

Such an impetuous beginning—abrupt for any eighteenth-century writer, and still more so for one as given to stylistic flourishes as Dodd—implies a previous acquaintance, a construction strengthened by the word "heretofore." Franklin must already have forwarded at least one earlier message to the unnamed young woman whom Dodd was thinking about at such a troubled moment of his life. Who was she? What led the distraught pastor to believe that Franklin could help him get in touch with her again?

It so happens that in the last days of 1775 Franklin had taken an unusual step in favor of a young woman who had suddenly and rather mysteriously appeared in Philadelphia with a baby daughter in her arms. Together with the wealthy merchant Robert Morris, he had placed an advertisement in the December 6 issue of the *Pennsylvania Gazette*, informing its readers that "Mrs. Brodeau, from England, takes this Method of acquainting her friends and the Public in general, that she has opened a BOARDING SCHOOL in Walnut-Street, near the Corner of Fourth-Street, where young ladies will be genteely boarded, and taught to read and speak the French and English languages, the Tambour, Embroidery, and every Kind of useful and ornamental NEEDLEWORK." The little piece concluded by asserting that Morris and Franklin would provide information concerning the lady's "Character and Recommendation."[6] This is, so far as we know, the only time that Franklin gave his personal backing to an enterprise of that kind, but two years earlier he had advised another woman, a protégée of his close friends Dr. and Mrs. John Hawkesworth of Bromley (Kent), to open a boarding school for young ladies in America.[7] Dr. Hawkesworth, himself a fairly well known literary figure and an intimate friend of Dr. Johnson, helped his wife run a school for girls in Bromley. Still another coincidence: William Dodd, who is known to have once given a dinner party in honor of Dr. Hawkesworth, also tried to set up a school for young women in Bromley, but that establishment was judged disreputable and had to be closed.[8]

In view of all this, one is led to surmise that Dodd had met Franklin in Bromley on one of Franklin's many visits to Hawkesworth, and that the "young woman" mentioned in Dodd's note was none else but the "Mrs. Brodeau" of the *Pennsylvania Gazette*'s advertisement.

Nothing is known about a Mr. Brodeau—did he ever exist?— but Anna Brodeau, the schoolmistress, certainly proved to be a lady of talent and distinction. When she died, on July 4, 1836, her obituary in the *Washington National Intelligencer* recalled that she had brought letters of recommendation "by persons of the first rank in London to the most prominent families in Philadelphia."[9] Her school thrived. Less than eight years after Franklin's advertisement, Sally Franklin Bache wrote her father that "Mrs. Brodeau . . . has made a handsome fortune."[10] A well-deserved fortune indeed, judging from the rapturous ode by an anonymous poet, published by the *Columbian Magazine*. The opening lines set the tone:

> How sweet the task to teach the infant heart
> The love of virtue and the charms of art!

The poet went on to thank Mrs. Brodeau for having spread culture "where late the savage stray'd—Or lay inglorious in his native shade." The curriculum, he pointed out, not only taught how to curb one's unseemly passions, but also included much

more than the embroidery-centered fare advertised at the
start: painting, literature, music, geography, and science "in
each flow'ry road." The climax was grandiose:

> These are thy charms, Brodeau. Thy studies these:
> O may they long thy gen'rous bosom please,
> Till time unfolds the blessings of thy reign,
> And art and manners to their summit gain;
> Till wisdom's queen shall thee her fav'rite own,
> And place thy name with Genlis and Chapone [11]

No faint praise, this. Mrs. Hester Chapone Munlo (*Letters
on the Improvement of the Mind*, 1786) and Mme Stéphanie-
Félicité du Crest de Saint-Aubain, comtesse de Genlis (*Lettres
sur l'Education*, 1782) were the most celebrated women writers
on female education in those days. Mrs. Brodeau's school
eventually moved to more spacious quarters at Lodge Alley and
attracted students from the best families in Philadelphia.[12] In
1790, her daughter, Anna, married the distinguished inventor
and architect William Thornton, who was to have a part in
designing the new Washington Capitol.[13]

The brilliant headmistress, however, had a skeleton in her
closet. When Anna Thornton, who had arrived in Philadelphia
as a baby, died at ninety on August 18, 1865, the *National Intelligencer* let it be known that the deceased lady, though probably unaware of it, was the daughter of "the unfortunate Dr.
Dodd of London who was executed for forgery in the year
1777," as the late Mr. Thornton himself had once confided to
a friend, one Colonel Bomford. To protect the mother's posthumous reputation, the obituary added that Mrs. Brodeau had
actually married Dr. Dodd but changed her name to Brodeau
after the catastrophe, an obvious misrepresentation since
Mary Perkins Dodd survived her husband by some years, albeit
in a state of insanity.

All the actors were dead, the presumed father was remembered less as an offender than as the victim of cruel punishment, the mother as legitimately wed to him, the unknowing daughter as one who had been accepted in the upper echelons of Washington society. Surely the editors of the journal were not looking for trouble when they printed what must have been whispered for a long time. Yet four days later, they had to publish an indignant rejoinder from "the friends of the late Mrs. Anna M. Thornton." The friends admitted the existence of a rumor that the deceased lady was Dodd's daughter, but ascribed it merely to the silence her mother, Mrs. Brodeau, had always maintained about her past. Since no explanation whatever was offered for Mrs. Brodeau's reticence, the denial is less significant than the admission of the rumor.

My guess is that the reverend, ridden with debts and obsessed by the thought of his lost mistress and baby girl, forged the bond in a desperate attempt to escape to America and use the money to start a new life away from his creditors and his inadequate wife. Franklin might help him do this as he had helped Mrs. Brodeau.

Back to Dodd's brief note of January 29, 1777, to Franklin in Paris. The second part is no less mysterious than the first:

> Anxious for the success of the grand struggle in which you are engag'd, I could have been happy in conversing with you, when I was at Paris; but you was not then arriv'd. If you shou'd see or converse with Mr. Mante who resides at Dieppe, but is frequently in Paris, He knows my sentiments, and wou'd be happy to communicate with you. I am Sir with very great Esteem Your obedient humble Servant
>
> W. Dodd
>
> It is not possible to effect a *reconciliation?* How happy wou'd I be to be any way instrumental in it!

Who was this Mante about whom the reverend thought in his hour of distress, ostensibly as a possible peacemaker between England and America? An entry for Thomas Mante in the British *Dictionary of National Biography* calls him a "military writer [who] described himself as having served as an assistant engineer at the siege of Havana in 1762, and as a major of brigade in the campaigns against the Indians" (though, as the *Dictionary* points out, his name does not appear in any British army list). His most notable work was a *History of the Late War in America,* published in London in 1772 Later, in France, he produced several translations, the latest appearing in 1807, probably after his death. Not a political figure, then, but a seemingly respectable historian and soldier.

Five letters from Mante to Franklin, however, reflect a very different image. All of them are pathetic appeals for money, with the special twist of having been written in France from behind bars.[14] Without context they would fall into the depressing category of the begging letters so abundantly represented among Franklin's papers, but some intriguing light is shed on them by other sources, especially the correspondence of the economist Anne-Robert-Jacques Turgot and the painstaking work done in the French archives by the American scholar Benjamin Franklin Stevens.[15]

The portrait of Mante that emerges is that of a shadowy figure indeed. Ever since 1769 he had been spending most of his time in Dieppe, the Normandy port that the French have always felt, not without reason, to be their most vulnerable spot for a British attack. Within less than one month, in June–July 1774, Mante is glimpsed in two incompatible postures: offering intelligence to John Robinson, British secretary of the Treasury, while pestering him for money; and being highly recommended to the French minister of war as someone who could provide information on a sensitive topic, the possibility of a British raid on Dieppe. The French officer who wrote the secret report about Mante stressed that the Englishman was brilliant but unscrupulous, *sans religion*.[16]

This disquieting character turned up in Paris in November 1776, one month before Franklin's arrival. He offered foreign minister Vergennes some salt purified by a new method that Vergennes, after ordering a chemical analysis, found unpromising.[17]

By January 15, 1777, exactly two weeks before Dodd's cryptic reference, Lord Stormont, the British ambassador in Paris, reported to his court that an English engineer by the name of Mante ought to be watched. He certainly was employed by the French court, but even the king's entourage had their doubts: "they suspect him to be a double spy."[18]

Yet if the French distrusted Mante at that time, they did not show it. One month after Dodd's execution, Mante received French citizenship and the title of comte—or at least so he said. More suspiciously, he was granted the use of some land on the Brittany coast, purportedly to raise three thousand sheep imported from England, their lambs to be sold to the adjacent counties at a preset price. Paul Wentworth, Britain's master spy, worriedly related the information to London, adding that Mante's contact in England was one Hicks, "Keeper of the Old Ship" in Brighton. That very summer, comte de Noailles, the French ambassador in London, was writing back to Vergennes that he felt uneasy about the presence of an Englishman in Dieppe, where Mante ran a business of undisclosed nature. Not to worry, was the minister's prompt reply: "the individual has long been known to me, and just as long held in suspicion."[19]

The next reference to *de* Mante (as he by this point styled himself) probably happened at the end of 1777. Wentworth relates to his superiors that the new count, whom he believes to be protected in England by the duke of Richmond and Lord

Amherst, spends most of his time in Paris; he is convinced that Mante has passed on to the French some maps of the coast of Sussex and Kent.[20] These are to England what Dieppe and Brittany are to France: the most likely targets for an attack from the opposite side of the Channel. They are also the parts of the English coast that Dodd had been sketching, innocently or not, during his lonely hikes.

The "count" did not thrive for long. On March 13, 1778, in great trepidation, he let the duke of Richmond know that the French had arrested him: "A lettre de cachet, my Lord Duke, has fulfilled your prediction."[21] Henceforth, he would insist to the English that the arrest was due to political reasons, but to the French authorities and to Franklin he told a different story. The comte de Boisgelin had made him the manager of a vast tract of land in Brittany. Instead of the three thousand promised English sheep, Mante had received only 166. In a fit of rage at Mante's disingenuousness, Boisgelin had him thrown into the St. Germain prison, where he was kept incommunicado for weeks before being transferred to For l'Evêque, a Parisian jail for actors and debtors.

Still, Mante was not at the end of his wits. He had apparently been acquainted for some time with Turgot, who made frequent references to him in letters to his fellow economist Pierre-Samuel Du Pont de Nemours. Turgot's attitude was one of detached amusement: good old Mante was a perfect crook, of course, but did Boisgelin have to be such a merciless creditor? Boisgelin was not to be moved. He turned down Turgot's appeal to let Mante out of jail. (Sixteen years later, the unforgiving gentleman was sent to the scaffold, and Mante, if he himself survived the Terror, would surely have appreciated the turn of fate.)

In the appeal that Mante sent to Franklin in the summer of 1778, Turgot's rather mild interest was magnified into deep concern.[22] The surprising fact is that Franklin, who normally reserved for his fellow Americans what little funds he could spare, doled out some money to this former English officer. Not much, to be sure (forty-eight livres, says his account book, dubbing the amount as ChY, for Charity), but he made another donation of two guineas nine months later. He was thanked profusely and presented with a copy of Mante's *Traité des prairies artificielles*, still extant at Yale in the Franklin Collection, a work that displays its author's considerable expertise in sheep raising. Trying to earn some money, the prisoner applied himself to translating Du Pont's *Tableau des principes de l'économie politique*, an undertaking that Turgot would not discourage but felt needed revision by Du Pont himself.[23]

After almost two years in jail, Mante finally obtained Boisgelin's permission to come out in order to be, in the language of the day, "cut for the stone." "A propos stone," chuckled Turgot, "Mante . . . recovered perfectly from a huge stone that broke during the operation. A hundred honest people would have died from this" (June 28, 1780).[24]

A free man again but as poor as ever, Mante, now living in Sceaux near Paris, launched one more piteous appeal on New Year's Day, 1781.[25] This time he offered his services to the American cause quite openly, but there is no indication that Franklin ever took him up on it.

William Dodd's name never appears in Mante's letters to Franklin, yet one is left with a number of interesting though unanswerable questions. What kind of bond existed between the preacher to lost sheep in England and the raiser of sheep across the Channel? Would it be conceivable that the parson, at a loss for cash and dreaming of running away to Philadelphia, considered selling to Mante or to the French his knowledge of the British coast? Was he, in his mysterious note, hinting to Franklin that he was amenable to becoming an

American agent? Might Dodd's contacts with the shady Mante have driven a suspicious British government, in 1777, to get rid of the divine by making the most of his forgery?

And what about Franklin's role, if any? In this, as in so many other instances, Franklin kept his counsel. Scheming and betrayal, human anguish and pain swirled about him, people cried out for help. He stood at the center of the maelstrom, calm, cautious, benign, and enigmatic.

7

Franklin's Most Baffling Correspondent

BRILLIANT spy or shameless blackmailer? Astute diplomat or embarrassing loose cannon? Sophisticated collector of books or debt-ridden raving paranoid? Valorous dragoon or pathetic subject ordered to retire to a convent? Poignant or ludicrous? Man or woman? Who was this creature?

This creature was the unfathomable chevalier d'Eon, whose name has given rise to what psychiatrists call "eonism," meaning a transsexual personality. Enormous numbers of books, memoirs, forgeries, confessions, novels, serious publications, and titillating fantasies have been written about him for two centuries and keep on being published. The reason for his appearance in this book is that one more facet of his complex life has been overlooked so far: he was, in some mysterious way, involved with Benjamin Franklin.[1] Let me first place his extraordinary career in its historical context.

No sooner had the ink dried on the peace treaty of 1763 that put an end to the Seven Years' War (known in America as the French and Indian War) than Louis XV started drawing plans for revenge against England. It had been a dreadfully humiliating peace, with France losing Canada, Senegal, Tobago, the left bank of the Mississippi, and most of its settlements in India. The king, dreaming of a glorious comeback as soon as he rebuilt and augmented his naval power, envisioned no less than an invasion of England. This, of course, would require enormous advance preparation and would entail the best efforts of the Secret du Roi—a super-clandestine outfit established by the monarch himself some ten years earlier. Accountable to him alone, its existence was never revealed to the regular government, especially not to the ministry of foreign affairs. Since the royal instructions to the ministry and the Secret were often contradictory, the king being a woefully indecisive man, the setup was a recipe for disaster.

D'Eon had been part of the Secret since its inception. Charles-Geneviève-Louis-Auguste-André-Timothée d'Eon de Beaumont (1728–1810) was born in Tonnerre, Burgundy, to a well-to-do family connected with the wine trade. He studied law and while still in his twenties was sent on a diplomatic mission to Russia, where he acquitted himself very well. This was followed by such valorous conduct in his regiment of dragoons that he was awarded the coveted cross of Saint-Louis. His next post, in his mid-thirties, was as secretary to the French embassy in London.

It was at that point that the king decided to have England's coasts and some of its interior reconnoitered for vulnerable spots. He took advantage of an interim between the departure of his current ambassador and the arrival of a new one to nominate d'Eon minister plenipotentiary, with the task of facilitating the work of a young French lieutenant, Louis-François de La Rozière, who was to make sketches along the beaches. And—what were his superiors thinking of?—d'Eon was entrusted, on June 3, 1763, with a letter handwritten and signed by Louis XV, detailing the invasion plans. If discovered by the British, this document was sure to set off a new war that France was bound to lose, given its state of unpreparedness. D'Eon kept it hidden in a brick of his basement that was wired in such a way that his whole house on Brewer Street would blow up if the document was touched.

In England, d'Eon soon became very popular in aristocratic and even in court circles, thanks to his lavish parties, which were flavored with his Gallic ebullience and flowing with the choice Burgundy procured by his Irish brother-in-law, the chevalier Thomas O'Gorman. He spent wildly—so wildly that the French foreign ministry, unaware of his special status, felt that he had to be reined in and told him so. But d'Eon paid no attention. His new role seemed to have gone to his head, and he saw himself as invulnerable.

The arrival in October of the new ambassador, Claude-Louis Régnier, comte de Guerchy, provoked a serious crisis. A well-meaning but obtuse man who had absolutely no preparation in diplomacy, Guerchy treated d'Eon with the condescension of a full-blooded aristocrat toward one who had just reached the lowest rank of nobility, and ordered him bluntly to return to his former secretarial duties. D'Eon reacted with such insolence and fury that Guerchy convinced the authorities back home to recall this recalcitrant subordinate. The order came, but d'Eon refused to leave.

Londoners, at that point, were treated to the entertaining spectacle of Frenchmen behaving according to stereotype, as a duel of sarcastic pamphlets, venomous rumors, and other tools of propaganda warfare was played out between Guerchy, a confused, enraged bull, and his merciless picador, the ever-inventive d'Eon, who now, perceived as the underdog, had most of the populace on his side.

Soon after, having been deprived of his post and salary,

d'Eon detonated a diplomatic bombshell. Just to remind his colleagues in the Secret that he could, and just might, blackmail them any day, he published in 1764 a hefty volume of private letters, memoirs, and negotiations, an exposé so indiscreet and gossipy that all of Europe, it seemed, was soon trembling with shock and shaking with laughter. It became a best-seller. Best friends stopped talking to each other after its revelations. Mme de Guerchy's infidelities became common knowledge.

Frustrated and furious, Louis XV tried to have d'Eon extradited and sent back forcibly to Paris, but was told, to his surprise, that British law would not allow such a procedure. The head of the Secret, trying to defend one of his best agents, represented to the king that those follies might be d'Eon's way of hiding the true purpose of his residence in England. (Whether this leader believed his own explanation is another question.) He also reminded the king that d'Eon still possessed that compromising letter about the proposed invasion of England. The king concluded that the best course was to do nothing, while sending d'Eon just enough money to keep him from succumbing to British blandishments. The sorry affair ended in court, at the King's Bench, and d'Eon lost the first round.

Then, in 1765, a sudden reversal: one of Guerchy's employees declared under oath that the ambassador had instructed him to poison d'Eon, and, after this plot failed, to ambush and assassinate the chevalier. D'Eon won in court this time, and Guerchy, who had become a diplomatic headache for George III, returned to France and died soon after. Franklin, once again living in London, must have followed the lawsuits with the same fascination as did the rest of the capital.

An interlude of calm followed, during which d'Eon kept his government informed of the ins and outs of English politics in a series of coded messages signed William Wolff. He was a first-class spy, always ahead of the regular diplomats. On July 10, 1766, as a gesture of good will, he surrendered the dreaded document to his superiors.

It was too peaceful to last. As early as 1770, a new wave of dismay swept over the Secret du Roi. Rumors from Russia, then from France and England, insinuated—no, insisted—that the chevalier was a woman. Consternation and disbelief followed. He, a captain of dragoons, how could that be? Well, look at his small, slender stature. Consider that, by his own admission, he has never had an affair with either sex, or even wished for one. Remember how, in St. Petersburg, he masqueraded as a woman at the Empress's costume balls? Indeed, it was whispered that none other than the Princess Daschkova, closely tied to the Russian court, had been the first to reveal the amazing fact on a visit to London.[2]

Why not ask d'Eon directly to disclose his sex? The London press questioned him, of course, but his reactions did nothing but deepen the mystery. He never gave a straight answer. In great secrecy he confided to a friend, then to another and another that, yes, he was a woman—yet he urged them not to tell anybody because such a revelation would be the end of his political career. Naturally, the story was promptly leaked. People recalled that Guerchy had accused d'Eon of being a hermaphrodite. When, in 1772, the king sent Jean Drouet, a former member of the Secret, to visit his old colleague d'Eon in London and find out the truth, the chevalier refused to undress but allowed Drouet to "palpate." After his examination by touch, Drouet reported "all the attributes of a girl and all the regular inconveniences."[3] On the other hand, when the betting on his sex began in London and grew to prodigious sums, d'Eon was enraged. He went around pubs challenging both bookmakers and betters, but his fencing ability was too well known for anyone to consider dueling against him. During all that time he never wore any but men's clothes, and he referred to himself in the masculine, but his library contained a large number of books about famous women.[4] Why did d'Eon choose to obfuscate the question in such a way? Many guesses have been offered, but none are convincing. Some think that his half-revelations came out of a desperate wish to be in the limelight again, some that he was tired of politics and corruption and of spying without ever receiving any recognition, and that he saw this ploy as the best means of retiring peacefully to France—in the guise of a modern Joan of Arc, of course.

As the betting fever mounted, the chevalier, fearing he might be kidnapped and killed, fled London and, for the following seven years, spent many months on the large estate of a British friend. There, in the calm of Leicestershire, near Derby, he read widely, for there also was an intellectual side to his personality. Buying ever more books, he ran into serious debt. He wrote on state finance and the history of taxation, beginning with the Babylonians and the Egyptians. His views often paralleled Franklin's: he, too, campaigned in favor of smallpox inoculation and wished to spread the technique of raising silkworms.[5] As the tension mounted between England and its colonies, he declared himself ardently pro-American.

It must have been during the early 1770s that Franklin became personally acquainted with d'Eon, probably through O'Gorman, the Irish brother-in-law who cultivated vineyards in Tonnerre. O'Gorman visited London during the winter of 1772–73 and told Franklin his dream: to start viniculture in the New World. Franklin saw no future for such a project in the existing colonies but held out some hope for its realization in the land that the Walpole Company hoped to obtain west of the Mississippi.[6] Back in France, O'Gorman thanked Franklin for his encouragement and asked to be kept informed "with

caution and in a neutral manner." Those happy schemes eventually came to nought with the collapse of the Walpole Company, but the two men remained on good terms and O'Gorman
was to become, during Franklin's mission to France, the source
of all the Burgundy served at American receptions.

D'Eon, meanwhile, became embroiled in a new affair that
would involve him with the Frenchmen whose names were
to appear in his first extant communication with Franklin,
namely Morande and Beaumarchais. Charles Théveneau de
Morande was a master of libel. He lived off a judicious combination of poison pen and blackmail, and had wisely taken
refuge in London after a stay in the Bastille. When he threatened to put on sale a large edition of his *Mémoires secrets d'une
femme publique,* revealing the sordid past of the king's mistress, the comtesse Jeanne du Barry, the Secret, in a panic,
instructed d'Eon to purchase all the copies and destroy them.
The Secret then changed its directive and sent the playwright
Pierre Augustin Caron de Beaumarchais, future creator of
Figaro, to negotiate with Morande. For a while, d'Eon, Morande, and Beaumarchais, those three geniuses of intrigue,
had fun together, outwitting one another with roguish abandon. D'Eon even confided to Morande that he really was a
woman. By late April 1774, the French government had agreed
to pay Morande a very large sum, plus a life pension, and the
whole slanderous edition was burned.

Three weeks later, as d'Eon was brooding about the immor-
ality of Morande's good luck compared to France's neglect of
his own loyal but ill-rewarded activities, the worst possible
catastrophe happened to him: Louis XV died quite suddenly of
smallpox. His grandson and successor, the twenty-year-old
Louis XVI, immediately abrogated the Secret du Roi, and
d'Eon went into free fall. Lampooned daily in the papers, he
was a political outcast without any prospects and with a moun-

tain of debts. In a final blow, d'Eon learned that Morande and Beaumarchais, now aware that the French government's official position would be to consider him a woman, were about to make a killing on the betting market. Never mind that they offered him part of the expected booty; d'Eon would have nothing to do with that scheme. He was hurt to the quick and would hate them both forever.

The early days of 1774 were dark for Franklin, too. Accused of having circulated some politically compromising letters written by Thomas Hutchinson, governor of Massachusetts, and of having refused to identify his source, he stood emotionlessly through hours of vituperation by Solicitor General Alexander Wedderburn. He lost his position of deputy postmaster general of the United States. He had to admit that his efforts at reconciliation with the mother country had been in vain. He, who had been loyal so long to "that fine and noble China vase," the British Empire, was turning into an American rebel who would have no choice but to seek help from the old enemy, France.[7]

The new king of France, for his part, had given up on his grandfather's plan of invasion, but was thinking of those restless Americans as a possible tool of revenge for the treaty of 1763. It is not impossible—it is even plausible—that Franklin and d'Eon held some conversations at that time.

While Franklin, back in Philadelphia as of the spring of 1775, was plunging into pre-revolutionary activities, d'Eon, in despair, deprived of his last bargaining chips, was tirelessly negotiating—through Beaumarchais, of all people—the terms of his returning to France. After fifteen years of absence, he aspired to see Burgundy again, and his old mother.

During the very long time it took to elaborate what became known as the Transaction, Louis XVI and his foreign minister, comte Charles Gravier de Vergennes, remained adamant:

d'Eon would only be allowed to come home, be put under the king's protection, and receive a pension plus enough money to pay his debts, if he would refer to himself in the feminine gender for the rest of his life, never wear any but women's clothes, behave with due modesty, and pledge not to bring up old grievances. The one remnant of his past life was to be the cross of Saint-Louis, which he was permitted to pin on his dress. A death sentence for his ego. But even as d'Eon eventually caved in, he surely believed that he would somehow finagle his way out of his ludicrous predicament and play a political role once more.

Franklin arrived in France in the closing days of 1776 to join Silas Deane, who had been there since the previous spring, making contacts and preparing the first shipments of military supplies to America. A brief anonymous message in English, sent in care of Deane, was awaiting him. It reads:

> Sir
>
> I congratulate your arrival with an intelligence of the first moment, which you will apply with your wonted caution. Mr. de morande is secretary to -m- beaumarchais, and brother to a refugee of the same name in London, lately acquitted *in the Kings bench*, of a Suit by chev. d'Eon, and known by every body to be a man *a tout faire*. There is also -m- Charles parker forth of somerset street portman sq. some time past and, now in paris intimate with all three, who conveys (by Lord Stormonts messenger) to lord mansfield all the transactions and equipiments of the court of france for america, the ships, description, name, force and cargo of mr. du Coudrays expedition at havre, &a. Mr. b-m- [Beaumarchais] was to have come to england, but it was found that mr. p-F- [Parker Forth] could more convenient go to france. You are too wise to neglect this because anonymous.

When the moment came to publish this document in the Yale edition of the *Papers of Benjamin Franklin*, we editors puzzled over its authorship.[8] I finally suggested that we assign it to Louis-Léon de Brancas, comte de Lauraguais, who hated Beaumarchais and knew Parker Forth. We did so with a question mark. Mea culpa. Now that I have studied d'Eon's career more in depth, I am convinced that he was the writer—especially since, as we shall see, there exists an answer from Franklin sent a few weeks later to an unnamed person who can only be d'Eon.

The anonymous message bristles with clues that Franklin could easily pick up. The Morande who was secretary to Beaumarchais was indeed the brother of the infamous Charles Théveneau de Morande of blackmail notoriety, the "man *a tout faire*" who would carry out any vile plan for money. But, unlike his sibling, Jean-Baptiste Théveneau de Francy proved to be a respectable person.

Nathaniel (not Charles) Parker Forth, a shady character, was known in Paris as the spy employed by the British ambassador David Murray, Viscount Stormont. He shuttled frequently between Paris and London, carrying messages from one government to the other. As to Lord Mansfield, he was William Murray, earl of Mansfield (a relative of the ambassador), who held for thirty-four years the position of chief justice of the King's Bench. D'Eon appeared more than once in his court, generally on the losing side.

Good spy that he was, d'Eon, still in England, knew exactly what was being prepared secretly in France: nothing less than the first shipload of arms and ammunition for the American colonies, procured by Beaumarchais in the name of his fictitious commercial company, Roderigue Hortalez, and loaded on the *Amphitrite*. If Franklin needed a course on the intricacies of sending clandestine military supplies to a country not yet recognized as a nation, the saga of the *Amphitrite* provided it. Apart from the obvious problems of getting together the money, the goods, and the ship, there were a number of prima donnas to be dealt with, notably the mercurial Beaumarchais who had to be kept silent—an impossible task—and the prickly Tronson du Coudray, a talented engineer who had been made an American general and authorized by Silas Deane to take with him a group of junior officers.[9] After many a setback, however, the *Amphitrite* and two other vessels of supplies did reach America and contributed to the crucial victory at Saratoga a year later.

A consequence of d'Eon's warning was that Franklin always kept his distance from Beaumarchais, with whom Deane had worked hand in glove. Beaumarchais eventually lamented that Franklin had never wanted "to partake of his soup" and had ignored his many gestures of friendship. He could not understand the reason for the American's coldness, and it is indeed surprising that those two men, who shared the same goal and were both endowed with an irreverent sense of humor, did not become friends.

Dated February 10, 1777, Franklin's answer to d'Eon was written in a French far too elegant to be his own. He had engaged a French secretary by then. The letter is obviously addressed to a man he already knew:

> Sir,
>
> I am grateful for your amicable congratulations upon my happy arrival in Paris. I hope to have the chance to do the same for you as soon as you will be lucky enough to return to your country. Allow me to add my own hopes to your good and patriotic ones in that respect, as much out of regard for your country which could use your presence and your talents as for the pleasure I would feel in meeting you here and conversing with you.
>
> I am glad to learn that my friend O'Gorman is in good health and that he shall soon be in France. If, since I arrived here, I had been able to drink his excellent Burgundy rather

than Bordeaux wine, I would not be suffering from an attack of gout so violent that it prevents me from writing you more than these few lines to wish you all kinds of happiness. I have the honor to be, with distinguished consideration, your most humble and obedient servant B. Franklin.

This letter, which contains some erasures, making it look more like a draft, lay for many years in the archives of Tonnerre, but I was informed in the late 1980s that it had disappeared.[10] What makes me believe that it is not a forgery is the allusion to Franklin's attack of gout. Two days earlier, in a letter to an English friend, he had written of such an attack, which had overtaken him with rare violence.[11] His style, too—bland, cautious—is exactly what one would expect under the circumstances.

On August 14 of that same year, 1777, d'Eon, now forty-nine, finally sailed back to France defiantly, in his uniform of captain of dragoons. But he was not allowed to wear it for long. He was promptly dispatched to his native Tonnerre, where they gave him a hero's welcome, and then he was called back to Versailles where the ultimatum was clear: dress as a woman, behave as a woman, or you will get into serious trouble. Queen Marie-Antoinette decided to have him outfitted in great style, at her own expense, by the celebrated Rose Bertin, her *couturière*. On the day of his reception at court, November 21, d'Eon was decked out in a long train, a huge powdered wig, white gloves, a fan, and a diamond necklace with matched earrings. The ladies at court vied with one another in teaching him the proper demeanor of an aristocratic lady. His social life was soon dazzling.

Hence, the "Mademoiselle d'Eon" who attended a dinner party at Franklin's home in Passy, in the early days of 1778, must have been elegantly attired. Franklin was in an exultant mood at that moment because a whole new diplomatic wind was blowing since the American victory at Saratoga. He was so ebullient indeed that, according to a story reported on January 10 in Bachaumont's *Mémoires secrets,* he came very close to committing a serious faux pas. The episode took place the day before Epiphany, and Franklin, bowing to French Catholic custom, wanted to procure a blessing for the bread in his residence. Consequently, he bought thirteen brioches, one for each American state, and planned to decorate them with little pennants, the first of which was to bear the word *Liberté.* The local priest, who had been invited to the dinner, expressed his doubts about the appropriateness of using that term. Another guest, the bishop of Saintes, told the priest in no uncertain terms that "Liberté" could not possibly be tolerated. The next guest to be consulted was Mlle d'Eon. She answered demurely that although she had nothing to add to what the eminent clerics had decided, there was an important political reason to keep in consideration: that "not even three leagues away from Versailles, it was a bad idea to use a word that was wholly out of favor there."[12]

The dinner must have taken place on January 5, the day before the feast called *la fête des Rois,* the Magi. On January 24, d'Eon sent Franklin a message in his own hand, in French, dutifully signed "La Chere D'eon" (Chere being his abbreviation for the feminine "Chevalière").[13] Translated, it reads:

> I came to Passy to have the honor of seeing you, and to congratulate you on the latest events in America; but you were in Paris and in your absence we drank to your health and to liberty with your friend, Mr. Rai de Chaumont. He received me most amiably as well as Madame his wife and Mademoiselle their daughter. I hope that a toast to Liberty offered by Mademoiselle D'Eon three leagues away from Versailles will be as beneficial as possible to America. My brother-in-law, the chevalier O'Gorman, is just about to arrive from Burgundy where he will return next week. He hopes that you will visit

Dijon next spring and that you will stay with him in Tonnerre. I would be delighted to be there at that time and to give you proof of my sincere and respectful attachment.

All this in the feminine gender when writing about himself, as prescribed. The reference to "liberty" being mentioned three leagues from Versailles is obviously an allusion to the above-mentioned report in Bachaumont.

Franklin did not visit Dijon the following spring but d'Eon did, albeit as a guest of the local jail for nineteen days. The opening of hostilities between France and England had driven him mad with excitement. He bombarded the ministers with petitions begging to be allowed to go and fight for America's freedom, but in vain. A duchess advised him to marry a powerful man—the only way for a woman, if lucky, to attain her goal. In spite of repeated injunctions to go back to Tonnerre and live there quietly, he tarried in Versailles defiantly wearing his uniform until Vergennes, exasperated, had him arrested and deported to Dijon. But how were the Dijon authorities to deal with this celebrity whose presence attracted hundreds of curious to the town, each begging for a private visit? The prisoner was let go on May 10, 1779.

Franklin himself was just as excited. Louis XVI now seemed keen on reviving his grandfather's project of invading England, and what was known as d'Eon's plan—that is, de La Rozière's sketches of the coasts—was brought out and studied. A feverish correspondence took place through the spring of 1779 between Franklin and John Paul Jones, who was to command the Franco-American naval force, and between Franklin and Lafayette, who was to command the ground troops. In his eagerness to avenge the burning of the coastal towns of New England, Franklin stressed that four thousand to five thousand men, landing unexpectedly, could destroy some rich English towns, or exact a heavy contribution from them, taking part of it in ready money and the rest in hostages. He suggested that 48 million livres tournois (or 2 million Sterling) might be demanded from Bristol or Liverpool, and other large sums could be wrung from Lancaster, Whitehaven, Bath, and so on.[14] All those grandiose schemes were eventually abandoned.

D'Eon, meanwhile, made short sojourns in various convents, ordered an astonishing number of dresses, and worked at restoring his vineyards, which had fallen into disarray. But he was a broken man.

An anonymous author, at that very time, was composing a repulsive booklet, a little over one hundred pages long, linking in a common pit of animosity Franklin, d'Eon, and Beaumarchais. This work did not appear until 1781, at which point it went through several editions and was even translated into German. It is titled *Histoire d'un pou français: ou, L'espion d'une nouvelle espèce, tant en France qu'en Angleterre* (The story of a French louse: or, A new kind of spy, both in France and in England). The narrator and hero is indeed an enterprising French louse *(pou)*, born on the head of a prostitute and well placed for spying in a novel way. His adventures force him to change residence frequently, hopping from the head of a countess to that of the queen, then on to a soldier and a laundress. Finally he lands on Mlle d'Eon, whom he accuses of being cowardly, loud, and frequently in bad company. Said demoiselle is invited to dinner by Franklin, and the description that the louse gives of the old man is downright cruel: a wrinkled forehead, warts all over his face, a prominent chin, teeth that look like cloves.

There is worse to come. After the dinner guests have offered thirteen toasts, one for each of the colonies, Miss d'Eon sits beside Franklin and sings to him some verses of her composition. The louse does not think highly of them, but Franklin applauds, kisses her, and whispers in her ear: "See you this evening, my divine one!" The next episode takes place in the residence of Beaumarchais, where the louse overhears a conversation between the playwright and his visitor, Franklin, the gist of which is that the American is the helpless dupe of Beaumarchais.[15]

In the years that follow, it was O'Gorman's turn to keep up the correspondence with Franklin, and he did it in a most amicable way, calling him "Dear Doctor and best of Excellencies."[16] Whereas Voltaire, upon hearing that d'Eon planned to call on him in Switzerland, referred to the chevalier as "a monster," and "an amphibious animal," Franklin, as far as we know, never poked fun at the man's strange personality.[17]

A meeting in Paris between Franklin and d'Eon was arranged for January 1785, but we do not know if it took place. During that same year Franklin returned to Philadelphia (in July) and d'Eon made his way back to London (in November). Strangely enough, d'Eon, once reestablished in England and free to dress as he wanted, decided to keep his female attire. It certainly gave some piquancy to his fencing exhibitions. This sexagenarian, as nimble as ever with his sword, challenged the best opponents in the country while wearing a black silk dress, white lace collar, and a bonnet sprouting pink feathers. He made some money that way, became a Freemason, and kept writing.

But with the advent of the French Revolution, d'Eon's luck changed once again. No more king to protect him. No more pension. In despair, he saw his precious library—all eight thousand volumes and manuscripts accumulated over forty years—auctioned off by his creditors at Christie's in May 1791. After his last jewels had been disposed of, he barely survived thanks to his fencing until, at sixty-nine, he was severely wounded and could fight no more.

D'Eon's last thirteen years were as obscure and miserable as his early days had been flashy. After he had spent five months in debtors' prison, an aging widow, Mary Cole, took pity on him. The two old ladies, living together, cared for each other until one day, in May 1810, Mary discovered that her friend had died. She discovered too, while washing the body, that Mlle d'Eon, her dear companion, was a man.

The results of the autopsy were published in the London press, but betting on the chevalier's sex had long since been outlawed and the public remained indifferent. This most enigmatic of Franklin's correspondents was buried, ironically, in Middlesex County, England.

The preceding three "enigmas" showed us Franklin on the periphery of the espionage world. Probably the target of assassination by a spy in the first story, inexplicably sending money to a double agent jailed in France in the second story, he is glimpsed in the third as having a cordial relationship with the most eccentric transvestite-cum-spy of his day.

These mini "detective stories" may inspire some future historian to take a closer look at the tantalizing mysteries of secret intelligence. Not everything has been discovered on that subject, and the Public Record Office in London still contains precious information for researchers equipped with the technology to make invisible ink reappear. Where to begin? The names of Van Zandt, Parker Forth, Hynson, Morande, Wentworth, and Bancroft come to mind.

8

Franklin and the Mystery Turk: The Morals of Chess

WHY WOULD a non-chess player like me choose to write on such a well-known facet of Franklin's life? Because of two new elements I would like to add to the chess legend developed around him. The first, a delightful period piece, shows the fascination with automata, as pervasive in the eighteenth century as our worship of electronic marvels is today. The second, following the story of that endearing Turk, contrasts Franklin's utopian view of the game, as expressed in his *Morals of Chess*, with the more realistic appraisal of his friend Dr. Barbeu-Dubourg, a fervent admirer for once turned critic.

Shortly after his arrival, Franklin's passion for chess became famous throughout Paris. His closest friends, the physicist Jean-Baptiste Le Roy and Dr. Jacques Barbeu-Dubourg, were always proposing games. To please him, his landlord's beautiful daughter, Mme Elise Foucault, took chess lessons along with her husband. And Franklin's captivating neighbor, Mme Brillon, proved a worthy antagonist, though her drive to win was less ferocious than his and her style more mildly mannered.

The episode of the chess game played while Mme Brillon was soaking in the bathtub has titillated countless people, but in reality it was less risqué than the telling of it. Franklin was engaged in an arduous match with their common friend and neighbor, M. Le Veillard, while Mme Brillon was following it from her bathtub, covered, in the fashion of the day, by a board. When Franklin apologized the next morning for having kept her up so late, she replied: "No, my good papa. . . . I am so happy to see you that the good it does me more than balances the little fatigue of overstaying in the bathtub."[1] Mindful of his health, she chided him for his sedentary habits in a little poem that he credited for being the inspiration of his famous "Dialogue between the Gout and Mr. Franklin": "You play chess when you should take a walk."[2]

A number of chess anecdotes have been passed down several generations of the Chaumont family, in whose mansion Franklin resided. They tell of him playing chess late into the night and sending out for fresh candles only to find out that dawn had long since arrived; of his refusing to open an important dispatch from America until the game had been concluded.[3] In turn, Jefferson relates that the Doctor, while playing with the old duchesse de Bourbon, succeeded in checkmating her king and removed it. "Ah!" said the Duchess, "we do not take kings so!" "We do in America," he replied.[4]

No wonder that Franklin's curiosity was piqued when, on Christmas Eve 1782, a friend who lived in Vienna sent him news that "a very ingenious Gentleman Mr. Kampl, Counsellor of his Imperial Majesty's Finances for the Kingdom of Hungary" was proposing to embark on a two-year tour of France, the Low Countries, and England, along with his family. The trip's purpose was to show off the gentleman's mechanical inventions and improvements, for which there was not much encouragement to be found in central Europe. To meet his expenses, Mr. Kampl planned "to exhibit the figure of a Turk, as big as life, playing at chess with any player; and answering, by pointing at the letters of the alphabet, any questions made to him." Franklin's correspondent had twice seen this mechanical Turk in action but could not discover what made it work. Yet "was there nothing but the organisation of his arm, hand, and fingers, besides the motions of his head, that alone would entitle him to no small admiration."[5]

The ingenious inventor's name, which appears variously as Kemple, Kempl, Kempel, and Kampl, was really Wolfgang von Kempelen—or Kempelen Farkas Lovag in his native Hungarian. Born in 1734, he became famous for his designs of fountains and palaces as well as for his talents as engineer and builder.

Von Kempelen arrived in Paris in the spring of 1783. On May 28, he wrote to Franklin, in excellent French, to apologize for the delay in showing him, as promised earlier, the chess-playing automaton. The reason, he said, was that he needed a little more time to perfect another very interesting machine he wanted the Doctor to see. This was undoubtedly his extraordinary "speaking machine" that simulated the human vocal system and took him twenty years to perfect, whereas his money-maker, the Turk, had been built in six months.

The Turk must have been quite a sight in his exotic outfit topped by a large turban. He sat on a chair fixed to a table mounted on wheels; the table itself was equipped with several doors. Leaning his right arm on the table, he held a pipe in his left hand, with which he played after removing the pipe. A chess board of eighteen inches was affixed to the table, which contained wheels, levers, cylinders, and other moving pieces, all publicly displayed before the game. The Turk's vestments were then lifted over his head, and the body was seen to be full of similar wheels and levers, with a little door in his thigh, also opened to the public. The whole contraption was wheeled around the room before its doors were shut and the play began, with the automaton always making the first move. At every motion, the wheels could be heard as the Turk examined the chess board, shaking his head twice when he threatened the queen, three times when he put the king into check.

The moment for appearing in Paris had been perfectly chosen: a chess club had just opened near the Palais Royal, under the patronage of Monsieur, the king's brother, who was a member.[6] We don't know whether Franklin accepted von Kempelen's invitation to meet him at his lodgings on the rue d'Orléans or whether a game actually took place between the real American and the counterfeit Turk, but we do know that Franklin was impressed, very impressed. The proof of his enthusiasm has been deduced from a letter that the minister from Saxony to the court of St. James, Count Johann Mauritius von Brühl, himself a celebrated chess player, wrote in reply to Franklin on October 8, 1783, to thank him for having introduced von Kempelen to chess aficionados in England.

Franklin's original letter to the count was presumed lost for well over a century.[7] Not any more. During her stay in the British Isles in December 1995, Barbara Oberg, the former editor of the Franklin Papers, discovered it at the Scottish Record Office in Edinburgh. It reads:

Passy near Paris

Augt. 22. 1783

Sir,

M. de Kempel, the ingenious Author of the Automaton that plays Chess, will have the Honour of putting this Line

into the Hands of your Excellency; and I beg leave to recommend him to your Protection, not merely on Account of that wonderful Machine, but as a Genius capable of being serviceable to Mankind by more useful Inventions which he has not yet communicated. With great Respect, I have the honour to be, Sir, Your Excellency's most obedient & most humble Servant   B. Franklin
His Excelly. Count Bruhl, Minister of Saxony

That very day, Franklin also wrote along the same lines to his young friend and editor in England, Benjamin Vaughan.

No more mention of the "ingenious" Hungarian is to be found among Franklin's papers after that. And yet the Turk kept earning money for his master, at five shillings a demonstration, even though doubts about the human character of his thinking process were raised in London as early as 1784. An eccentric and cantankerous writer by the name of Philip Thicknesse—whose claim to fame is that he was Gainsborough's patron for twenty years—suspected a trick. The complicated machinery shown to the spectators before the chess game, he wrote, was meant solely "to misguide and delude the observers." Thicknesse also branded as a clever ruse the various activities carried out by the assistant, who periodically wound up the automaton, or locked and unlocked a cabinet.[8]

The Turk, nevertheless, pursued his colorful career well into the nineteenth century. It is said that Napoleon played against him in 1809 and lost. He became known as "Maelzel's chess-player" after the name of his new owner, the Bavarian inventor of the metronome, who purchased him in 1804 from the late Kempelen's son. Johann Maelzel brought the Turk to New York in 1826 and exhibited him in Boston, Philadelphia, and Baltimore. The excitement was intense and the press coverage enthusiastic.

Yet Edgar Allan Poe, who saw the automaton in Richmond,

Virginia, commented that it was impossible for the chess player to be a pure machine performing without any immediate human agency. He concluded: "The only question is of the *manner* in which human agency is brought to bear."⁹

It was not until 1834 that the full extent of the deception was revealed by a Frenchman, M. Mouret, who had been in the employ of the exhibitor. Thicknesse, it turned out, was right in believing that the play-acting with the automaton was no more than a ploy to divert the public's attention. In fact, a gifted chess-playing child or dwarf concealed within the counter followed the game with the aid of a looking glass fixed to the ceiling. Mouret's revelations, published in Paris in the *Magasin Pittoresque*, did not reach America for a few years. Meanwhile, Maelzel had died at sea while crossing from Cuba to Philadelphia. At the time of his death, he was deeply in debt in spite of some great inventions of his own, such as an automaton trumpeter who played military music and an automatic orchestra of many instruments.

All this equipment, along with the Turk himself, came into the possession of Dr. John Kearsley Mitchell, a professor of medicine in Philadelphia. He published a long paper in the first issue of the *Chess Monthly* in which he explained how the hidden human player kept abreast of the game:

> On the under side of the chest there appeared a chess-board, directly beneath that upon the upper surface, upon which the game was played. Each square was excavated so as to make the board between the opposite squares very thin. The squares were numbered from one to sixty-four, under each of which hung a little lever, well balanced, to which was attached a small disk of iron. These disks, when attracted by magnets placed on the top of the box, swung up into the excavations and remained there quietly until liberated by the removal of the magnets.¹⁰

The eventual installation within the machine of a seat gliding on rails allowed a man of normal size to hide himself with a modicum of comfort.

Dr. Mitchell finally deposited his turbaned Turk in the Chinese Museum of Philadelphia where he stayed fourteen years, abandoned in a dusty corner, until 1854 when he was destroyed by fire along with the museum. So forgotten was he that not the slightest notice was taken of his disappearance. And yet, as Henry Ridgely Evans observes, "the first chess club to be founded in Philadelphia owed its existence to the excitement caused by the performance of the Turk."[11] And even before that he had fooled none less than Benjamin Franklin, who on August 14, 1999, was inducted into the U.S. Chess Hall of Fame in Reno, Nevada.

Two Views on Chess

> Playing at Chess is the most ancient and the most universal game known among men; for its original is beyond the memory of history, and it has, for numberless ages, been the amusement of all the civilized nations of Asia, the Persians, the Indians, and the Chinese. Europe has had it above 1,000 years; the Spaniards have spread it over their part of America, and it begins lately to make its appearance in these northern states.[12]

Such are the opening lines of Franklin's much admired bagatelle *The Morals of Chess.* It has been highly praised for being vivacious, well informed, ethical, and radiating kindness. It has also been lauded for its claim that "life is a kind of chess" and its list of the qualities that ensure victory in both chess and life: foresight, circumspection, caution, hope for a favorable change when things are going wrong, perseverance in search of resources, and lack of presumption at the moment of success, lest inattention follow.

The rules Franklin lays down to guarantee a fair and proper game sound perfect. No false move to extricate oneself from a difficulty or to gain an advantage; no expression of impatience such as singing, whistling, picking up a book, tapping one's feet on the floor or one's fingers on the table; no endeavor to deceive one's adversary by pretending to have made a bad move; no undue gloating in victory. Franklin told Mme Brillon that he should have dedicated the piece to her because its best advice was based on her magnanimous way of playing.

But was Franklin himself really a magnanimous player? According to the Chaumont family lore, Franklin was not famous for the courtesy and fairness advocated in his bagatelle. He grew impatient at the slowness of his partners, was prone to rearranging the board if his opponent left the room, and often drummed his fingers on the table. In other words, like all other chess fanatics, he played to win.[13]

If Franklin ever had a devoted friend and admirer, it was Dr. Jacques Barbeu-Dubourg, the first French translator of his works and one who never failed to assure him of his inviolable attachment. Yet Dubourg, for once, dared to differ. With deferential disclaimers to his "dear and respectable Master," he brought to Franklin's Fourth of July party (1779) a refutation of Franklin's *Morals of Chess*. Here are his remarks, appearing in English for the first time:

> Rather than an amusement, the game of chess is an empty occupation, a painful frivolity that does not exercise the body, that tires the mind rather than refresh it, that dries up and hardens the soul. . . . It is the simulacrum of war, that cruel game whose only excuse must be its unavoidability. The greatest good or the least harm it can produce is to inflate one person's arrogance and mortify the self-esteem of another.

Chess players are almost always anxious, suspicious, unapproachable, fussy and contemptuous. Success has an inebriating and swelling effect on them, adversity destroys them. They are totally unforgiving toward each other and forever distrustful of onlookers when the boredom they inspire is not sufficient to keep people away.

A strange medical observation is that playing chess diminishes perspiration and increases urination whereas most other games have the opposite effect, which is much more conducive to good health. But that is the least of its drawbacks. What I cannot condone is that far from developing useful talents, chess seems to smother any seed of public virtue in human hearts. So many bright minds are fascinated by the sight of a chess board that the Fatherland loses the potential of some of its best citizens.

It is a delusion to imagine that this game is in the image of human life. On the contrary, how many disparities!

1. In chess, time counts for nothing. In life, it may be essential to be able to make up one's mind quickly. To know the value of time is one of the most important human sciences.

2. In chess, the fight is always one on one. In life, one often has to defend oneself against various people simultaneously, and one always has a chance to be helped by several and to help them in turn.

3. In chess, the outcome is always winning or losing, with nothing in between. In life, one can suffer little losses or great ones, little gains or great ones.

4. In chess, there are indeed thousands of possible combinations, but they are all of the same kind, depending solely on calculation and not at all on luck. In life, fate never fails to play a role in human affairs . . . producing an infinity of gradations and an infinity of nuances. . . . No game is meant to teach us how to live; their only point is to fill, harmlessly, some gaps. The happiest of all mortals is the one with the fewest gaps.[14]

Who gave the better appraisal of the game, Dr. Franklin or Dr. Dubourg? Let the reader decide.

9

Franklin and Mesmer: A Confrontation

I N THIS case, as in the previous one, I was lucky enough to
find in the French archives a document hitherto unknown
to the American public: the report in French of the Académie Royale des Sciences on their investigation of Mesmer. I
thought it psychologically fascinating and wrote the following
paper, which appeared in the *Yale Journal of Biology and Medicine* 66 (July 1993). Fifteen foreign scholars asked me for a
reprint, which led me to believe that the piece, with minor
revisions, might be of interest to readers of this book.

In the year 1784, the population of Paris watched with
mounting excitement as the two most celebrated foreigners in
its midst confronted each other in a debate that pitted medicine against humanism. Medicine in this case was wrapped in
a mystical cloak, while humanism clung to the cool rationality
of the Enlightenment—albeit Enlightenment on the wane.[1]
On one side, Franz Anton Mesmer, the Vienna genius, the
savior of humanity—or was he really a charlatan? On the other,
Benjamin Franklin, the apostle of liberty, the great inventor,

the propagandist for smallpox inoculation—or was he, at this late stage, too fixed in his views to accept new ways?

The French, to be sure, were tiring of the ultra-rational philosophers who had given them the *Encyclopédie*, and many of them were ready for something different. As the historian Robert Darnton so aptly puts it, "They buried Voltaire and flocked to Mesmer."[2]

Yes, they buried Voltaire, the very soul of skepticism and clarity, in the spring of 1778, just after he had embraced Franklin *à la française*, on both cheeks, at a public ceremony. And the pendulum lost no time in swinging back in the opposite direction, toward the supernatural, the mysterious, and the occult. In the absence of Voltaire, Franklin stood as the embodiment of solid, scientific thinking, a bastion of stable logic in shifting times. He could not have offered a greater contrast to the man whose views he was called upon to evaluate. Franklin in his seventies, Mesmer a whole generation younger, in his forties. Franklin taken out of school at the age of ten and acquiring by himself, after that, a wealth of knowledge; Mesmer a graduate of the prestigious medical school in Vienna.

After practicing medicine in Vienna for a few years, Mesmer ran a "magnetic clinic" with a Jesuit professor of astronomy. Their clinic was founded on the theory that magnetic fluid, flowing from the stars, permeated all living beings and that every disease was due to an obstruction of this flow. At some point, Mesmer had discovered that he could—or so he thought—manipulate that magnetic fluid without magnets, thus launching the concept of animal (as opposed to mineral) magnetism. This brought him into conflict with the medical faculty, and in February 1778 he decided to leave Vienna for Paris.

He could not have chosen a more propitious moment. Paris,

in the late 1770s and early 1780s, was the mecca of the marvelous, a city truly besotted with the wilder claims of science. People felt surrounded by wonderful, invisible forces: Newton's gravity, made intelligible by Voltaire; Franklin's electricity, popularized by a fad for lightning rods; the miraculous gases of the balloons that lifted man into the air. The natural philosophers hypothesized enough fluids in the air, the earth, and the human body to make their readers' heads spin. Wealthy amateurs collected instruments displayed in their homes and bombarded the Académie Royale des Sciences with their discoveries.

Everybody's mind focused on the mysteries of nature. Even when Robespierre and Marat wrote to Franklin, it was not to discuss politics. Robespierre merely requested information on the lightning rod, while an extremely polite Marat urgently sought Franklin's endorsement of his theories on the nature of fire.[3] "Never have so many systems, so many theories of the universe appeared as during the last few years," sighed the *Journal de Physique,* adding that many of these provocative theories were mutually contradictory. People were so intoxicated with the power of science that an avalanche of hoaxes found wide acceptance, and the line dividing science from pseudo-science was almost erased. Darnton places mesmerism "somewhere near the middle of the spectrum in which science shaded off into . . . occultism."[4]

Mesmer soon established the first of his famous tubs, or *baquets,* in an apartment on the place Vendôme. Since he spoke with a heavy German accent, he expressed himself mainly through disciples who produced literally hundreds of pamphlets. Thanks to a compelling personality enhanced by robes and rituals, he soon became the talk of the town. Expressions such as "a magnetic personality" and "a mesmerized audience" were born at that time.

Thirty or more persons could be magnetized simultaneously around a covered oak tub about one foot high, filled with powdered glass and iron filings, as well as a number of "mesmerized" water bottles, symmetrically arranged. The lid was pierced with holes through which passed iron branches, to be held by the patients. In subdued light, absolutely silent, they sat in concentric circles, bound to one another by a cord. Then Mesmer, wearing a coat of lilac silk and carrying a long iron wand, passed through the crowd, touching the diseased parts of the patients' bodies.

Mesmer was a tall, handsome, imposing man. Every now and then he would place himself *en rapport* with a subject seated opposite him, foot against foot, knee against knee. This practice, often provoking a trance-like state, is thought to have been the germ of what would become hypnotism. Those who fell into convulsions were carried to a room where they were protected by padding.

Mesmer's reputation grew. By 1779, Paris was polarized over him, and Franklin had good friends in both camps. Mesmer's theories were debated in the salons and the cafés, investigated by the police, patronized by the queen (Marie-Antoinette was, of course, Viennese), ridiculed on stage, burlesqued in popular songs and cartoons, and widely practiced in secret societies called Sociétés de l'Harmonie, whose members were pledged to clean living and abstention from tobacco. Those twenty-four societies, flourishing all over France, made Mesmer a very rich man, for the entrance fee was stiff. He was doing so well that he moved his establishment to the elegant Hôtel de Coigny and lived in luxury.

Eventually Mesmer aroused enough attention for the Académie des Sciences to permit the reading of a letter explaining his views, though they refused to verify his cures. His proposal for investigation by the Société Royale de Médecine would please a modern epidemiologist: twenty-four patients, twelve for traditional medicine, twelve for his own cures, all picked at random. Any disease but venereal ones, and an impartial jury of educated outsiders. But the society turned him down. Still, he made an important convert at the Paris University faculty of medicine in the person of Dr. Charles Deslon, physician to the king's brother. Deslon became Mesmer's mouthpiece and medical stand-in, since foreigners were not licensed to practice. For this apostasy he was expelled from the faculty.

Mesmerism, six years after its introduction in France, was beginning to be considered a threat. This new, universal remedy to prevent and cure illness was still cloaked in mystery. Wouldn't it be a scandal for Europe, thought the authorities, to see a people as enlightened as the French forget the lessons of Descartes and stand bitterly divided between those who considered magnetism a useful and sublime discovery, and those who believed it to be a dangerous and ludicrous delusion? When dealing with influences possibly deleterious to both body and mind, shouldn't a good government destroy error? It should, decided the king.

By the early spring of 1784, mesmerism, now the hottest topic of the day, reappears in Franklin's papers. "Reappears" because soon after Mesmer's arrival, Franklin had been warned against him by his good friend Dr. Jan Ingenhousz, who had written from Vienna, where he served as physician to the Empress: "I hear . . . the Vienna conjuror Dr. Mesmer is at Paris . . . that he still pretends a magnetical effluvium streams from his finger and enters the body of any person without being obstructed by walls or any other obstacles, and that such stuff, too insipid for to get belief [sic] by any old woman, is believed."[5]

Franklin and Mesmer had met and dined together in late 1779, but their encounter turned out to be at cross-purposes: the American was interested in the glass armonica (as he spelled it) that Mesmer used as musical background for his séances, while Mesmer wanted to talk only about animal magnetism.[6] Franklin's endorsement would have been of enormous value to Mesmer, but all his efforts to obtain it were in vain.

Franklin's initial skepticism is reflected in the answer he sent a sick man who had asked him whether it would be worthwhile to travel to Paris to submit to Mesmer's cures:

> There being so many Disorders which cure themselves, and such a Disposition in Mankind to deceive themselves and one another on these Occasions . . . I cannot but fear that the Expectations of great Advantage from the new Method of treating Diseases will prove a Delusion.
>
> That Delusion may, however, in some cases, be of use while it lasts. There are in every great rich City, a Number of Persons who are never in health, because they are fond of Medicines, and always taking them whereby they derange the natural Functions, and hurt their Constitutions. If these People can be persuaded to forbear their Drugs in Expectation of being cured by only the Physician's Finger or an Iron Rod pointing at them, they may possibly find good Effects tho' they mistake the Cause.[7]

Given the state of orthodox medicine in those days, Franklin may well have been right, and Mesmer's unorthodox methods may have saved some lives.

Still, Franklin wanted to keep an open mind. He asked a Frenchwoman whose judgment he respected whether she had ever heard of a real cure obtained by the new method. Indeed she had. Magnetism had just saved from certain death their mutual friend, M. de Breget, whom the regular doctors had despaired of curing. In extremis, the patient was subjected to magnetism administered by Dr. Deslon. He was given barley water and lemonade the first day, broth and meat jelly the second, and solids after that. After nine days, he had been able to get up and dress. Whereupon the French lady expressed her perplexity: "It is very hard for me to believe what I cannot understand. I have no opinion on this prodigious happening, but I would be charmed to hear yours. Versailles is buzzing with this miracle, and I wish that some doctor had followed the treatment and written a report. . . . What I have said so far comes from a level-headed man who does not believe in magnetism any more than I do."[8]

The king soon appointed two commissions, the first consisting of four prominent doctors—including one whose name would acquire a sinister ring, Dr. Guillotin—the other made up of five members of the Académie des Sciences, headed by Franklin whom we see plunging into a purely French affair. In the absence of a state department to set limits or impose guidelines on his conduct, he pioneered in the field of diplomacy by following his instinct. And his instinct told him to keep on good terms, on very good terms, with the much-needed French. If they wanted his advice on a scientific problem, why not give it?

In deference to his age and lack of mobility due to a painful kidney stone, the meetings took place at his residence in Passy, then a lovely village a few miles from Paris. Soon, Franklin and his fellow commissioners were bombarded with advice from all sides. Mesmer sent a cleverly worded letter dissociating himself from Dr. Deslon and asserting that even though Deslon had stolen some of his ideas, he still was ignorant of the true core of animal magnetism. Lafayette wrote in the same vein, calling Deslon a traitor and Mesmer an honest man.[9]

The commissioners obviously had a jolly time planning and carrying out the inquest, more often than not outdoors in the vast gardens of the Hôtel de Valentinois, America's first diplomatic seat. A graphic account of one of their sessions is to be found in the diary kept by Franklin's grandson, Benny Bache, at that point fourteen and just back from his four years at the

Geneva boarding school. Living at a time when adolescence had not yet been "discovered," Benny allowed himself to be good-humored, and his diary is a delight. Under the dateline of May 22, 1784, he notes:

> The commissioners are assembled today with M. Deslon, who, after having magnetized many sick persons, they are gone into the garden to magnetize some trees. I have been present at it. It thus occurred: M. Deslon has made many passes toward a tree with a cane, then they brought a blind-folded young man, whom M. Deslon brought with him. . . . They made him embrace several trees for two minutes. At the first three trees which he held in this way, he said that he felt a numbness which redoubled at each tree; finally, at the fourth, he remained by the tree and no longer answered; then he fell, and they carried him upon the turf, where he made many singular contortions; then he suddenly arose.[10]

The commissioners also experimented with cups of magnetized and plain water, and they tried their skills at impersonating Deslon to see if they were capable, when wearing his clothes, of magnetizing people. They were.

Two reports appeared in the course of the summer, one for the public, of which 20,000 copies were eagerly snapped up, and one for the eyes of Louis XVI only, which remained in manuscript form for fifteen years. This secret report dealt with the impact of animal magnetism on matters of a sexual nature. With great emphasis, and not a little condescension, it made the point that women, having less stable nerves than men, a more inflammable imagination, and a greater tendency to copy one another, were the predestined victims of such a system. "Touch them in one point, and you touch them everywhere," it said. There was furthermore the suspicion that older women patients were simply put to sleep, while the younger ones were submitted to *titillations délicieuses*. Hence, concluded the secret report, the practice of magnetism should be condemned on moral as well as medical grounds.

The report to the Académie des Sciences, read aloud by the astronomer Jean-Sylvain Bailly and published in September 1784, opens a window on the methodology used by the commission, in the days when clarity, reason, and light were still— though not for long—the ultimate arbiters of truth.

The first thing that struck us was the discrepancy between the means employed and the effects produced. On the one hand, violent convulsions, long and repeated; on the other, simple touchings, a few gestures, a few signs. It was like fairyland. How could one man, disposing only of a wand, have such an effect on so many people?

Our role was to keep cool, rational, open-eyed. To define in some way the nature of a fluid that escapes all our senses. The proof of its existence, we were told, is its action on live bodies, its power of curing. But Nature, as we know, also cures, often without remedies.[11]

The experiments we carried out on ourselves demonstrated that if we stopped concentrating, the effect evaporated. Children, devoid of preconceived notions, had no reaction and neither did the mentally disturbed, which is strange since they are often prey to convulsions and upset nerves. Magnetism missed the mark when we tried to use it to warm up cold feet or when we requested it to diagnose some ailments.

Thus forced to give up on our search for physical proof, we had to investigate mental circumstances, operating now no longer as physicists but as philosophers. Examining subjects who had been blindfolded, we discovered we could influence them ourselves so that their answers were the same, whether they had been magnetized or not. This means we were dealing now with the power of imagination. . . . We succeeded in manipulating the imagination. Without being touched or signalled, the subjects who thought themselves magnetized felt pain, felt heat, a very great heat. In some cases, we provoked convulsions and what is known as crises. The subject's imagination could be brought to the point of the loss of speech. It allowed us to produce all the so-called effects of magnetism, even the calming down of convulsions.

Whereas magnetism appears nonexistent to us, we were struck by the power of two of our most astonishing faculties: imitation and imagination. Here are the seeds of a new science, that of the influence of the spiritual over the physical.

The conclusion of Bailly's report—which, it is often thought, was really written by Lavoisier—sounds as if its author were almost in awe. In awe of this tremendous power that they have stumbled upon, the power of one man's charisma to carry with it the enthusiasm of thousands of others, often, alas, for the worse. After Hitler and Stalin this needs no elaboration, but in the days of the Enlightenment, the unleashing of such a power seemed overwhelming: "When the imagination speaks to the multitude, the multitude will ignore dangers and obstacles. One man commands and the others are only his instruments. . . . Man has the capacity to act on his peers, to shake their nervous system to the point of convulsions, without the help of any fluid. This is a dangerous phenomenon."[12]

Dangerous indeed. Lavoisier and Bailly, valuable, brilliant, rational scientists, would both lose their lives to the passions soon to be inflamed by a handful of charismatic orators. Bailly, otherworldly intellectual that he was—his specialty nothing less than the moons of Jupiter—threw himself with zest into revolutionary politics, became the first mayor of Paris, tried to remain moderate, but was eventually engulfed. Lavoisier kept clear of politics, lending only technical assistance to the new order, but he too was sent to the scaffold for having been a tax collector, even an honest one, under the old regime.

Days after the report's publication, Franklin wrote about it to his grandson Temple, who was then in London. Well aware that Temple, age twenty-four, had joined one of Mesmer's

Sociétés de l'Harmonie—whether out of conviction, curiosity, admiration for Lafayette, or a desire to assert his independence—Franklin was careful not to gloat too much:

> The Mesmer report . . . makes a great deal of Talk. Everybody agrees that it is well written; but many wonder at the Force of Imagination describ'd in it, as occasioning Convulsions, etc. and some fear that Consequences may be drawn from it by Infidels that will weaken our Faith in some of the Miracles of the New Testament. . . . Some think it will put an end to Mesmerism. But there is a wonderful deal of Credulity in the World, and Deceptions as absurd have supported themselves for Ages.[13]

Mesmerism had certainly been dealt a blow. An engraving of the time shows Franklin surrounded by his colleagues and carrying the report, whose rays cause the mesmeric *baquet* to tip over. A blindfolded, scantily draped woman is about to fall out of it, while people flee in confusion. Mesmer and Deslon are flying away, one on a broomstick, the other on a winged donkey.

Mesmer, of course, protested vigorously to the Parliament and the faculty, and offered to mesmerize a horse or two as irrefutable proof. Mesmerism remained in practice in France for a while, especially in the provinces. Its guru held the allegiance of a number of famous people—Lafayette, for instance, who would attempt some years later, to Jefferson's undisguised horror, to introduce the doctrine of animal magnetism into the United States. ("A compound of fraud and folly" Jefferson called it.)[14] But the élan had gone out of the movement. A schism developed among its practitioners, and new leaders captured it, moving the practice from healing to spiritualism, in which guise it would last well into the nineteenth century. Mesmer, in disgust, set off for England and Italy in hopes of a new start that never came about. He died in obscurity in 1815, not far from where he was born, near Lake Constance in Germany. As to the unfortunate Dr. Deslon, a true martyr to the cause, he dropped dead soon after the 1784 report, ironically while being magnetized.

A pro-Mesmer versifier made sure that his hero had the last word. His poem proclaimed that by inventing his famous rod Franklin had indeed snatched lightning from the heavens; but Mesmer, a bolder man, had gone right into the abode of the gods and brought back to mankind the secret of their divine wisdom. Safely back in Philadelphia by then, Franklin must have remained unaware of this latest move in partisan one-upmanship. As far as he was concerned, the affair was closed, and he refused to have his name connected with any more polemics on the subject. A little-known consequence of his rejection of Mesmer's claims may have been Franklin's election to the Medical Society of London, an institution whose membership has otherwise been restricted to physicians.

Had he lived in an age of satellite dishes, Franklin would have heard and seen, in January 1790, a few months before his death, the production of a new opera in Vienna. He would have chuckled at the scene where a doctor, who is really a chambermaid in disguise, miraculously revives two dying men, who are really not dying at all. And how does this fake doctor do it? By waving a wand and singing in Italian:

> This is the piece of magnet,
> The mesmeric stone,
> Which originated in Germany
> And then became so famous in France.

Then come the convulsions:

> How they writhe about, twisting and turning,
> They're almost banging their heads on the floor.

And finally the cure:

Ah, hold up their heads!
. . . Hold tight, hold tight,
Tight, tight,
Go on, now you are freed from death.

Was this a belated tribute to Mesmer, a friend of Mozart's father? Or, the opera being *Così fan Tutte,* where all is deception and trickery, was it a joke at Mesmer's expense? We shall never know.

PART III

His Country's Envoy

10

Outfitting One's Country for War: A Study in Frustration

M Y FIRST piece of original writing after I joined the Franklin Papers dealt with the best way to prevent copper saucepans from poisoning their users. I happened to notice that the man who gave Franklin sound advice on the subject, a man whose name had been read in all previous editions as Lavinier, was in reality Antoine Laurent Lavoisier, the celebrated "father of modern chemistry." His advice was to use pure tin totally devoid of lead and to employ a skilled—even if expensive—boilermaker to do the plating.

This modest contribution to a bit of domestic technology was published in June 1960 in the *Annals of Science* and earned me no less than an invitation to write for a German scientific magazine. Enough to addict me for life to the joys and pains of publication! So I started looking for another topic.

When I ran into a message signed in 1778 by all three American commissioners (Franklin, Silas Deane, and Arthur Lee), I could not help being amused at their bewilderment over the French verb *entreposer*—to put in storage—and marveling at the miracle of winning a war in spite of such an incompetent start.

Here is their answer to a French merchant's query:

We can give you no Directions about the Articles "entreposed" for the Coast of Guinea. Because We understand nothing about the Matter. We neither understand why they were entreposed nor what entreposing is. It is impossible for us to apply to the Minister, without understanding that subject and knowing what Minister We are to apply to, and what Favour We are to apply for. We leave it to your Judgment, to remove the Salt Petre in the cheapest and best Manner for the Interest of the States.[1]

Think of saltpeter, that key ingredient of gunpowder, lying idly in some "entrepôt" instead of helping the American Revolution.... At that moment I found my mission and my topic: to track down the odyssey of those bags of saltpeter—fifteen hundred bags, as it turned out.

Little did I know that the quest would take me almost two years and that I would need to learn about cannon, anchors, rope, uniforms, light weapons, shipping practices, maritime insurance, and financing—information woven into documents that still vibrated with the intensity of clashing French and American egos. Furthermore, the work had to be carried out surreptitiously because I was still a mere transcriber who was supposed to confine myself to documents in French, whereas this research demanded that I study every scrap available at the Franklin Papers for the relevant period. I slipped my suggestions on re-dating and annotation in the appropriate folders—a tentative step toward my hoped-for career as an editor—and there they remained for the following thirty years until the edition finally caught up with this episode and my colleagues were happy to find it already disentangled (yes, I had become one of the editors by then).

Beginner that I was, I could not bear to omit any detail of the painful saga, and when the piece was published in the *Proceedings of the American Philosophical Society* 108 (June

1964): 181–223, it was as long as a dissertation—a subconscious atonement, perhaps, for not having completed my Ph.D. thesis in classics at Columbia. I present it now in a radically shortened version.

The year 1780 was a low point of the American Revolution. And the Franklin who toiled through its vicissitudes was not the triumphant scientist, the wily diplomat, the charmer of women, or the benign patriarch of history, but an embattled man in his mid-seventies, enfeebled by gout and kidney stone, beset by new problems and old enemies, groping his way in an alien culture, improvising and fumbling as he went, yet moving on—the very opposite of the crafty hedonistic roué so embedded in the national folklore.

When 1780 began, the chief aim of Franklin's mission to France had been accomplished: the Treaty of Amity and Commerce had been signed, and France was at war, fighting the British at sea, gathering the expeditionary force that was soon to sail under Rochambeau. Franklin's fellow commissioners had been recalled. His chief responsibility now, as he saw it, was to procure more loans, to keep working toward the exchange of prisoners with England, and especially to mobilize Europe's good will toward his struggling countrymen.

But, as it turned out, Franklin was to be plunged into a series of commercial and maritime transactions that completely baffled him, buffeted as he was between French merchants eager to make a quick fortune from the war and an American Congress that foiled their schemes by not paying its debts, a practice that eventually plunged many of those merchants into bankruptcy. A major episode of this turbulent period has to do with the ventures, or misadventures, of a ship called the *Marquis de Lafayette*.

In mid-1779, Franklin received from Congress an order

calling for a staggering quantity of military equipment. The order was bewildering. Some years later, when advocating a French-English dictionary of commercial and technical terms, Franklin remarked that if an American merchant should send a request to France for a variety of goods he formerly ordered from England, the terms he used would be unintelligible. "This I experienced when at Paris," he reminisced. "The Congress sent me an Order for a great Quantity of Merchandise, I show'd the Invoice, but it was not understood, and I could not explain it. At length I took the Resolution of sending to England for one of each Article, which would not only explain what was wanted, but serve as a Model for your [French] Workmen to imitate."[2]

Not only was the order bewildering, but he was also expected to persuade France to pay the bill, a mind-boggling 12 million livres tournois. He obtained 3 million and decided to concentrate on cloth and uniforms. Indeed, the marquis Gilbert de Lafayette, back from his first expedition to America, never ceased hammering that Washington's troops were "Nacked, Schockingly Nacked."[3] Ammunition and weapons were to make up the balance of the enormous cargo.

In the early days of 1780, Franklin enlisted his team, which consisted of one Frenchman and one American. The American was his grand-nephew, Jonathan Williams Jr., then a merchant in the Brittany port of Nantes. Still smarting from the accusations of dishonesty made against him by Arthur Lee in the course of 1779—of which he was exonerated by a committee of merchants—Williams was so afraid to make a false move that his efficiency did not always match his good will. The Frenchman on the team, Jacques Leray de Chaumont, who was Franklin's landlord in Passy, had the very opposite attitude. Buoyed by his success as a merchant-prince in the East India Company, glorying in his new name of *de* Chaumont—which he owed to his recent purchase of the château of Chaumont-sur-Loire—he tended to be rash. An immensely ambitious man, less flamboyant but fully as important to the American war effort as Beaumarchais, he assumed the financial side of the undertaking while Williams was to carry out negotiations with the suppliers.[4]

The enterprise seemed off to a dynamic start, what with Lafayette buzzing around Versailles, wheedling arms from the royal arsenals and pressing for speed. He was to sail in March and wanted to bring Washington a first batch of goods.

In February, Franklin's private horizon was darkened by the unexpected return to Paris of John Adams, whose appointment as sole peace commissioner was a blow to his own status as minister plenipotentiary. Did Congress really not trust him to carry out the peace negotiations when the moment came? The previous year, when Franklin and Adams had labored together as commissioners, their relationship had been outwardly correct—though cool and strained—but now the prospect of an Adams without any outlet for his energies and ambition, since peace seemed further than ever, was truly an appalling one.

The momentous shipment suffered an initial blow when the first ten thousand uniforms missed Lafayette's departure by a few days. The next best chance would be with Rochambeau's expeditionary corps, scheduled to sail from Brest later in the spring.

A new character enters the team at this point: the intrepid, glamorous John Paul Jones, fresh from his naval victory at Flamborough Head (off the coast of Holland). Jones, it seemed, had everything working for him: his friendship with Franklin, his friendship with Chaumont who had financed his squadron, a roaring popularity in Paris, and undeniable navigational talent. But he also had an overwhelming ego and a fiery temper. He was soon embroiled in a bitter dispute with Chaumont over the question of prize money. This took him so frequently to Paris that when Rochambeau was ready to set forth in early May, Jones—who should have joined him on board the *Alliance* loaded with uniforms, the bales of cloth, the arms (old and new), and the cannon so painstakingly assembled during the previous months—was not there. As the French ships were already packed to the gills with their own men and equipment, only a tiny fraction of the congressional goods left Europe.

When Franklin learned of this second setback, he was already distressed by the news, trickling back from the States, of the devaluation of the continental paper currency. Forty old dollars for one new one! The French merchants were aghast. They rushed to Franklin, entreating him to do something, protect their investment, save his country's credit. His first reaction was disbelief—he had never been officially warned of this dramatic step—but when France's envoy to Philadelphia filed report after report describing the impact of the devaluation, Franklin, at a loss for a reply, merely let it out that America's allies, to be sure, would be accorded preferential treatment. Not so Adams, whose reaction was that France needed America more than the Americans needed the French.[5]

During the spring and summer of 1780, Franklin was plunged into a situation he particularly loathed: caught up in the conflicts of other people. Caught, right in Paris, in the Adams-Vergennes dispute, which led to Adams's storming off to Holland while spreading the word that Franklin was subservient to French interests. Caught in the Chaumont-Jones battle still raging between Paris and the coast. Caught, worst of all, in the bitter contest taking place in Brittany between John Paul Jones and Pierre Landais. Landais was a highstrung French captain accused by Jones of having deliberately fired on the *Bonhomme Richard*, his flagship, in the heat of battle at Flamborough Head. Ordered to submit to court martial in

America, Landais took advantage of one of Jones's many absences from the coast to seize back the command of the *Alliance,* his former ship. Arthur Lee, waiting for passage back home, happily fanned the flames of discontent and helped Landais in his coup. "That restless genius," fumed Franklin, "wherever he is, must either find or make a quarrel."[6]

After the *Alliance* had stolen away half empty, another ship had to be found for Jones. The French government yielded to supplication and lent a corvette called the *Ariel*—unfortunately not capacious enough for the six hundred tons of merchandise still awaiting shipment. When urged to petition the king for a larger vessel, Franklin exploded: "I will absolutely have nothing to do with any new Squadron Project. I have been too long in hot Water plagu'd almost to Death with the Passions, vagaries, ill humours and Madnesses of other People. I must have a little Repose."[7]

What he got was not repose, but more frustrations. While John Paul Jones was refitting the *Ariel,* at great length and expense, Chaumont came up with a new and apparently brilliant scheme: he would buy a ship himself, rechristen it the *Marquis de Lafayette,* and charter it to Jonathan Williams. Franklin did not care for the idea but accepted it. He was growing despondent, desperately aware of his ignorance in maritime affairs. He kept begging Congress to send him a consul, a naval expert; but all he received was wave upon wave of bills, pushing him into ever more frantic applications for still more loans from an increasingly reluctant French Treasury. And now, with Arthur Lee's return to America, he was certain that attacks against him were being intensified back home. Indeed, in those early days of August 1780, Congress had moved to send Henry Laurens, its former president, to the Netherlands to negotiate a loan and a treaty of amity and commerce.

But Franklin's star was not fading in French eyes. They

revered him as much as ever and rushed to lend *him* some money as soon as they heard, in September, that Laurens was on his way. Not only did Laurens fail to get the loan; he did not even land in Continental Europe. He was captured at sea and imprisoned in the Tower of London.

In early October, Jones, who had tarried through the summer, finally sailed away, only to return five days later, the *Ariel* badly mauled in a storm. All hopes of getting the stores across the ocean before winter were now dashed.

A few days after that new setback, Franklin was laid low, in the fall of 1780, with the worst attack of gout he had ever suffered. He fought pain in his usual way, by irony. In the short intervals of respite, he composed, in that rickety, jaunty, impudently ungrammatical French of his, one of his most amusing little pieces, "A Dialogue between the Gout and Mr. Franklin," in which his gout berates him for his lazy habits, sedentary life, and gastronomic self-indulgence.

Still, the problems of that cargo had to be faced. If the *Ariel* had been too small, the *Lafayette* was too large—providing a chance and a moral obligation to ship all that stray merchandise purchased by the American commissioners in the first flush of arrival and languishing ever since in odd warehouses. Most crucial among those goods was the saltpeter, and the time had obviously come to ship those 1,500 bags still *entreposed* somewhere—whatever that meant. But saltpeter was a royal monopoly, jealously guarded. Hence an urgent exchange of letters between Franklin and his friend Lavoisier who, in his double capacity of farmer general (tax collector) and manager of explosives (*régisseur des poudres*), was the man best qualified to cut through red tape. It took a lot of doing, but an export permit was finally obtained.

By the time November had cast its gloom over Paris and Franklin had entered his long convalescence—somewhat comforted by the widely held belief that gout was good for one's health—the affairs of his ill-fated cargo took a dramatic turn for the worse. In the course of a government crisis, the French minister of the navy, Antoine-Raymond-Gabriel Sartine, was suddenly dismissed. Chaumont, who was known to be Sartine's man, saw his credit plummet from one day to the next. In a panic, Jonathan Williams begged his great-uncle to pay the *Lafayette's* bills promptly in case Chaumont defaulted. His own credit was at stake.

The weeks that followed, up to the New Year (1781) and beyond, were sheer nightmare. Chaumont, who had over-extended himself but was too proud to admit it, turned nasty. He kept changing the terms of his contract with Jonathan Williams, refused to accept an arbitration award, demanded another one, turned it down too, and bombarded Franklin with financial schemes so complex that a director of the French Treasury confessed that they were all Greek to him.

Bewildered, frustrated, trying to keep a semblance of peace between Chaumont and Williams, Franklin, hardly out of bed, went to consult his banker and then proceeded to Versailles to confer with foreign minister Vergennes, who told him he was being too hard on Chaumont. After a dinner with Chaumont, whom he found indeed cold and dry, Franklin offered to put his private funds, if need be, at the disposal of the public to stave off the Frenchman's bankruptcy. At his banker's suggestion, he presented Congress with an intricate plan for bartering Chaumont's debts against some of the expenses incurred by the French troops in America.

Congress, that very week, was sending Franklin an additional order for arms, clothing, and ammunition, a request for a new loan, and a reproachful comment on his handling of the previous shopping list. His recall, as he well knew, was being pressed for in Philadelphia. On Christmas Day, Arthur Lee wrote that Dr. Franklin, "whose conduct I consider as injurious to the honor and the interests of the United States," should be removed. Lee alluded to considerable supplies having been furnished Franklin a year previously and stated that "not having expedited them has every appearance of designed neglect."[8]

Designed neglect! Franklin's journal for that Christmas season is a muffled cry of pain. His entry for December 26 reads: "Went to Versailles to assist at the Ceremony of Condolence on the Death of the Empress Queen [Maria-Theresa]. All the Foreign Ministers in deep Mourning, flopp'd Hats and Crape, long black Cloaks. . . . Much fatigu'd by the going twice up and down the Palace Stairs, from the Tenderness of my Feet and the Weakness of my Knees."[9]

Around the same time, he tried to pay a visit to the old and ailing comte de Maurepas, the king's mentor, but the count lived on an upper floor of the palace, and Franklin's legs just could not negotiate the steps. On January 17, 1781, he noted: "My birthday" and then crossed out the words, judging them perhaps too frivolous. He had indeed turned seventy-five that day. He simply jotted, once more, that he had accepted many bills. "They come thick."

Almost every entry of his diary carried dismal information about some new creditor of Chaumont jumping into the act, while the *Lafayette* remained blocked in Bordeaux and expenses mounted.

The deadlock broke, almost miraculously, in late January 1781, when Chaumont received unexpected remittances from America. The wheels started turning again, albeit very slowly. It took all of February to get the ship around to Lorient, and almost all of March to load it with the largest, costliest, most troublesome cargo ever to leave France for America. When the *Lafayette* finally set sail, Franklin decided that he would rather step down of his own accord than be recalled, and he sent a letter of resignation to the president of Congress.

The last episode in the *Lafayette* saga was the only one to move fast. After three weeks at sea, the ship was captured and hauled to England where its contents—those fifteen hundred bags of saltpeter heading the list—were auctioned off by candlelight on September 27, 1781.[10]

At his darkest moment of Christmas 1780, Franklin had written: "I, in all these mercantile Matters, am like a Man walking in the Dark. I stumble often and frequently get my Shins broke."[11] But he did keep walking, and by the time of the auction he was already beginning to assemble a new shipment. It would be done, with Vergennes's help, by a new cast of people amid as much tension and quibbling as ever, but with a huge difference. A new term had entered history's vocabulary: Yorktown.

11

Franklin's Choice of a Dinner Set

In memory of John Harris,
so generous in sharing his knowledge.

I BECAME obsessed with this quest for well over a year because of a dream: the dream that some day, when a state
dinner was given at the White House, the tableware would
be ever so simple, pure white, with no more ornamentation
than a sprig pattern in relief around the rim—and, on each
table, a little card would tell the guests that they were to be
served on reproductions of the dinner plates that Benjamin
Franklin had chosen while he was minister plenipotentiary to
France. Franklin's popularity is such, all around the world, that
the room would soon be buzzing with anecdotes about him,
true or imaginary, and with the upbeat mood that the mere
mention of him never fails to create.

But I have stopped hoping that this will ever happen. Despite my search, I have not been able to discover a single remnant of Franklin's dinner set that can be proved authentic. In
the 1970s, while the museum called Franklin Court was being
built in Philadelphia on the site of his house, a quarter million
shards were excavated. Whether they date back to his day or to
the nineteenth-century row houses subsequently built there,

nobody can tell. All one knows is that a great many people threw a lot of broken crockery down a pit.

At first sight the folder dated June 3, 1780, looked like any of the hundreds of other documents that cross our desks. It was a two-page account of items to be dispatched to Franklin's residence in Passy, along with a one-page letter advising him about the shipping procedures. The total sum he was expected to pay was 333 livres tournois and 3 sols. On the fourth and last page, a notation in Franklin's hand: "Acct. of Pottery 333 *l.t.* 3.o."

Pottery? Not war matériel, for once, or any of the vast multitude of items that Congress ordered its emissary to send from France? No, pottery in large quantities: soup tureens, twelve dozen plates, platters of various shapes and sizes, oil cruets, butter dishes, plenty of dessertware, glasses, and buckets, as well as enough implements to serve tea to many people.

The date of the purchase makes sense. By 1780, Franklin was the minister plenipotentiary of a sovereign nation officially recognized by France. He was finally free of his censorious colleagues, John Adams and Arthur Lee, and it would be his decision, and his alone, to entertain foreign diplomats and distinguished guests in any way he wished. He was also aware that it would take years for the American Revolution to reach its goals, and being of a thrifty disposition, he must have felt that the time had come to invest in a set of dinnerware rather than pay the caterers' high rental fees. The previous Fourth of July celebration in 1779 had been a lavish banquet for forty, featuring chicken, duck, turkey, veal, lamb, quail, two varieties of pigeon, artichokes, carrots, turnips, onions, cauliflower, cabbage, lettuce, peas, mushrooms, cucumbers, green beans, grape leaves, *fines herbes,* gooseberries, strawberries, raspberries, cherries, pears, apricots, lemons, melons, and figs, followed by rhapsodic toasts whose eloquence was fueled by many a good bottle. Subsequent parties, given by Franklin alone, were less elaborate.

Under those circumstances, the bill for the dinnerware obviously deserves a closer look. Where did it come from, this first set of dishes ordered for America's just-born foreign service—if one can call it that when it consisted only of one aging minister and two young secretaries? (The secretaries were grandson Temple and a recently hired Frenchman.) The new set did not originate from Sèvres, or from Limoges, the best known manufactories of fine china. It came from the little town of Montereau, sixty miles southeast of Paris, famous only for a political assassination on its bridge in the fifteenth century and for the gracious confluence of the Seine and the river Yonne in its midst—hence the name Montereau-faut-Yonne, meaning "in the fault (disappearance) of the Yonne," given it in the document under study.

The real surprise comes from the stationery's letterhead. Under an ornate design of branches and a crown decorated with fleurs-de-lys, it reads "MANUFACTURE (crossed out: ROYALE) DE FAYANCE ANGLOISE, Des Sieurs CLARK and Companie, éstablie à Montereau-faut-Yonne, en vertu d'Arrêt du Conseil du 15 Mars 1775, sous la dénomination de QUEENS WARE, ou Marchandises de la Reine."[1] Not only does Clark & Co. sound English, but "fayance angloise" is astonishing, and, to make it still more puzzling, the man who signed the invoice was called Mackintosh. Why on earth would Franklin be buying British goods in the midst of the American Revolution? And given the French ban on imported English ceramics, how does one explain the existence in France of an English-sounding firm and the undoubtedly English "Queen's Ware"? What was going on?

In the absence of any documentation about this purchase either at the White House or the State Department, I wrote to the curator of the Musée de la Céramique in Montereau. He was delighted to receive the copy of a document that would become, he said, one of the highlights of his museum, but regretted having to inform me that as far as he could tell, no Montereau piece from the 1780s has survived. Furthermore the manufactory, which had been active until 1955, has now totally disappeared, along with its archives. The only information he could give was that the making of Queen's Ware in France had started in 1775 with capital provided in equal parts by partners called Holker and Garvey.

Were these, finally, the clues? Garvey is the name of an Irish family that emigrated to Normandy in the mid-eighteenth century because they were Jacobites, supporters of the Catholic line of Stuarts in England at a time when Protestants were in the ascendancy. Established in Rouen, the brothers Robert and Anthony Garvey made a fortune there and were eventually admitted to the ranks of the French nobility. (Incidentally, it was their nephew, Plowden Garvey, who shipped back to America, in 1785, Franklin's 128 crates of belongings.)[2]

As to the Holkers, both the father, John (1719–86), and the son, Jean (1745–1822), played an important role in the history of French manufacturing as well as in Franco-American relations. Holker *père,* a native of Manchester, was a close friend of Franklin, to whom his wife sent pots of apple jelly from their orchards. His chief business had to do with textiles, but he took an active interest in several other fields, such as pottery. Holker *fils* became the very first French consul in the United States.[3]

The group of English and Irish émigrés in the region of Rouen commonly practiced what is referred to in our day as industrial espionage. They "debauched" (the opposite verb of the French *embaucher,* to hire) English workmen whose knowledge of advanced technology was far superior to that of their French counterparts, and lured them to France with the promise of better wages. The French government, eager to catch up with its perennial rival across the Channel, offered these men a bonus if they converted to Catholicism and an attractive dowry if they married a Frenchwoman.

After a disappointing visit to the ceramics museum in Montereau—the only positive feature of the day being that the Beaujolais nouveau had just arrived—I came back to Paris feeling discouraged. The curator had shown little, if any, interest in the search and would not reveal the location of the one document he knew of, the one that concerned the creation of the manufactory.

The Sèvres museum, which I visited next, is rich in specimens of porcelain and pottery through the ages and offers many examples of a line of white pottery (ca. 1760) made in Paris, and called Pont-aux-Choux, after a bridge next to which the inhabitants grew cabbage. Mme Madeleine Ariès, one of the foremost experts in the field, assured me that Pont-aux-Choux and Montereau were practically indistinguishable, because Montereau was fabricated by the very workmen who had moved there after Pont-aux-Choux closed down. This stimulated me to buy, in the museum's shop, a white plate with a pattern in relief on its border, an excellent replica, I trust, of Franklin's set.

My lucky break came as I was having tea with history professor François Crouzet and his wife. "The one person you have to see," they told me, "is John Harris at the University of Birmingham. He is the great expert in the field of what is euphemistically called 'the borrowing of technology.'"[4] Since I was planning to visit my English relatives on my way home, I stopped for a day in Birmingham. It turned out to be a delightful day with a learned and generous man who spared no effort to enlighten me and steer my research in the right direction.

And this is what I learned.

In 1774, John Holker, who had recently taken charge of the Montereau works, convinced the French superintendent of finance, the forward-looking Jean-Charles Trudaine de Montigny, that it would be a good idea for France to increase its production of a new line of pottery recently launched in England. He felt sure that a market would soon develop for it. Trudaine agreed quickly and granted him his patronage.[5] A company was founded to run the manufactory under the direction of William Clark of Newcastle and George Shaw of Burslem, both defectors from England.[6] Within months, the firm was petitioning the government, through Trudaine, to facilitate their expansion, since the Montereau clay had proved perfect for the making of Queen's Ware—it turned out a still whiter product than the original English one, and demand for it was indeed growing throughout Europe. The English expatriates asked for exemption from a number of taxes and from military duty for their children, as well as additional subsidies for ten years. France accepted all of those conditions by March 14, 1775—hence the heading of the letter Franklin received five years later, minus the word *Royale* (probably because the royal patent had expired by then).

This Queen's Ware that was becoming so popular—known in France as *faïence fine*—had been perfected during the 1760s by Josiah Wedgwood. One of his innovations was to replace the usual tin glaze by a transparent lead glaze. Known at first as creamware, it was renamed Queen's Ware after Wedgwood had obtained the patronage of Queen Charlotte. Its success was such that it soon was "to be found in every inn from Russia to Spain" and was a factor in the eventual collapse of traditional earthenware-making markets in England, France, and Holland.[7] Its advantages were a refreshing neoclassical simplicity after a surfeit of rococo, easier handling because it weighed less, and greater resistance to chipping; its drawback, in some people's eyes, was that it marked the beginning of industrialization.

Traveling in France in the summer of 1776, Wedgwood's friend and partner Thomas Bentley spotted in the rue St. Jacques (the very street where Franklin's order was to be shipped four years later) some French imitations of Queen's Ware and bought two *compotiers*. He sent Wedgwood a reassuring letter and remarked with satisfaction that the models and glaze were "very indifferent, and the workmanship bad."[8]

Wedgwood did not take the French stratagems lying down. In his "Address to the Workmen in the Pottery on the Subject of Entering into the Service of Foreign Manufacturers," printed three years after Franklin's purchase, he pointed out the misadventures that English workmen could expect if they listened to the siren song of foreign entrepreneurs.[9] He turned his wrath on George Shaw (Clark's partner in Montereau) and exclaimed that the wages this man—by the way, a deserter from the army—was promising his prospective dupes were six times higher than those paid to French workers. The catch was that as soon as local apprentices had learned the tricks of the trade, those splendid wages would be replaced by low ones that "would afford but miserable subsistence to Englishmen, brought up, from infancy, to better and more substantial fare than frogs, hedgehogs, and the wild herbs of the fields." (So much for French cuisine!) It would be too late then to think of going home, for the wily French had ways of blocking such a move, leaving the imported workers outcasts in a strange land. Anyway, how could Englishmen be such traitors to their country? The appeal ended with the promise of a fifty guineas' reward for anyone who caused the apprehension of a vile seducer.

Luckily for their long-standing friendship, Wedgwood does not seem ever to have become aware of Franklin's patronage of

Montereau, just as Franklin may not have known that his dinner set was pirated from Wedgwood. Wedgwood had made a
medallion of Franklin in profile back in 1766, the two of them
remained on good terms, and eventually they became partners
in the fight for the abolition of slavery.

What could have been Franklin's reason for choosing this
particular line? The pleasure of harming British industry, it
seems, as well as the satisfaction of pleasing the French, particularly the Holker family. And Franklin was in his mid-
seventies at the time, a very busy man, a widower who probably
did not want to devote much energy to the choice of tableware.
He may have remembered the request that his daughter Sally
had made seven years previously, when he was still living in
London, to send a set of Queen's Ware for the family's use in
Philadelphia. She thought that the pattern of raised sprigs
around the border was particularly elegant, and in the absence
of any indication to the contrary, I imagine that was the design
he chose.[10]

Jefferson, as soon as he took over Franklin's post in Paris in
1785, ordered fine chinaware that reflected his own taste and
refinement, but Franklin, the printer, the man of the people,
had preferred to represent his country with dinnerware that
was pure white, simple, and modestly priced.

12

Franklin and the Nine Sisters

THIS piece is based on a talk I gave in French at a Masonic lodge in Liège, Belgium, on an occasion when women were invited. The apprehension I felt at finding myself in such an unfamiliar milieu was soon dissipated by the custom of universal hugging and kissing that preceded the talk. And luckily, I had been warned not to expect applause at the end, but two minutes of respectful silence, to be followed by questions.

It was Franklin's custom, when he reached a problematic point in life, to make a list of pros and cons, what he called his moral algebra. There is no proof that he drew up such a list upon his arrival in France in December 1776, but he certainly had time, during his six weeks' crossing on *The Reprisal*, to count his few assets and many liabilities before tackling his vaguely outlined mission of obtaining whatever help he could for his sorely pressed country.

Worst of all, among his liabilities, was his distaste for begging. And yet that was the purpose of his mission. Begging for arms and munitions, for money, ships, for an eventual alliance.

Convincing one monarch to help some faraway shaky self-proclaimed states to overthrow a fellow monarch. Endeavoring to make a good impression on the most snobbish and sophisticated court in Europe—he, the fifteenth child of a Boston candlemaker. Sticking to his Protestant faith in an overwhelmingly Catholic country where Protestants were treated as pariahs.

His assets must have seemed few and fragile. Yes, he had some good friends in the scientific circles of Paris. Yes, electricity was his passport all over Europe. Yes, the cause of his "insurgents" might be sparking a flame in some French hearts, but how many? And yes, the French had detested the British ever since Joan of Arc, but their last confrontation with "perfidious Albion," the French and Indian War, had ended in a stinging defeat.

Still . . . he had to begin somewhere. His first power base, so to speak, was the Académie Royale des Sciences, for which he had been a foreign correspondent for a number of years, and where he was warmly welcomed. His second affiliation, some months later, was to be with the French Freemasons.

Freemasonry had been part of Franklin's life ever since 1731 when, at the age of twenty-five, he was inducted into the lodge of St. John in Philadelphia. Rooted in Scotland and England, American Masonry had started roughly ten years earlier. His ascension was rapid. Within four years he had been made grand master of the Grand Lodge of the Ancient and Honorable Society of Free and Accepted Masons, and a few years later grand master for the province of Pennsylvania.[1] Always looking for improvement, he had suggested, while serving on a reform commission, the serious study of mathematics and architecture, along with the purchase of books and tools.

As it happened, Freemasonry in France had undergone a deep transformation shortly before Franklin's arrival. Under the leadership of the king's cousin, the duc de Chartres, a central directorship called the Grand Orient had been created and the lodges totally reorganized. They became a meeting place for that slice of high society increasingly open to the new ideas emanating from the *philosophes*. Although the atmosphere within the lodges was perfectly democratic, the membership was not, because dues remained very high. Still, new ground was broken since the aristocrats invited to join were no longer chosen on the basis of their birth but for their outstanding character and talent.

Relations between the Masonic Temple and the Church were marked by courtesy. A large number of abbés belonged to lodges; Protestants could be admitted; Sephardic Jews were given entry on rare occasions; and atheists were hardly ever allowed. One may wonder at the high proportion of Catholic clergy involved, since Masonry had been forbidden to Italian Catholics by bulls from two different popes, but the situation was different in France, where it was necessary to secure a ratification of those bulls by the Parlement, and this never happened. Thus the ritual invocation continued to be to the Great Architect of the Universe. The two unassailable principles were the respect due to the king and the supremacy of human reason. Tolerance and liberalism were slowly making their way.

The famous philosopher Claude-Adrien Helvétius had long dreamed of a lodge composed of particularly gifted brothers, a kind of superlodge that would comprise the best representatives of all disciplines and arts. He suggested calling it the Nine Sisters in honor of the nine Muses. He died too early to see his idea become reality, but his close friend, the astronomer Joseph-Jérôme de Lalande, powerfully helped by Helvétius's widow, managed to launch such a lodge in 1776. During her husband's lifetime, Mme Helvétius had kept one of the most brilliant salons in Paris, nicknamed the "Estates-General of European philosophy." After his death, she bought the house of painter Quentin de La Tour in Auteuil, just off the bois de Boulogne, and a bevy of artists and writers soon gathered there. They formed the nucleus of the Nine Sisters, a lodge often referred to today as the UNESCO of the eighteenth century.

Lalande, author of the entry on Masonry in the *Encyclopédie*, was the guiding spirit of this new lodge. A colleague of Franklin at the Académie Royale des Sciences, he probably acted as sponsor at the American's induction in the spring of 1778. The exact date of the initiation is unknown, but since Voltaire had been initiated as number 97 on April 7, and Franklin bore number 106, the event must have happened shortly after that date. Furthermore, Franklin was made Venerable on May 21, 1779, and since one had to have belonged at least one year before attaining that rank, the big day must have fallen at some point between April 7 and May 21.

A splendid feast soon took place in the newcomer's honor. "Preceded by their music," reports the *Journal de Paris*, "the brothers will leave in little boats from the Pont Royal at 8 a.m. to reach their destination." Their destination was the Ranelagh, a replica of the famous establishment of that name near London.[2] Both a restaurant and banqueting hall, the French Ranelagh had opened its doors in 1774 and enjoyed the patronage of Queen Marie-Antoinette. The high point of the celebration was the presentation to Franklin of the apron that had belonged to Helvétius and, after him, to Voltaire, who had recently died.

There always seems to be a sarcastic voice in the midst of rejoicings, a bad fairy at the baby's crib. An anonymous memoirist out of sympathy with Masonic practices remarked: "It was a surprise to see Dr. Franklin, entrusted with matters of the utmost gravity, fritter away a whole day among a bunch of so-called poets who turned his head with their puerile incense."[3]

Flowery invitations from other lodges started pouring in, each more laudatory than the next. We may smile at the thought of our reticent New Englander so often adorned with laurel wreaths, but this adulation must have been a powerful support for Franklin during the many discouraging hours of his long and arduous mission.

Franklin's papers include a voluminous pile of Masonic documents. Most of them are invitations elegantly printed on elaborate stationery, but they reveal precious little about what happened at the events. Their style is brisk and no-nonsense. They invoke "the sweetness of mutual friendship," to be sure, but also firmly remind members to arrive on time if they want to be admitted, to bring nine pounds—plus six on the rare occasions when they would be escorting ladies—and to dress according to regulations.

The Nine Sisters sailed through the summer and early fall of 1778 in high spirits, but serious problems arose in late November because of a decision to hold a grandiose commemoration of Voltaire six months after his death. The French Academy had already paid him tribute in August and had consequently run afoul of the Church's displeasure. It is surprising to see Franklin, generally so cautious in his role of recently accredited foreign diplomat, take an active part in a ceremony that was bound to contain an element of rebellion.

The event opened with the initiation of a few new members, the most famous of whom was the painter Jean-Baptiste Greuze, who had recently done a portrait of Franklin. Seated in a vast auditorium that was draped in black and dramatically lit, the guests listened to eulogies of Voltaire, alternating with music by Rameau, Glück, and Piccinni.[4] By an extraordinary exception, two women had been admitted. One was Voltaire's niece, Mme Denis, who presented the lodge with Voltaire's bust by the already famous Jean-Antoine Houdon. The other was the deceased's great friend, the marquise de la Villette. Stanzas, including some flagrantly anticlerical passages, were read by Jean-Antoine Roucher, a poet much appreciated at the time. Finally, a huge painting of the apotheosis of Voltaire was unveiled, and Franklin, flanked by two assistants—one of whom was Count Stroganoff, whose chef created the famous dish that bears his name—removed the laurel crown that had been placed on his head and deposited it under the painting.

The assembly then moved, in a complete change of mood, to a brilliantly lit room full of flowers, where the banquet was served. More verses were read by Roucher. One of these, obviously meant for Franklin with its allusion to the captive thunder dying at his feet, provoked an ovation. Franklin had become the focus of the proceedings.

All hell broke loose within a few days. The Church was still refusing permission for Voltaire to be buried, and his embalmed corpse was lying in the vaults of an abbey in Champagne. (Not until 1791 would it be transferred to the Pantheon.) Louis XVI, both a fervent Catholic and a Mason—he belonged to the lodge of the Three Brothers—was furious at the Nine Sisters. He directed the duc de Chartres to restore discipline to the wayward lodge, already notorious for its autonomous tendencies.

Under the pretext that those two ladies never should have seen the Masons in full regalia, the Grand Orient ordered the expulsion of the Nine Sisters from their temple, a majestic building that had previously belonged to the Jesuits. All of their furniture was roughly removed, along with Houdon's bust of Voltaire. The lodge came close to being abolished. While all of Paris, intent and amused, followed a war of memoranda and counter-memoranda, an agreement was suddenly concluded on May 20, 1779, exactly one day before Franklin became Venerable. This was certainly no coincidence: his personal prestige had carried the day. He behaved with his usual calm, and passions quieted. In the words of a contemporary: "The inventor of the lightning rod knew, here too, how to protect us from thunderbolts."

Franklin stipulated two conditions before accepting the high honor: he would not be obligated to attend all meetings, and he would not be asked to speak in public. He read French without difficulty, but speaking was arduous for him. In his battle with modes, genders, and tenses, he infallibly went down to defeat.

The first event of his Vénéralat, as it was called, took place on August 18, 1779, and it was an academic feast. Two hundred and fifty people were invited. They were treated to a speech by the president, a symphony, an encomium of Montaigne, and chosen excerpts of verse and prose. Artists had been asked to exhibit their work in the upper gallery. Houdon happily obliged, as did Greuze. The big novelty was a scientific one: a very sophisticated barometer. The banquet lasted late into the night. Although Franklin did not attend the feast, he was not much missed, because what the lodge wanted most was the luster of his name.

At other times, however, his presence was urgently requested. Writing on the tenth day of the eleventh month of the Year of the True Light 5779—that is, on January 10, 1780, since the Masonic year begins on March 1—Lalande told his colleague that, as the main ornament in a public celebration, Franklin could only blame himself for their Respectable Lodge's insistence on his attending. Well aware of his many obligations, his brothers nevertheless begged him to come, even if he chose to remain silent. How much better, though, if they could have the privilege of listening to him! Lalande was not at liberty, he wrote, to tell Franklin why his presence was so crucial, but it was. The signatures affixed to this invitation illustrate the French Enlightenment at its most scientifically advanced and humanly generous. They include that of lawyer Elie de Beaumont, the wonderful pleader of lost causes and tireless defender of people unjustly persecuted, as well as that of Pierre-Jacques Le Changeux, the inventor of the earlier-mentioned barometer. Let us hope that Franklin, always keen on technological innovations, made an appearance, if only to study that barometer.

The American's influence is confirmed, too, by the sudden appearance of Anglo-Saxon names on the membership list of the Nine Sisters: not only his grandson William Temple, but also John Paul Jones, who had been the toast of Paris since his naval victory off the coast of Holland, and Dr. Edward Bancroft, Franklin's close friend and confidant.

Intellectually speaking, Franklin's most notable contribution to the lodge was the part he took in creating the Société Apollonienne, a systematic effort to revamp higher education, which had gone into a precipitous decline since Louis XIV. This was an organization for diffusing newly acquired knowledge—an echo of what Franklin had done half a century earlier in Philadelphia when he had founded the American Philosophical Society. The Société Apollonienne offered literary and scientific lectures to audiences of both sexes. Its president, Antoine Court de Gébelin, widely considered the father of linguistics, was the most illustrious member of the Nine Sisters after Voltaire, Franklin, and Lalande. The Société was so successful that after two years it moved to a handsome new locale and took the name of Musée de Paris (back to the Muses!).

The inaugural session in the new building, held on March 6, 1783, was a celebration of American independence,

six months before the Treaty of Paris that would mark the end
of the Revolution. Franklin, once again, was crowned with
myrtle and laurels. His bust, also the work of Houdon who had
become a member of the Nine Sisters, was unveiled. It may
well be the very one that was recently bought at auction by the
Philadelphia Museum of Art for $3 million.

Franklin's state of health was in decline as of 1784. A kidney
stone was tormenting him. Riding in a carriage was extremely
painful, and he remained mostly confined at home until his
departure in July 1785. Houdon sailed on the same ship on his
way to sculpt Washington's statue, but his joy at having received such a glamorous commission was tempered by the
contretemps of his luggage reaching Le Havre too late for em-
barkation. Temple lent him shirts and other necessaries, but
what is an artist to do without the tools of his craft?

The Nine Sisters, meanwhile, were trying to keep Franklin's presence alive among them. By March 1786 they were
proposing two gold medals worth six hundred livres tournois
each, as prizes in honor of Benjamin Franklin *vivant*: an oratory prize for the best prose essay about him, to be at least half
an hour long; and an art prize for an allegorical drawing two
feet high and one and a half feet wide, showing Franklin's
contributions to the sciences and to American freedom. The
competition was to close at the end of February 1787. It was
open to everyone except members of the lodge, and the prizes
were to be announced on the first Monday of the following
May. Unfortunately, I have not been able to discover its results.

Franklin's Masonic adventures seem to us odd for a diplomat. Today, an ambassador who would allow himself to become embroiled with a contentious local group and, still worse,
accept to head it, would surely invite protest from the host
country and possibly recall by his own nation. But Franklin, in
the absence of formal guidance, was following his instincts. By

doing so he not only provided himself with the cocoon of affection he needed so badly, but also strengthened the spiritual and intellectual ties between his nation and its ally.

Those ties may have reached beyond France. As Robert Palmer remarked: "The fact that Washington and other American leaders were Masons made European Masons feel akin to them. . . . The network of Masonry . . . created an international and interclass sense of fellowship among men fired by ideas of liberty, progress, and reform. At Budapest the Masons called themselves the American Lodge."[5]

13

The Duchess, the Plenipotentiary, and the Golden Cap of Liberty

FRANKLIN'S admirers—and they are legion across the country as well as in Europe—take pleasure in seeing objects he owned; they even try to touch them if the owner or curator is not looking. Imagine then the even greater thrill of discovering an object of Franklin's that is described in the letters but everyone thought had disappeared.

Ellen Cohn and I had gone to the Butler Library of Columbia University with a completely different purpose in mind when we stumbled upon a tiny piece of paper in a scrapbook. It showed an elegant silver pitcher with the following caption: "Cream Jug made by Smith & Sharp, London, 1765. Presented by Dr. Fothergill to Franklin on his departure from England. Left in his will to his executor, Henry Hill. Now in the possession of Mrs. Francis Gummere, of Haverford, Pennsylvania." The "now" in question unfortunately referred to the 1930s. Where could the cream jug be today?

Back at Yale, we rushed to have a look at Franklin's will. It informed us, in his own words, that he had received the jug "from good Dr. Fothergill, with the motto *Keep bright the*

Chain." Keep the chain of friendship bright and shiny! That was a formula I remembered having seen more than once in Franklin's writings, a saying that he had adopted from the treaties of peace concluded with the Indians. He had even taught it to his French friends, who learned to say: "Il faut garder la chaine de l'amitié claire et brillante."

Dr. John Fothergill (1712–80) was a Quaker physician with whom Franklin had collaborated in trying to find a way to reconcile the differences between the colonies and Great Britain. He was a man of broad medical reputation, a collector of rare plants, shells, and insects, a philanthropist of whom Franklin said: "I can hardly conceive that a better man has ever existed."

So now we knew that this was the very object that Franklin had asked his former landlady, Mrs. Stevenson, to forward to Paris. We knew that it was somewhere in the United States, but where? As we were discussing our next move, another scrap of paper slipped out of the folder holding the will. The Yale professor who had scribbled it on an otherwise unspecified August 14 said that he knew "how oddments of information may be useful" and indicated that a silver jug having belonged to Franklin was on display at the Sterling and Francine Clark Institute in Williamstown, Massachusetts.

Ellen promptly got in touch with the curator in Williamstown, Beth Carver Wees, who supplied a photograph and details about the peregrinations of the pitcher.

Part of the beauty of the piece is the engraved chain that undulates along the lower edge of the cover and the upper edge of the base, gracefully linking them. The inscription appears above the handle. One can dream about all the hands that touched that pitcher while being served tea in Passy: those of Jefferson, Lavoisier, Condorcet, Lafayette, John Paul Jones, and so many others.

Which brings me, as usual, to France, and to another precious token of friendship that Franklin, this time, bequeathed straight to history, via George Washington.

A less impressive but equally valid title for this piece could be "The Dancer, the Printer, and the Crabapple Walking Stick." A year or two after he arrived in Paris, Franklin met a charming, middle-aged widow whose name alternated between comtesse de Forbach and dowager duchess of Zwei-Brücken (or duchesse douairière de Deux-Ponts). Born Marianne Camasse, she had been a dancer in her youth and had danced her way into the heart of Duke Christian de Deux-Ponts Birkenfeld, who ruled over a small German principality not far from the French border. Such a marriage, between royal blood and a commoner, had to be a morganatic one—that is, any children born from it were automatically disbarred from reigning. Still, the two sons of this union managed to cut a figure in society. Christian and William, after distinguishing themselves at Yorktown, married into French aristocracy.

Franklin often received little gifts from the duchess—a walking stick and a pair of scissors, for example. About the scissors she wrote: "As you see, I multiply as much as I can the means of remaining in your mind. Forgive me, dear man, the little tricks that my heart suggests. They are the only tricks I am capable of. Now, whether you are walking, writing, or changing your shirt, you are bound to think of me."[1] Walking (the stick) and writing (the scissors to cut his quill pen) are easy to understand. But changing his shirt? Franklin makes no allusion to that particular activity in his reply, so we are left to guess. Studs? A batch of new shirts?

His reply was as gracious as her note:

I received my dear Friend's kind Present of the Scissors, which are exactly what I wanted, and besides their Usefulness to me have a great additional Value by the Hand from which they came. It is true that I can now neither walk abroad nor write at home without having something that may remind me of your Goodness towards me; you might have added that I can neither play at Chess nor drink Tea without the same Sensation: but these had slipt your memory.[2] There are People who forget the Benefits they receive, Madame de Forbach only those she bestows. But the Impression you have made on my Mind as one of the best, wisest, and most amiable Women I ever met with, renders every other means to make me think of you unnecessary.

After which he had added: "That Impression will remain as long as the Heart on which it is stamped," but erased those words, perhaps judging them too sentimental. The draft that we have shows numerous other corrections and allows one to appreciate the trouble that Franklin went to in order to convey the exact nuance of his feeling.

Still, he lost the walking stick. Four years later she gave him another, which now rests at the National History Museum of the Smithsonian Institution in Washington, reverently wrapped in acid-free tissue paper. Franklin bequeathed it to George Washington: "My fine crab-tree Walking Stick, with a gold Head curiously wrought in the form of a Cap of Liberty, I give to my Friend, and the Friend of Mankind, General Washington. If it were a Sceptre, he has merited it and would become it." Washington, in turn, left it to his nephew, who presented it to the Smithsonian. It is a knobby, shiny black stick ending not in a curved handle but in a solid gold sculpted Phrygian cap—the cap that would become a sanguinary symbol during the French Revolution but in the 1780s still signified merely liberty. In exchange, the duchess asked for one of the peace medals that Franklin had commissioned to celebrate the end of the war.[3]

The walking stick inspired a poem, of course. Almost any occurrence did, in the genteel circles of eighteenth-century France, when people seemed to write verse as easily as prose. In this case, the French rule of putting stress on the last syllable was a great help, since it allowed Washington to rhyme with Trenton and even with Marathon in an evocation of the rocky history of freedom.

Two years after his return to Philadelphia, Franklin sent the duchess a last message:

> Dear Friend, There is no one of that Character whom I left in Europe, that I think of so often as you. . . . I am now past 81 Years of Age, and therefore tho' still in tolerable Health cannot expect to survive much longer. We are at a great Distance, and I can never again have the Pleasure of seeing you. I write this Line then to express my sincere Wishes of Health and Happiness to you and your good Children, and to take leave. Adieu, most respectable and most amiable of Women, and believe me while I live, Yours most affectionately B.F.[4]

There was true fondness and understanding between Franklin and the dowager duchess. They had both risen from humble origins to an exalted rank in society, he through intelligence and hard work, she through beauty and charm. Was it the duchess, perhaps, who taught him the French saying that little gifts nourish friendship (*les petits cadeaux entretiennent l'amitié*)? Franklin, in his later years, became almost prodigal in that respect. While in Paris, he distributed the medals celebrating American freedom as well as books that he had published in France: the constitutions of the thirteen states that he had helped La Rochefoucauld to translate, plus his own *Bagatelles*. Back in the New World, he proudly dispatched red cardinals for Mme Helvétius, some recently composed music for

Mme Brillon, Virginia hams, squirrel skins for special lady friends (such as the duchess's daughter Elisabeth, who was advised to "line her mantle" with them), Newton Pippin apples, cranberries, and the "Crown soap" that his sister Jane made according to their secret family recipe. Except for the birds, which died in transit, all of his presents arrived safely and inspired enthusiastic responses, along with presents in return—such as dolls for his granddaughters, little French mittens, and finery for Sally. All of this created on both sides of the Atlantic a whirl of memories, affection, and nostalgia, reminding him once again that in Paris he had truly belonged and was not forgotten.

14
Franklin Plays Cupid

THIS slight, amusing little story intrigued me because it shows that despite his love of France and his rapid assimilation to the country, Franklin did not have a real grasp of the formality that underlay, like a rock, the charming surface of social intercourse. His unawareness of this fundamental fact of French life—that tradition played a larger role than human emotions—led him to make the same psychological mistake when he proposed a marriage between Temple and the daughter of his close friends, the Brillons. His suggestion was based on the attraction that the young people obviously felt for each other, on his own desire to end his days in France, and on the assumption—how mistaken!—that Congress would reward his efforts by granting Temple an honorable career in foreign service. What the Brillons saw, from their point of view, was that Temple, being neither French nor Catholic, was disqualified from taking over his father-in-law's administrative position—reason enough, in their eyes, for turning down the proposal. Abashed and hurt as he must have been by their refusal, Franklin had no choice but to accept it in good grace.

In the case of Mlle Desbois, he lost face, somewhat, with

the French authorities, but the episode must have eventually made for a good story, a story of misunderstanding—à la Henry James—between the wily European and the ingenuous American.

In November 1779, Franklin received a visit from a young Frenchwoman in distress, a Mlle Desbois. She had brought with her a recommendation from a man he knew well, the treasurer of Brittany, M. Beaugeard. The purpose of her trip to Paris was to plead her case, or rather that of John Locke, the American sea captain with whom she had fallen in love. Locke, a whaling master, had been seized by the French while serving on an English vessel, and was currently languishing in prison in Nantes. Could Franklin help them?

To the plenipotentiary, the plight of John Locke was a routine case. When the French captured an English ship, they had no way of distinguishing the British crew from Americans who had been "pressed" into service, generally, though not always, against their wishes. Everybody was thrown in jail together, and it was up to the Americans to convince Franklin of their nationality and patriotism. If persuaded, Franklin turned to the French minister of the navy, Antoine-Raymond-Gabriel Sartine, to obtain their release.

Love and a prospective marriage were the novel elements in this case, and they imbued Franklin's appeal with a special fervor: "As your Excellency will see by the enclosed, by the Letters that have passed between this Captain and the Lady and by her Earnestness in her sollicitations, I perceive they are passionate Lovers, and cannot but wish the Obstacles to this Union removed, and that there were a great many more Matches made between the Two Nations, as I fancy they will agree better together in Bed than they do in Ships."[1]

Those were the days when the fight between John Paul

Jones and the French captain Pierre Landais was reaching its
climax and every mail brought the unfortunate Franklin some
belligerent memorandum from one party or both. Clashes
within crews on ships had become so frequent that efforts had
to be made to keep the "allies" separated.

The prospect of a transatlantic rapprochement made
Franklin grow lyrical: "You may lose a Prisoner by granting this
Grace, but I hope the king will gain by it some good young
Subjects."

Sartine must have been flabbergasted. A former police commissioner, he viewed life with circumspection. Did France's
American partners have no grasp of matrimonial laws and cus-
toms? Did people marry just like that in their country, for love?
Come to think of it, the revered, beloved Doctor himself had
demonstrated a rather cavalier attitude toward the sanctity
of institutions, what with his common law marriage and illegitimate grandson. All of this called for an answer as firm as it
was courteous:

> I would be glad to grant the man his freedom, but allow me to
> observe that the English Court is claiming him because, by
> escaping, he broke his word of honor, and furthermore ab-
> ducted a demoiselle who is probably the very one you met. You
> will understand, Sir, that I cannot possibly help join those two
> people without knowing the intentions of the young lady's
> family. A premature release on my part would give the impres-
> sion that I approve of the prisoner's conduct, whereas in fact
> society requests that I do not grant him lightly the means of
> abusing her parents' trust and perhaps even the trust of the
> girl he has seduced. I shall look further into this affair.[2]

He did. Two weeks later he reported that the governor of
Nantes strongly suspected Locke of being already married in
America. Sartine also forwarded a letter from Mlle Desbois's
mother, referring, as he says, to her daughter's abduction and

plans to flee to England. (This last document does not appear in Franklin's papers; it was sent back to Sartine, at his request.) Alas, poor Franklin, what a faux pas! The worst of it is that if his files had been kept in Passy with the same care as they are at Yale, he too would have known that Locke was already married. One year earlier, while begging for his release, Locke had informed him of the fact: "Most honrabil docktor Sur, Thease lines comes to In form you that as I am hear and a Marican and a poor prisner & have a wife and famyly In a maricah."[3] In fact, the Nantucket records show that John Locke, native of Cape Cod, had married Abigail Mayo on July 9, 1775—only four years before Mlle Desbois began her campaign for his freedom.[4]

The wisest course for Franklin, of course, was to keep quiet and let Mlle Desbois slip out of his life. But she did not. A little over three years later, a letter arrived from Lorient—again from Brittany and again from a respectable source: the rector of the Royal Church, Monseigneur Brossière. The young woman was nothing if not well connected. After the usual apologies for taking up Franklin's time, the cleric informed him that when Locke was eventually exchanged and went back to England, she had followed him there and lived with him for two years under the name of "Madame Loch." Everybody thought they were married, but in fact they were not. After returning to France, she met a most suitable party but cannot prove that she has never been married to "Loch" unless Franklin helps her make it clear that Locke already has a wife and child in Nantucket. It would be better still if he could attest that the wife is still alive.

Franklin's answer, if he sent one, has disappeared. All that remains of this obscure episode is an endearing glimpse of an unexpected facet in our celebrated polymath: shall we say naïveté?

15

Was Franklin Too French?

A SYMPOSIUM was held in Philadelphia in 1990 to mark the two hundredth anniversary of Franklin's death. Its theme, "Reappraising Franklin," gave me a new impetus to explore one part of his life that I feel needs reconsideration: his final years. In most biographies, this period is presented as the glorious climax of a great career: Franklin signing the Constitution, just as he had signed the Declaration of Independence and the Treaty of Paris. A good journalist who was always there when history took a turn.

But what I see in Franklin's letters is an old man whose private dreams have been shattered. For a good part of his life, he had hoped for a grant of land in the West. He never received one, though many of his contemporaries did. Nor was he given any tangible token of appreciation for his long and often arduous mission to France.

After their return to Philadelphia, the bright youth he had whisked off to Paris, his beloved grandson Temple, vegetated for years on a farm in Rancocas, New Jersey, his hoped-for foreign service career over before it had begun. Benjamin Franklin's enemies could always invoke the role that Governor

William Franklin had played during the Revolution to block any appointment that came William Temple Franklin's way. In spite of Franklin's efforts, his son-in-law Richard Bache was not reinstated in his position as postmaster general, a position he had lost for purely political reasons. And finally, whereas Washington is generally thought to have been an admirer of Franklin, that admiration was always confined to polite words, never translated into deeds.

All those disappointments stem, I believe, from the many years that Franklin spent abroad, especially in France. It seems that he absorbed the culture of the French, so different from his own, to a degree that may have disturbed his fellow Americans.

My musings on this topic have appeared in J. A. Leo Lemay, ed., *Reappraising Benjamin Franklin: A Bicentennial Perspective* (University of Delaware Press), 143–53.

Franklin was an inspired alien. It is not an easy task for anybody, being an alien, yet he managed, in his seventies, to adapt to an entirely new environment, the Gallic world so deeply different from the Anglo-Saxon culture he had lived in on both sides of the Atlantic.

He used every key the alien has to open the doors of his or her new world. The first of these is one's profession. His passport to France was electricity. It was in Marly-la-ville, three leagues from Paris, that his hypothesis on the electrical nature of lightning was verified experimentally for the first time, in 1752, making it unnecessary—had he but known—for him to launch his famous kite during a storm and risk his life in the process.[1] The French were proud to have been the first to become fascinated by his theories, especially since the Royal Society of London had been apprised of them earlier. Louis XV sent him congratulations and had some electrical experiments performed at his court. Franklin's fellow philosophers debated his views and corresponded with him long before he would set foot on French soil, as a summer visitor, in 1767 and 1769. He was much acclaimed during those two visits: he had the honor of being presented to Louis XV and even invited to the Grand Couvert, the evening meal that the royal family ate in public. "Invited" is something of an exaggeration. He was allowed to stand between the queen and Mme Victoire, one of the king's sisters, and watch them eat. The occasion pleased him so much that he drew a sketch of the seating arrangement and sent Polly Stevenson a detailed account of all that he had observed.[2]

By 1772 he was elected a foreign correspondent (*membre étranger*) of the Académie Royale des Sciences, and when he reached Paris in the closing days of 1776, no longer an illustrious traveler but an envoy pleading for help, the first base he touched was the academy. "Mr. Franklin est venu prendre séance," wrote Condorcet in his minutes for January 15, 1777. Judging by the numerous academicians of all categories present on that day, he must have received a warm welcome. His colleagues did not waste time before putting him to work. He was asked to serve on a commission to protect the Paris powder magazine, the Arsenal, from lightning and to study a memoir suggesting the best way to do the same for the spire of the Strasbourg cathedral. He also took part in Antoine Parmentier's efforts not only to gain acceptance for the lowly potato and its byproducts, but also to build a new kind of oven in which bread could be baked more efficiently. He encouraged the attempts of an ambitious young man, Claude Pahin de la Blancherie, to establish an international community of artists and scientists based in Paris.

A paper that Franklin wrote on the aurora borealis was read to the academy. He also sent a report on toads that had been found alive in the masonry of his residence in Passy. Leafing through the minutes of the Wednesday and Saturday meetings of the academy, one is touched by the many admiring, affectionate references made to Franklin by his learned colleagues. The abbé Alexis Rochon, for instance, credited the new kind of printing press he had devised to an ingenious system Franklin had invented in America.[3] Every meeting that Franklin attended must have boosted his morale, which flagged more than once between his arrival in Paris and the signing of the Treaty of Amity and Commerce fourteen months later. Even after that moment of triumph, his spirits would sink again when his much younger American fellow commissioners, Arthur Lee and John Adams, did their best to make him feel old and irrelevant.

Franklin's immersion in French scientific life was to carry him well beyond the confines of the academy. Not only did he help investigate Mesmer, but it was to him that the aeronauts of both schools—that of Jacques Charles and that of the Montgolfier brothers—gave the first accounts of their balloon flights.[4] He supported them both, morally and financially, and took delight in chiding Sir Joseph Banks, president of the Royal Society, about the fact that the balloons were progressing so much faster in France than in England. In so doing he used the word *we* to refer to the French and himself: "Your Philosophy seems to be too bashful. In this Country we are not so much afraid of being laught at. If we do a foolish Thing, we are the first to laugh at it ourselves and are almost as much pleased with a *Bon Mot* or a good *Chanson* that ridicules well the Disappointment of a Project, as we might have been with its Success."[5] Can identification go much further?

The second key at the outsider's disposal is that of his church or the spiritual group to which he or she belongs. In Franklin's case, as we have seen, this was Freemasonry.

The alien's third key is the hardest to describe. It is a combination of personality, congeniality, and good luck—and it can
result in entrée to the new country's social life, the ultimate
manifestation of one's acceptance. Franklin had no problem in
this respect: he was lionized throughout his entire stay in
France, as he had been during his previous visits. His only difficulty was in finding enough days to accept the invitations that
poured in. As the ever acidulous, ever quotable John Adams
put it: "He was invited to dine abroad every day and never declined unless when We had invited Company to dine with
Us. . . . Mr. Franklin kept a horn book always in his Pockett in
which he minuted all his invitations to dinner, and Mr. [Ar-
thur] Lee said it was the only thing in which he was punctual."[6]

Franklin's influence on French society went far beyond the
world of dinner parties. The disenfranchised in France, people
who had never seen him, who did not even know how to spell
his name, created a mythical Franklin both omniscient and
benevolent, one who was not only a bridge between themselves
and the powers that be, but also a beacon of hope. As Adams
put it in his bitterly clairvoyant way, even the scullion in her
kitchen thought Franklin would bring back the golden age.
The letters that reached the American plenipotentiary's desk
every day, whether from country priests, runaway adolescents,
would-be emigrants, anxious parents, idealists with schemes to
improve America, convicts who heard he had rescued one of
them, or merchants on the edge of bankruptcy, represent not
only a cross-section of France's anxieties—and a fascinating
page of prerevolutionary history—but the greatest tribute of
trust and love that a foreign diplomat had ever received.

And what did Franklin think of the French? In the early
stages of his stay, he was extremely careful never to criticize
them. He, who had at times written and spoken harshly about
them during the French and Indian War, had nothing but good

things to say once he lived in Paris. "They are a most amiable Nation," he declared, "without a national Vice." When he compared France to other countries, it was to fault the pride of the English and the insolence of the Scots. He granted that the French indulged in some frivolities, but they were harmless ones such as carrying their hats under their arm because their hair was so elaborately coiffed that no hat could stay on it.[7] He praised the ladies for their eagerness to please, the thousand ways they had of rendering themselves agreeable, and their willingness to be embraced—or rather, to have their necks kissed, so as not to rub the paint off their cheeks.[8]

Toward the end of his stay—after the Treaty of Paris had been signed in 1783—Franklin allowed himself some deeper criticism of French society. He was irritated by the pervasive system of patronage in Europe. Self-reliance was still a cardinal virtue in his canon, and in the bagatelle entitled "Information to Those Who Would Remove to America," he lashed out at the arrogance of the nobility, at hereditary honors and undeserved privilege. It was not advisable, he said, for a person to go to America "who has no other Quality to recommend him but his Birth. In Europe it has indeed its Value, but it is a Commodity that cannot be carried to a worse Market than that of America, where People do not inquire concerning a Stranger, *What is he?* but *What can he do?*"[9]

In spite of his admiration for French women, Franklin also reported with distaste the habit that had spread among the wealthier ladies of sending their children to wet nurses, a practice that truly shocked him. He went so far as quoting the prediction made by a surgeon of his acquaintance that women's *bubbies* would eventually disappear for lack of use. Were the Parisiennes not ominously flat-chested already?

Excessive luxury also bothered him—the only point, perhaps, on which he and Adams saw eye to eye. One likes to imagine them spending a few harmonious moments over a supper of cheese and beer, reminiscing about the bracing rigor of their youth in Massachusetts as opposed to the hedonism flourishing all around them in Paris.

None of this, however, prevented Franklin from falling in love with France and declaring, on at least two occasions, that he might settle there for good. The first time was when, as we have seen, he tried to arrange a match between his grandson and Mlle Brillon; the second, when he proposed to Mme Helvétius. The earnestness of his proposal has been much discussed. I tend to believe that, even though it was part of a facetious piece, he meant it seriously.[10]

The obvious reason why Franklin adapted to France so quickly and so well is that his love for England had turned to implacable hatred, a reversal that included a change of heart about his son William, whom he came to consider a renegade and eventually disinherited. He was also quite intensely a man of the present, not given to nostalgia or daydreaming. The only fault his French friends saw in him was that he tended to forget the absent: *loin des yeux, loin du coeur* being their slightly more sentimental rendering of "out of sight, out of mind." And finally, he was temperamentally suited for France. The irreverent streak, which surfaced throughout his life, found a congenial reception in Paris, as did his love of laughter and desire to amuse. His mischievousness did not shock the French. Nor did his interest in women, which was considered perfectly normal.

So Franklin was very French. In fact, he was too French for his own good. The higher his popularity soared in Paris, the lower it sank with his colleagues John Adams, Arthur and William Lee, and Ralph Izard. Whereas Franklin's policy was not to press the French too hard for an alliance, but to wait for them to discover where their interests lay, Adams was inclined to barge in.

After Franklin's policy of alleged passivity had borne fruit in the shape of treaties of commerce and alliance, loans amounting to millions of livres tournois, a French expeditionary corps, and finally, peace negotiations, he was accused of excessive gratitude where little, if any, was required. So much has been written on the reasons for Adams's hostility to Franklin that I can only suggest that Adams must have felt toward him the way Salieri did toward Mozart, if we are to believe the author of *Amadeus*. Adams knew himself to be an intelligent, hard-working, God-fearing, and patriotic man, which he truly was. But there, right beside him, lived that unworthy genius who enjoyed himself, indulged himself, and possessed all the charisma. It was galling.

Some excerpts from letters to third parties tell the story of this animosity with the raw power of their unchecked anger:

Adams on Franklin: "If I was in Congress and the Marble Mercury in the Garden of Versailles were in Nomination for an Embassy, I would not hesitate to give my Vote for the Statue, upon the Principle that it could do no Harm."[11]

Franklin on Adams: "[Mr. Adams] is always an honest Man, often a wise one, but sometimes . . . absolutely out of his senses."[12]

Adams on Franklin: "You may depend on this, the moment an American minister gives a loose to his passion for women, that moment he is undone; he is instantly at the mercy of the spies of the Court, and the tool of the most profligate of the human race."[13] (Considering that Franklin was seventy-seven when this passage was written, it betrays at least a grudging admiration for his enduring powers.)

Franklin on Adams (on the possibility of having to collaborate with him on treaties of commerce with various European nations): "I can have no favorable opinion on what may be the Offspring of a Coalition between my Ignorance and his Positiveness."[14]

Adams on France: "All I ever suffered in public life has been little, in Comparison with what I have suffered in Europe, the greatest and worst part of which has been caused by the ill Dispositions of the Comte de Vergennes, aided by the Jealousy, Envy and selfish Servility of Dr. Franklin."[15]

Franklin on France: "[I believe] that this Court is to be treated with Decency and Delicacy. . . . and that such an Expression of Gratitude is not only our Duty, but our Interest. A different Conduct seems to me what is not only improper and unbecoming, but what may be hurtful to us. . . . It is my Intention, while I stay here, to procure what Advantages I can for our Country, by endeavouring to please this Court. . . . [Mr. Adams] thinks, as he tells me himself, that America has been too free in Expressions of Gratitude to France; for that she is more oblig'd to us than we are to her."[16]

Gratitude toward France was to be the bone of contention from then on. Franklin never wavered on this point. He tended to see countries as characters in allegorical dramas: England was the cruel stepmother, America the virgin bride, France the husband and protector. Translated into iconographical terms, his vision was transmuted into the medal called Libertas Americana, in which America is symbolized by the infant Hercules strangling two serpents at a time (the British armies defeated at Saratoga and Yorktown), while England appears as a leopard ready to attack. France has become Minerva, with some fleurs-de-lys on her tunic, shielding little Hercules.[17] Congress was cool toward the medal and did not finance it on the ground that Minerva loomed too large, considering that France had had nothing to do with the victory at Saratoga (nothing, of course, if one discounts the large quantities of supplies sent surreptitiously by Beaumarchais). Franklin went ahead anyway and distributed the medal to those whose help had been crucial in his country's hour of need.

Britain, in Franklin's view, was still to be feared: "Britain has not well digested the loss of Its Dominion over us, and has still at times some flattering Hopes of recovering it. . . . A Breach between us and France would infallibly bring the English again upon our Backs; And yet we have some wild Heads among our Countrymen, who are endeavouring to weaken that Connection!"[18]

The price to pay for this attachment to France would be very high. The most embittered letter the Doctor ever wrote, I believe, was sent on September 10, 1783, exactly one week after the signing of the Treaty of Paris. He had heard from his Boston friend, the Reverend Samuel Cooper, that "It is confidently reported, propagated, and believed by some among us, that the Court of France was at bottom against our obtaining the Fishery and Territory in that great Extent in which both are secured to us by the Treaty; that our Minister at that Court favoured, or did not oppose this Design against us; and that it was entirely owing to the Firmness, Sagacity and Disinterestedness of Mr. Adams, with whom Mr. Jay united, that we have obtained those important Advantages."[19]

Franklin did not react to this astounding accusation until the peace treaty had been signed. Then, on that September 10, he sent identical letters to Adams and to Jay: "It is not my Purpose, to dispute any Share of the Honour of that Treaty which the Friends of my Colleagues may be disposed to give them; but having now spent fifty Years of my Life in public Offices and Trusts, and having still one Ambition left, that of carrying the Character of Fidelity, at least, to the Grave with me, I cannot allow that I was behind any of them in Zeal and Faithfulness. I therefore think that I ought not to suffer an Accusation, which falls little short of Treason to my Country, to pass without Notice."[20]

How devastating for a man as proud as he was to write, in effect, "Your ambassador is not a traitor." He, who had always striven to present himself as impervious to calumny, unruffled under attack. As early as 1757, he had advised: "Act uprightly and despise Calumny; Dirt may stick to a Mud Wall but not to polish'd Marble."[21] He used the image of the marble wall more than once in his life. But with enough acid even polished marble will become porous, and the aging Franklin could no longer keep his Olympian composure. He was deeply hurt.

This was only the first installment of the price to pay for loyalty to one's ally in war. The next was paid by Franklin's grandson Temple, who had served the peace commission as secretary, filling reams of pages with his clear hand that resembles his grandfather's so much that we editors have trouble distinguishing between them. When the moment came to bring the peace treaty to Congress, the honor did not go to Temple, who had been Jay's choice, and for whom this would have been an important stepping stone (since, as the son of a Loyalist, he was ever under a cloud). The honor went instead to John Thaxter, a protégé of Adams who had had nothing to do with the clerical work involved in the negotiations. Right after that disappointment, in the summer of 1784, Temple renewed his ties with his disgraced father, now in exile, and began to make pleasure his way of life.

Franklin must have grown worried at that point. He had meant to have Temple study law in Paris but had used him instead as his secretary, confidant, and stand-in as his own health grew worse and he no longer could go to Versailles himself. Now the best years for studying had passed. Temple was twenty-four and could offer only the goodwill of the court as well as his knowledge of the French language and French ways. Indeed, he knew his way around so well that Jefferson would often turn to him, in his early days in Paris, for help on points of etiquette. But this skill could not substitute for professional training.

In his anxiety, Franklin made an unusual move. He asked Congress to take Temple under its protection and, in view of his own experience and past services to the public, to name the young man secretary to the commission soon to be appointed for the conclusion of treaties of commerce with various European nations. He also mentioned that Sweden had expressed an interest in having Temple serve as American minister in Stockholm.

What a mistake! It took no time for Franklin's enemies to escalate the Swedish possibility into a French certainty and to tell each other, in agitation, that the wily old diplomat proposed to install his bastard grandson in Paris while grabbing the London embassy for himself. All this, of course, with the complicity of the foreign minister of France, whose chief aim, as they saw it, was to clip America's wings. From William Lee to his brother Arthur to Elbridge Gerry to John Adams, the imaginary plot was repeated and embellished as it went round. Now, at last, Franklin had revealed his vulnerable spot: the way to hurt him was through Temple. A triumphant Gerry was able to report to Adams on June 16, 1784, that Temple had not been chosen as secretary to the new commission precisely *because* he was related to Franklin:

> I think, your friend the D—r, when he finds . . . that his Grandson has not only no Prospect of Promotion but has actually been superseded. . . I say, I think he will have no reason to suppose that his Conduct is much approved. Indeed, we have not been reserved in Congress with respect to the Doctor, having declared in so many Words, that so far advanced in Years and so tractable is he, that it has become a Matter of Indifference to Us, whether We employ him or the Count de Vergennes to negotiate our Concerns at the Court of Versailles.[22]

The news of the appointment of Colonel David Humphreys, Washington's personal protégé, was a serious blow to

Franklin. He was, as he told his trusted friend Charles Thomson, secretary of Congress, "sorry and ashamed" to have solicited in favor of his grandson. "Ashamed." A word he had never applied to himself, not even when admitting the errors of his youth.

From then on Franklin never obtained anything he wished on a personal level. The population of Philadelphia gave him a hero's welcome on his return, but the authorities were, and remained, cool. He may have had the trappings of prestige, such as towns and counties named after him—even the first state west of the Rockies (though only for a few years)—but real power had slipped from his hands, and he was too politically astute not to know it. As sole recompense for his mission to Paris, he asked that his son-in-law, Richard Bache, be reinstated in his former job as postmaster general. The request was ignored. Washington answered every paragraph of Franklin's letter except that one.

And what about the old dream of some land in the West? In a rare outburst of bitterness, Franklin confided to Thomson: "I must own I did hope . . . The Congress would at least have been kind enough to have shewn their Approbation of my Conduct by a Grant of some small Tract of land in their Western Country, which might have been of Use and some Honour to my Posterity."[23] But while the Lee brothers were recompensed for their services in France (what services?), Franklin was not.

Still, the love of France lived on in his grandsons. Temple settled in Paris around 1800 and never left. He is buried there. Benny Bache, who had been set up as a printer by his grandfather but became a journalist as soon as Franklin died, defended the French cause in his newspaper, the *Aurora,* at a time when doing so was growing increasingly unpopular because America was throwing itself into the arms of England. He attacked Washington in the columns of *Aurora* and locked horns with John Adams. Accused of being "a French agent in treacherous correspondence with the Directory," Benny was threatened with jail. In spite of a yellow fever epidemic, he spent the summer of 1798 in Philadelphia in order to prepare his defense. He caught the disease and died at age twenty-nine.[24] The price for loving France had been heavy indeed for both grandfather and grandsons.

PART IV

Back at Home

16

Innocents on the Ohio: The American Utopia of Dr. Guillotin

W HEN I heard, a few years ago, that a symposium on utopia was to be held in Pisa, Italy, I promptly submitted a paper in French that involved Franklin, Dr. Guillotin, and a utopian scheme. The reason for my alacrity was the hope that my Italian in-laws, who live in Tuscany, would attend.

After listening to a full day of theories about an impressive variety of utopias—with every speaker going well beyond the allotted fifteen minutes—I was informed that my paper, postponed until the next morning, did not qualify to be presented. Why not? Because the term *utopia*, which in its original Greek means a nonexistent place, cannot apply to an actual location, still less to an actual endeavor to settle in it, no matter how idealistic the motive or imaginative the plan.

And that was that, said the professor in charge of my section. I tried to argue that one of the speakers had suggested that utopia did not derive from "no place" but from *eutopia*, "good place," as in *euphoria* or *eulogy*. To no avail.

I became angry at that point and asked him why, being such a stickler for the rules, he had let so many people speak

overtime while a good part of the audience was obviously doz-
ing. Before he recovered, I offered to give my paper in five
minutes, pledging to stop in the middle of a word rather than
exceed that limit. He accepted in exasperation.

I kept my word and delivered at full speed an abridged
version of the events. Led by the loyal Italian clan, well versed
in the custom of applauding the diva halfway through her last
high note, the audience responded with cheers. Whether they
were cheering the contents of my tale or its brevity, I made no
effort to discover. Here is the full version, in English, of what I
had planned to say.

Eighteenth-century France produced an immense variety
of utopian schemes and schemers, but few utopians willing to
translate their words into action. Dr. Ignace Guillotin's American utopia was an exception to the rule. It proposed to bring
men from France to the American wilderness.

The recorded history of Guillotin's utopia begins in the
summer of 1787, when two young Frenchmen presented themselves at Franklin's home in Philadelphia. Franklin, then
eighty-one and president of the supreme executive council
(that is, governor) of Pennsylvania, had been back from France
exactly two years. He received the visitors with pleasure. Just
as he had been the *point de ralliement* of the Americans in
Paris, he was now the rallying point of the French in America—
and it was as true as ever that he was more important in the
eyes of the French than in those of his countrymen.

The two Frenchmen had come to talk about a tract of land
in the West: they wanted to reconnoiter down the Ohio as far
as they could. Their project revived an old dream of Franklin's.
Although he had not gone there himself, he had been affiliated
for many years, as we have seen, with societies aiming at new
establishments on the far side of the Alleghenies. His vision

was of an expansion of American power that would enrich both his compatriots and himself.[1] But when Dr. Guillotin took up the same idea, he transferred it to the ethereal level of utopias. The older of Franklin's two visitors, M. Picque, was a botanist; the younger, *un jeune homme de bonne famille* named Antoine Saugrain, was a medical doctor and mineralogist. He had brought a number of letters of recommendation from Franklin's friends. If there was one facet of French society that Franklin disliked, it was the patronage system—the flow of empty, futile recommendations. In this case, though, the letters did not come from the idle aristocrats for whom his contempt was barely concealed, but from his peers—active, intelligent members of that dynamic, liberal bourgeoisie with whom Franklin felt at ease: inventors, those who tinkered with objects and ideas, champions of the dignity of work. Longest and most effusive was the introduction written by Saugrain's own brother-in-law, Dr. Guillotin, not yet notorious for the instrument of death he eventually came to abhor—the guillotine—but esteemed enough in Paris to have been chosen as a fellow commissioner of Benjamin Franklin, three years earlier, in the *enquête Mesmer.*[2]

After evoking those happy memories, Guillotin's twenty-eight page letter, written in florid French, eventually came around to the matter at hand: "We mean to start an establishment on the banks of the Ohio. You may contribute much to our success through your good offices; indeed, your powerful protection in itself would guarantee a happy outcome." (What music to Franklin's ears! The French really thought him omnipotent!) The translation of a single sentence gives a whiff of Guillotin's style:

> Vexed with the noise, the agitation, the intrigues and the luxury of our cities; revolted by the chasm between our laws and our customs which often oblige one to choose between being

ridiculous or criminal; afflicted by the disheartening spectacle of vice triumphant and of virtue despised and humiliated; frightened by the horrors coldly spawned by Despotism and Superstition, we have resolved to flee this poisoned land where an honest man encounters nothing but anguish and disgust and we have decided to establish ourselves near the Ohio River because, beyond the general assets to be found in the thirteen states—a secure asylum to enjoy peace and freedom—that part of America offers both a mild climate and great distance from the large cities and the seacoast, those founts of commerce and riches, to be dreaded as the sources of luxury and corruption.

The proposed settlement was to comprise about twelve men, some with families, some bachelors; some rich, some not so well off; but all of them friends, willing to share, endowed with "some knowledge of sciences useful to mankind, such as agriculture, architecture, mechanics, physics, chemistry, medicine, surgery, and even belles-lettres, drawing and engraving." They wanted to settle either near Louisville or between the Mississippi and the northern bank of the Ohio, where three French settlements had already been established.

The rest of Guillotin's letter and other recommendations bestowed special praise on young Saugrain.[3] He came from an old family of printers, related not only to the Guillotins but also to the Didots and the Vernets, and he was well connected with the gifted craftsmen and artists who had been Franklin's true circle in Paris. While still very young, Saugrain had gone to Louisiana, then to Mexico, where he had worked for the viceroy, Don Gálvez, who had sent him back to France to buy scientific instruments. While in Paris, he had learned of his protector's death—hence his interest in Guillotin's utopian colony. Of the obscure M. Picque, it was only pointed out that he had "beaucoup de douceur"—but although sweetness is certainly a virtue, it was perhaps not the best attribute for plunging into the wild West.

And that is the heart of the matter: how much *did* those people know about the untamed American West? What makes their adventure typically utopian is not its tragic dénouement, which has been described more than once and is not altogether unique, but the gap between assumptions and reality.[4]

To justify still further the atmosphere of euphoria in which the two young men set forth, there was a French success story awaiting them five miles from Pittsburgh. A lawyer from Normandy who had consulted Franklin in Paris and been encouraged by him had found bliss working on a little plantation in the Pennsylvania woods with his beloved young wife.[5] Picque and Saugrain met that happy man when they reached Pittsburgh after an eighteen-day trip in October 1787. They visited his home and found everything idyllic—especially his wife: "Pretty, well-bred, well-educated, and yet a real housewife. . . . The husband sold his produce in town and read for relaxation. They lived on bread, potatoes, beef, eggs, and drank whiskey." This jolly description is by Brissot de Warville, who had it from Saugrain.[6]

The only sober note in all of this ecstatic oratory had been struck by Jefferson, back in Paris, in a message written in support of the travelers. He had begged a friend to give them "counsel and protection against imposition in their purchases to which as strangers they will be exposed."[7] Difficulties—if not exactly of that kind—started as soon as they reached Pittsburgh. Picque's letters to Franklin (none by Saugrain is extant) sound dispirited. The travelers did not find upon arrival the money they expected, indeed no mail at all. Inns were expensive, they would have to settle in the country. "We procure a little game from the Delawares who hunt around here. And the

few savages who come every day into town provide some entertainment for the foreigners. This small town is really very dull.
Everything seems dead."[8] Obviously, Pittsburgh was no Paris.

But was the Pittsburgh of the late 1780s—not quite two
hundred houses, including the brand new academy from which
the University of Pittsburgh would later develop—really so
deadly? True, "the Town at that time was the muddiest place
that I ever was in," reminisced an American traveler, "by reason of using so much coal, being a great manufacturing place,
and kept in so much smoke and dust, as to affect the skin of
the inhabitants." An early instance of environmental pollu-
tion. Yet the town had its charms: "It was noted for handsome
Ladies. . . . I had some letters of introduction from ladies of
New Jersey to ladies in Pittsburgh. These duties are to business
what dessert is to a dinner, it keeps up the spirits, for they are
the life of life."[9] One of those very ladies, Mrs. Dewees, who
was preparing to sail down the river that fall, took note in her
journal of our two Frenchmen with whom a third, M. Ragant
(Raguet?) had joined forces. On November 3, she wrote that
the three of them had come to dine on board her boat, and four
days later she remarked on the excellent pike they had all eaten
together. She added wistfully that the young men had come to
invite them to a ball held at Colonel Butler's, where thirty ladies
and gentlemen were to assemble. "It is hardly worth while to
say we declined going, as it was out of our power to dress fit at
this time, to attend such an Entertainment or else (you know)
should be happy to do ourselves the honour."[10] Not Paris, but
some social graces.

While Mrs. Dewees and her party pushed on down the
Ohio on November 18, 1787, Picque and Saugrain inexplicably
tarried in Pittsburgh. When the river froze, they were trapped.
Their morale sank still lower. In January 1788 they moved to
Hamilton's Island, two miles downstream of the town, where

"Our amusement consists in felling trees to make fire." Their boat, recently purchased, was "swept away in a debacle." They were told, as every traveler who has ever ventured from home is told by the local population, that this was the worst winter in more than twenty years. Meanwhile Guillotin, more loquacious than ever, was bombarding Franklin with messages in which he yearned to be with his two pioneers "sous un ciel superbe." To top it off, M. Picque was grounded for three weeks by a terrible attack of sciatica—an endemic ailment in that part of the country, he said. Luckily, a wonderful local root called dejejonkona relieved him of both the sciatica and his—ever so French—liver trouble.[11]

On March 19, Guillotin was still daydreaming in blissful ignorance: "Our two young travelers will have found an ample harvest. . . . One of them must be on his way back to Europe by now. . . . He will share the treasures of America with us."[12] Actually, March 19 was the day on which Guillotin's young travelers were finally setting out.

Six days later their dream turned into a horror:

As we were navigating between the Little and the Big Miami, we were attacked by savages who, after killing one of the horses we had on board, climbed aboard a flat boat and soon caught up with us. Then they fired. I killed one of them but they soon had their revenge since they killed one of ours and broke two fingers of my left hand. As we were close to the bank, two of my remaining companions threw themselves into the river and swam ashore. Left alone, I had no choice but to follow suit. The savages swam faster than us and just as I was reaching solid ground, I saw with horror my companion, M. Picque, knifed to death.[13]

Writing this to a friend one month after the event, Saugrain goes on to tell how he, too, was caught by the Indians, had his arms tied and was expecting the worst, when he managed to escape, let himself be carried by the current and eventually joined up in the woods with the lone American survivor, a Virginian named Pierce. After four harrowing days, they were picked up by a boat and brought back to civilization—to Louisville.[14]

In the fuller account he put down later in his *Journal et Notes de Voyage,* Saugrain included more gory details, such as the scalping of poor Picque, and unwittingly revealed how terribly unprepared the expedition had been. Among the four of them (three French, one American), they had only three fusils (light flintlock muskets), one of which was not loaded. They committed the blunder of shooting after they had raised a white handkerchief, against Picque's advice and entreaties— remember his *douceur?* Saugrain was informed, too late, that no one had ever been killed who had surrendered to the Indians without resistance.[15]

How, one wonders, could those two "explorers" have been such innocents abroad? Hundreds of boats criss-crossed the Ohio. According to the *Pittsburgh Gazette,* 454 boats, carrying 9,516 people, went downstream between June 1787 and June 1788, the very time of the utopian expedition. It was widely known that in the late 1780s the dangers of Indian attacks were greater than ever. The Ohio River had been very unsafe throughout the Revolution. Peace had brought a respite between 1784 and 1788, but tension mounted at the end of that period. As the Rev. James Finley put it in his *Autobiography,* "the Indians, fearful of losing their immense hunting grounds from the great tide of immigration pouring in upon them, were wrought up to the highest pitch of fury." It really was a high tide: the first American census, in 1790, gave the population of Kentucky as 73,677; nearly all of those inhabitants had arrived in a twelve-year period.

Possibly because he was ashamed of his rashness, Saugrain did not write to Franklin during his convalescence, and it was from an article in the *Kentucky Gazette* that Franklin eventually learned of the disaster.[16] The information was badly garbled. Except for the drowned M. Raguet, the newspaper did not give the names of the unfortunate Frenchmen, but only stated that one of them had been murdered and the other seriously wounded.

Franklin forwarded the clipping to Guillotin on May 4, with the following embarrassed comment: "It seems they were unprovided with Arms to defend themselves. Indeed, Travelling on the Ohio has for some years past been thought as safe as on any River in France, so that there was not the least Suspicion of Danger, many Thousands of People having gone down that way to the new Settlements at Kentucke. . . . They were two young men of uncommon Knowledge and most amiable Manners." One month later, Franklin informed Guillotin that he had heard a report to the effect that "the one who escaped was in a fair way of Recovery," but he still had no direct news and no idea of which one had survived. Guillotin and the other members of his group, Franklin supposed, "would now be discouraged and drop their Project."[17] They did drop it, but Saugrain, after his return to France, declared that America was his country of choice, in spite of all, and that he would go back to it. Franklin's kindness to him never failed to "elicit tears from his eyes."[18]

One could end the story on the upbeat note of Saugrain's successful medical career in Missouri. Or one could end it on the somber irony provided by still another traveler who, telling of his own capture by the Shawnees, two days after Saugrain's, mentioned "several rich suits of clothes" gaped at by the Indians who had taken them from the French gentlemen.[19] But I would rather close by turning to the unfortunate M. Picque,

whose sciatica must have flared as he plunged in vain into the
Ohio's icy waters. He had, in his will, left his whole modest
estate to a Mme Lombardie, about whom one likes to believe
that she was his *amie* and had given him some happy hours. In
order to collect her inheritance, however, she needed a death
certificate in perfect legal shape. Urged to procure such a document, Franklin protested: "This death happening in a wilderness country where there was no settled inhabitants, it is not
possible to obtain such a thing as an *extrait mortuaire*." But the
French bureaucracy was not to be thwarted by such trivial
excuses, not even after the fall of the Bastille. Writing two
weeks after that momentous event, a Parisian lawyer, Maître
Delaunay des Blardières, insisted politely that he needed not
only "a notarized death certificate, but the authentication of
said document by two persons."[20]

We do not know which of the cultures eventually prevailed.

Was Franklin in any way responsible for this tragedy? Had
he, perhaps, painted too rosy a picture of race relations in
his country? He had written once that the editor of a newspaper should consider himself to some degree the guardian of
his country's reputation and refuse to insert such writings as
might hurt it. The French had questioned Franklin eagerly
about the "savages," and as well as extolling America's moral
and physical climate—its good laws and fertile soil—he had
spoken about the Indians in very favorable terms. As a contribution to Antoine Court de Gébelin's work, *Le Monde primitif*,
he had procured from America a grammar of the language of
the Delawares. Franklin had signed several peace treaties with
the Indians and had been a friend to them when he lived in
Pennsylvania. His only criticism related to their occasional
drunkenness. In Paris, spreading propaganda for his country,

he gave a strongly sweetened account of the tension that in fact created real dangers for white immigrants back home.

In a slim volume called *Bagatelles,* printed in 1784 on his Passy press, Franklin presented the Indian culture's perspective on white Americans. Witness, for instance, his delight in recalling the Indians' reply to an American offer of raising some young Indian men among the whites: "Several of our young people have attended college in your Northern Provinces, and been instructed in all of your sciences. But when they came back to us, they no longer knew how to run, how to live in the woods, how to bear cold and hunger. They were incapable of building a hut, of catching a deer, or killing an enemy. . . . They were absolutely good for nothing."[21] Whereupon the Indians politely made a counter-proposal: "If the principal inhabitants of Virginia care to send us twelve of their children, we shall educate them with great care in all the things we know and we shall make *Men* out of them." Indeed, it is generally claimed now that more whites raised by Indians remained with them, when given a choice, than Christianized Indians elected to stay in the white world.

Franklin, to be sure, did not deliberately mislead the two Frenchmen, but it may well be that by the late 1780s, when he was old, infirm, and preoccupied with the Constitution, he could no longer keep up with the grimmer side of what was happening along the Ohio.

17

Franklin and Slavery: A Sea Change

WHEN the Macmillan Reference Company decided to publish the *Encyclopedia of World Slavery*, they asked me to write the entries on Franklin and Condorcet. After re-reading the chapter on slavery that my co-author Eugenia Herbert, a historian of Africa, had contributed to *The Private Franklin*, I felt that the only new element I could bring was the influence that the French Enlightenment—especially in the person of Condorcet—had on Franklin's thinking. I submitted a joint entry on both men's crusade for the abolition of slavery. It was accepted, but in a radically abridged version. What I offer here is the fuller one.

It is well known that Franklin's attitude toward slavery evolved from contemptuous indifference in his youth to passionate engagement during his later years. But when did this metamorphosis happen and why? Nobody seems to know. This essay is no more than a hypothesis, an educated guess as to the climate he was exposed to in the circles of the French Enlightenment. No written texts, unfortunately, corroborate my guess. Nonetheless, it is interesting and fruitful to explore the

dreams and ideals that may have fired his soul during his almost nine years in Paris (1776–85).

Not-So-Benign Neglect

During Franklin's early career, slaves were among the many
commodities that he sold in his general store, and he published
advertisements for such sales in his *Pennsylvania Gazette*. For
instance: "A likely Wench about fifteen Years old, has had the
Smallpox, been in the Country above a Year and talks English.
Inquire of the Printer hereof."[1] Franklin owned slaves for
thirty years, while holding both the blacks he knew and the
institution of slavery itself in contempt. Almost every slave
was, he wrote in *Observations Concerning the Increase of Mankind, Peopling of Countries,* by nature a thief. "By nature a
thief" became, in a later edition (1769) "from the nature of
slavery a thief."[2]

In a letter to his mother on April 12, 1750, Franklin made a
cryptic allusion to the financial loss he had suffered because of
a Negro couple. He was currently renting out the husband's
services for a dollar a week but planning "to sell them both the
first Opportunity, for we do not like Negro Servants."[3] One
cannot help feeling that blacks, in his eyes, were nothing more
than unsatisfactory units of labor. Still, when Franklin and his
son William sailed to England in 1757, they took along their
respective slaves, Peter and King. In a will written shortly before departure, Franklin stated that he wanted "my Negro Man
Peter and his Wife Jemima" to be freed after his decease.[4] After
their arrival in England, Peter was employed occasionally in
scrubbing the moss-covered tombstones of the Franklin ancestors in Ecton while William copied the inscriptions.

When Franklin's wife Debbie inquired about the slaves, he
replied that "Peter continues with me and behaves as well as I

can expect in a Country where there are many Occasions of spoiling Servants, if they are ever so good. He has a few Faults as most of them, and I see with only one Eye and hear only with one Ear, so we rub on pretty comfortably."

As to King: "He ran away from our House while we were absent in the Country; but was soon found in Suffolk, where he had been taken in the Service of a Lady that was very fond of the Merit of making him a Christian, and contributing to his Education and Improvement. As he was of little Use, and often in Mischief, Billy [i.e., William Franklin] consented to her keeping him while we stay in England. So the Lady sent him to School, had him taught to read and write, to play on the Violin and French Horn, with some other Accomplishments more useful in a Servant. Whether she will finally be willing to part with him, or persuade Billy to sell him to her, I know not. In the meantime he is no Expence to us."[5] A coolly detached outlook.

And yet it was in England, under the influence of a group of people very similar to that lady in Suffolk, that Franklin entered the second phase of his attitude toward slavery, a more humane phase, if still predominantly one in which Franklin stayed intellectually and emotionally aloof.

A Measure of Involvement

The group, called the Associates of Dr. Bray, was an off-shoot of the Anglican Society for the Propagation of the Gospel that had been promoting the conversion to Christianity of blacks in the American colonies by sending books and catechisms to their pastors. After twenty-five years of disappointing efforts in that endeavor, they thought of establishing "Negro schools" in America to imbue the minds of the young slaves with moral principles, and they turned to Franklin for help. Unable to resist a project that involved organization and education, he endorsed the plan: "At present few or none give their Negro Children any Schooling, partly from a Prejudice that Reading and Knowledge in a Slave are both useless and dangerous; and partly from an Unwillingness in the Masters and Mistresses of common Schools to take black Scholars, lest the Parents of the white Children should be disgusted and take them away, not chusing to have their Children mix'd with Slaves in Education, Play, etc. But a separate School for Blacks . . . might probably have a Number of Blacks to it."

This was written on January 3, 1756. On February 17, Franklin sent a detailed proposal, including ways to set up and finance such a school in Philadelphia, with the hope that the idea might spread to other colonies.[6] Indeed, other black schools were opened in Williamsburg, New York, and Newport, each with Franklin's help and advice. When he eventually visited one of them after his return to America, he was pleasantly surprised, and conceived, he said, "a higher Opinion of the Natural Capacities of the black Race than I have ever before entertained. Their Apprehension is as quick, their Memory as strong, and their Docility in every Respect equal to that of the White Children."[7]

Debbie was enthusiastic about the project. For an emotional reaction to the slaves, one has to turn to her—with her occasionally quick and noisy temper but her unfailingly warm heart. She thought that the children answered "so prettily" and behaved "so decently" that she decided to enroll her own little slave Othello when the moment came. Her letter was entered as a testimonial in the minute book of the Bray Associates. When Othello died too soon for his education to begin, Debbie's grief was such that her husband felt compelled to allude to it: "I am sorry for the Death of your black Boy as you seem to have had a regard for him. You must have suffered a good deal in the Fatigue of Nursing him in such a Distemper."[8] Later she would relate the ups and downs of her relationship with George (invariably spelled "Gorge"), a slave whom Franklin had acquired as part payment for a debt. George lost his wife and was much afflicted—"a dredfull creyer"[9]—Debbie reported, but none of this ever elicited the slightest comment from her absentee husband.

Debbie died, the Revolution broke out, and Franklin, now in his seventies, went off to Paris in 1776, without a slave this time—a good thing, too, since owning slaves became illegal in mainland France as of the summer of 1779.

The Sea Change

One of the harshest things John Adams wrote about Franklin was that he frittered away his time—and the American commission's—in frivolous gatherings, dinners, and soirées in opulent French salons. To say that Franklin partook deeply of French intellectual life would have been closer to the truth. Salons were the Internet of the eighteenth century. People did not frequent them merely for chitchat but for a serious exchange of ideas; it was there that they listened to and discussed, sometimes quite heatedly, each other's writings. The salon of Mme Helvétius, in nearby Auteuil, which the Doctor frequented assiduously, attracted mostly people of liberal views, both aristocrats and *grands bourgeois*.[10] In her house and in the many others to which he was invited, Franklin met the lawyer Elie de Beaumont, defender of the oppressed; the economist Anne-Robert-Jacques Turgot, whose views were too advanced for his day; and the admirable jurist Chrétien-Guillaume Malesherbes, who would go to the guillotine one day for having sustained Louis XVI's right to a defender, even though he was personally a committed anti-royalist.

Most importantly, Franklin met the marquis de Condorcet,

one of the great mathematicians of his day who was also the *secrétaire perpétuel* of the Académie Royale des Sciences, one of the anchors of Franklin's Parisian life.[11] Condorcet's entourage sometimes dubbed him "the snowy volcano" or "the enraged sheep," because he was a man of passionate convictions but diffident exterior. Yet over time he became more than a colleague to Franklin; he became a friend and grew closer to this American, old enough to be his father, than to most other people.

Although the luminaries of the Enlightenment (Montesquieu, Voltaire, Rousseau, the abbé Raynal) were decidedly anti-slavery, none was more vocal, eloquent, or relentless than Condorcet, a self-appointed champion of the oppressed—Jews, women, blacks, or Protestants. His campaign in defense of the slaves had started as early as 1777, with a series of articles in the *Journal de Paris* that had exasperated the West Indies French sugar planters, a powerful lobby. They had convinced a number of Frenchmen that their country's economic future and gastronomical well-being were tightly bound to slavery and that a philosopher like Condorcet could not help being impractical and irresponsible. Still, Condorcet forged ahead. His crusade culminated in 1781 with the publication in Switzerland of his *Réflexions sur l'Esclavage des Nègres*—at a time when Franklin was already familiar enough with French to follow his arguments, written and spoken, and when he was not yet totally absorbed in the peace negotiations.[12]

Condorcet's short work opens with a letter to the slaves supposedly penned by a pastor with the transparent pseudonym of Joachim Schwartz:

My friends,
    Even though I am not of the same color as you, I have always considered you my brothers. Nature shaped you with the same spirit, the same reason, the same virtues as the

whites. I have only the European whites in mind. As to those of our colonies, I will not insult you with such a comparison. I know how often your fidelity, your honesty, and your courage have caused your masters to blush. If one went looking for a real man in the American islands, it is not among the white-skinned people that one would find him. . . . Your vote does not procure positions in the colonies; your protection does not insure pensions; you do not have the money to pay lawyers: hence it is not surprising that your masters can find more people willing to dishonor themselves in defending their cause than you have found willing to honor themselves by defending yours. . . .

I know that you will never read this work of mine and that the sweetness of your blessing shall never be granted me. But I will have satisfied my heart, which is now torn by the sight of your misfortune and revolted by the absurd insolence of your tyrants' sophistry.[13]

After this rousing prologue, Condorcet uses moral, economic, and political arguments to support his case. From a moral standpoint, the act of buying and selling a human being and keeping him in servitude is worse than theft. Yet theft is punished by society, whereas owning slaves, a far worse crime, has no name. The excuse for buying those Africans on the pretext that they are criminals already condemned to death, or prisoners of war destined to be put to death anyway, is invalid. It is a fact that the prospect of such profitable sales provokes many wars between Africans, wars often fomented by the Europeans themselves. And to keep in captivity the children born to slaves? Isn't that a still greater crime?

Turning to economics, Condorcet sets out to prove that slavery is not in the best interest of commerce and that the sugar and indigo plantations could just as well be cultivated by white people. The whites, he asserts, have been so corrupted by liquor and fornication with black women that they have become lazy. The land should be divided into small parcels cultivated by free men, white or black. Whereupon he declares that, according to calculations made in the United States, it takes five slaves to do the work of three free men—an estimate that may have been given him by Franklin. And Franklin, by the way, will echo in later years the argument that slavery as an industry corrupts white society. The greatest part of the trade of the world, he will write, is carried on "for Luxuries, most of which are really injurious to health or society, such as *tea, tobacco, rum, sugar* and *negro slaves.*"[14]

When it comes to politics, Condorcet's argument falters. He admits that his principles would spell the immediate end of a man's political career, but then he asks his readers to consider what kind of opinion posterity will have of them, they who believe themselves to be the very incarnation of reason and humaneness. Could the colonists really believe, he wonders, that 22 million whites can survive only if 300,000 to 400,000 Negroes perish under the whip?

Intelligent and eager as he was to perfect himself, Franklin cannot have failed to grasp that, like it or not, this topic was of huge importance. Condorcet's high emotionalism may have reminded him of the saintly Anthony Benezet, who also looked upon slaves as human beings, as brothers. I have the feeling that Franklin never went that far. He hated slavery but, unlike Benezet and Condorcet, he could not quite bring himself to like the slave.[15]

Furthermore, as long as he was in France—representing a country that desperately needed French help—he could not afford to antagonize the planters, one of whom, a rich and influential man, was his own host's son-in-law. Also, the very first French merchant to have extended financial help to the American insurgents was a *négrier* named Jacques Gruel, who was deeply involved in the slave trade in Nantes.

Full Commitment, at Last

After going back to Philadelphia in 1785, Franklin kept in touch with Condorcet's Société des Amis des Noirs and assumed the presidency of the Pennsylvania Abolition Society. He did not present a petition to the Constitutional Convention against the slave trade, for fear that South Carolina and Georgia would then refuse to join the Union, but he drafted and signed a plan for the integration of the freed slaves into white society, a thorny problem.

Franklin's plan for blacks proposed to advise those who had been freed, to place young people in trades, to provide schools for promising children, and to offer employment to adults.[16] He sent it to the Société des Amis des Noirs for comments. On January 20, 1790, he received an enthusiastic reply from its current president, Brissot de Warville.[17] The liberal philosopher assured his American ally that the plan had been translated and sent to all the French newspapers. He in turn enclosed copies of a memorandum of his own and asked Franklin to convey them to the New York and Delaware societies. A friendly race was on, it seems, between Paris and Philadelphia, as to which government would abolish slavery sooner.

Eventually, Franklin did sign a memorandum to Congress asking for an end to slavery in the United States. The blessings of liberty, he said, should be granted to all people without distinction of color, since they had all been created by the same Almighty Being.[18]

The memorandum, needless to say, aroused an intensely hostile reaction in various quarters; it particularly infuriated James Jackson, senator (later governor) of Georgia. In a supreme effort, less than one month before his death, Franklin rallied his energies and called one last time upon his sense of humor to help him produce his final hoax: the speech sup-

posedly delivered by Sidi Mehemet Ibrahim to the divan of
Algiers in defense of the traditional custom of enslaving the
Christians captured by Barbary pirates. In a biting parody of
the pro-slavery rhetoric, Sidi Mehemet wonders how his country could obtain the necessary produce without the Christian
slaves. Who will cultivate the land in the heat? Who will labor
in the homes and city? Must we not then be our own slaves? he
asks. Isn't more compassion due to Muslims than to Christian
dogs? Just as Jackson had justified slavery by the Holy Writ,
Sidi Mehemet now invokes the Koran in its defense. And wins
his case, of course.

And Condorcet? Embroiled in the French Revolution, he
fought for his ideals with such a rage that he ran afoul of
Robespierre and had to rush into hiding. One can only hope
that in the little room where he had found refuge during the
Terror, he learned that on February 4, 1794, the French Republic had abolished slavery in its colonies—in practice, only
Guadeloupe and Guiana. One month later, Condorcet was arrested and died in jail the following morning, probably by his
own hand. In 1802, both slavery and the slave trade were reestablished by Napoleon.

The battle had been lost on both sides of the Atlantic—but
the crusade was not over.

Epilogue: Around the Table, They Remember Franklin

I WAS invited in 1990 to deliver the Penrose Lecture at the American Philosophical Society. What, I wondered, could I possibly tell those eminent scholars and scientists that they did not already know? After considering and rejecting several topics, I decided that the only facet of Franklin's life on which I have some special expertise has to do with the French Enlightenment, which over there they call les Lumières, the lights. How much was he influenced by it, and vice versa?

And what about the format? I wanted the substance of this talk to be solid, but the presentation lively and light. Inspiration struck as I was riding my bicycle: a conversation! But then between whom, where, when, why? The idea of a dinner party slowly emerged, a dinner to commemorate the first anniversary of Franklin's death, which had occurred in the spring of 1790. The hostess obviously had to be Mme Helvétius, the woman he had hoped to marry, the one to whom he wrote his last letter in faltering French.[1]

Since this was a party I did not have to prepare myself, I gave free rein to my ambition and drew up a guest list of twelve people, including Lafayette, John Paul Jones, the duc de La Rochefoucauld—why not a duke, a marquis, and a naval hero?—and nine distinguished others. But reality set in when I remembered this was to be an oral presentation, and that I also needed a narrator to tell the audience who all those people were. The list was whittled down to six.

All I had to do, then, was to read a biography of each guest to discover his preoccupations in March 1791, and re-read his correspondence with Franklin so as to let him speak in his own words, whenever possible, at the imaginary table.

Let us suppose, dear readers, that Mme Helvétius decided one day that she wanted a verbal, multidimensional portrait of Franklin, one last collective evocation before the door on the past was closed forever. From the vast number of people whom Franklin had known during his eight and a half years in France, she selected six—all men, because it was not her custom to invite women to her dinner parties.[2] Two of them had been his colleagues at the Académie Royale des Sciences, Condorcet and Lavoisier, and another two, Robespierre and Marat, were political figures rapidly moving toward the center of the revolutionary stage. For the sake of obtaining the presence of Mirabeau, who was the lion of the moment, she moved up her party from April 17, 1791, which would have been the first anniversary of Franklin's death, to mid-March, because she had been warned that Mirabeau was dangerously ill and that his days were numbered. Finally, the abbé Morellet, that old and comfortable fixture of her household, Franklin's devoted admirer and friend, would act as co-host and, if need be, a moderating influence.[3]

Mme Helvétius was an accomplished hostess. For years, the most interesting people in Paris had met, talked, and laughed in her lovely house in Auteuil, on the edge of the bois de Boulogne, amid a profusion of animals and flowers. Relaxed and irreverent, they had enjoyed the somewhat bohemian atmosphere she knew how to create. Franklin had spent his happiest hours there: "Often, in my dreams, I dine with you, I sit beside you on one of your thousand sofas, or walk with you in your beautiful garden." In this, one of his very last letters, he even made the effort to write in his peculiar brand of French, losing his final battle with the genders but managing to convey his feelings with his own blend of irony and tenderness.[4]

He had proposed to her, back in 1781. At least we like to believe that he had. The idea had been broached in such a playful way that, as often happens with Franklin, one is never quite sure. Their friends, at least, saw it as a serious proposal. The comte d'Estaing once interrupted the lady's lament about Franklin's return to America: "Your fault, Madam, for not having fixed him here among us!"[5]

Even though she belonged to an old aristocratic family, Mme Helvétius's heart was with the Revolution. She had greeted the fall of the Bastille with as much enthusiasm as did the rest of Franklin's circle of liberal friends. That euphoric summer of 1789—the summer of the Declaration of the Rights of Man—had cooled into the wet October day when the women of Paris forcibly brought back the royal family from Versailles to the capital, in the vain hope of obtaining bread. As the winter dragged on, it had become obvious, then as today, that the first act, the act of liberation, is a hard one to follow when the economy is in shambles and the apparatus of government is slow to change its ways. The flight of the rich had left many poor people without employment. Even the confiscation of the assets of the Church—one-fifth of the riches of France—would not, it seemed, be enough. Unease was in the air.

Mme Helvétius had asked her guests to bring along, in any form they wished, their memories of Franklin. They took their seats around the table, on the center of which glittered a little landscape made of frost and snow on tiny evergreens.

As soon as the soup had been served, the hostess turned to Condorcet. In his late forties but prematurely stooped, never one to dress stylishly or cut a figure in society, Condorcet, hampered by a weak voice and a hesitant delivery, was more a man of the pen than the podium. The word "unworldly" might have been coined for him. Still, he was a great mathematician, the last of the *Encyclopédistes,* a spiritual heir of Voltaire, Turgot, and d'Alembert. He had embraced the Revolution with fervor and, long before France was ready to shed its king, was calling for a republic and dreaming up plans for free public education.[6]

"Haven't you known Franklin longer than anybody else at the table?" asked the lady.

"I think I have. My first letter to him was in 1773. Franklin was living in London at the time, and I asked him many questions about fossils. Are the fossils of fish, shells, and plants to be found in the seas near Philadelphia or in faraway seas? How deep under the earth? How high up in the mountains? I also wanted to know, year by year, what observations had been made in Philadelphia about the magnetic needle, in order to compare those oscillations with the ones measured in Paris. I wondered whether barometers in America react to changes in weather in the same way as our European ones. Meteorology, you know, is still in its infancy."[7]

"And what did he say?"

"Franklin referred all those questions, and one concerning volcanic stones, to the society he had founded, the Philosophical Society, but my final query he answered himself. I was curious about the Negroes. I asked him whether Negro children, born free and raised free, would keep the Negro character, or become European—and whether there had been distinguished minds among them. 'The Negroes who are free,' said Franklin, 'live with the White People but are generally improvident and poor. I think they are not deficient in natural Understanding, but they have not the Advantage of Education. They make good Musicians.'"[8]

Condorcet paused for a moment. "In later days, the Negroes would be a strong bond between Franklin and myself. We had many a talk about the injustices of society. The way it treats women, the way it treats Jews. It was finally the plight of the slaves that moved him to seize his pen. Imagine: only one month before Franklin died, he wrote a piece that Voltaire would not have disavowed, a sarcastic hoax in which he 'defended' the custom of enslaving Christians captured by Barbary pirates."[9]

This, thought the other guests, would be the perfect place to stop. But Condorcet is a poor orator and he won't sense that. He'll drone on.

Condorcet was hesitating. Almost in a whisper, he added: "We were close friends, Franklin and I. After he had gone back to Philadelphia, I wrote to him about my marriage. . . ."

The whole table perked up. Condorcet's marriage was much talked about. A confirmed old bachelor, he had, to everybody's astonishment, married a dark-haired, vibrant young woman named Sophie de Grouchy.[10] Tongues had wagged all over Paris: this would be, of course, *un mariage blanc*, unconsummated, the bridegroom too gauche, the bride probably in love with someone else but forced into this union by her family. When a little girl was eventually born to the couple, the same gossipers remarked that the birth had occurred nine months to the day after the fall of the Bastille. Obviously, it had taken such an earth-shaking event, etc., etc. . . . By now, Condorcet's enemies knew only too well that the way to hurt him was through hints to Sophie's alleged infidelities, a campaign that would sink eventually to the depths of scurrility.

He looked defiantly around the table. "I informed Franklin in 1788 that I had married a lovely, spirited young woman, endowed with many talents. I told him that she had decided to overlook my age and my modest status in society because she loved literature and philosophy. She could have made a far more brilliant match, but she was kind enough to give me the preference. I told Franklin that her first present to me was his portrait, which she had copied from the one by Greuze."[11]

"My wife also paints very well—she studied with David—and she, too, did a portrait of the Doctor...." It was Lavoisier speaking. He had jumped into the awkward silence that followed Condorcet's profession of love and happiness. Even if they did not see eye to eye on current events—and who, in those days, could be said to see eye to eye with anybody else?—they were colleagues, after all, and courtesy should prevail. "We sent the portrait to Philadelphia," pursued Lavoisier, "and Franklin said he was ever so pleased. His own had been carried away by the British when they occupied his house, and his late wife, whose portrait was hanging by itself, seemed glad, he thought, to have a partner again."[12]

Mme Helvétius, however, was not giving this party in order to hear the praise of wives.

"Tell me, Lavoisier," she cut in, "apart from your stand on phlogiston, about which I understand nothing, what *was* your link with Franklin?"[13]

"So many links, dear lady. First of all, I would say, saltpeter. The Americans needed it desperately for making gunpowder. We had plenty here, but it is a royal monopoly, as you know, and Franklin could not have exported it unless I had been able, as *régisseur des poudres,* to circumvent the laws a little. He, on his part, helped me install lightning rods at the powder magazine, the Arsenal, where we live, my wife and I. We could sleep in safety, thanks to him, and our fellow-Parisians too."[14]

"Lucky you, to have been dealing with Parisians smart enough to accept the lightning rod!" broke in another guest. "Does anyone here know the trouble that the lightning rod, that sublime invention, gave me?"

The others may have been tempted to exchange winks around the table, for that so-called trouble had been the springboard of the man's career. But time was running out for anyone to wink or smile when the lawyer from the northern city of Arras passed judgment on anything; his icy brilliance was beginning to send shivers down people's spines. Maximilien Robespierre—his name now stripped of the particle *de* that he had still used in his letter to Franklin—explained that, back in 1779, a man in St. Omer had installed a lightning rod on his house, only to be sued by a neighbor who felt that lightning would now fall on *his* house. The town magistrates ordered the removal of the offending object within twenty-four hours. Two days later, the owner presented a petition accompanied by a scientific report meant to enlighten the judges. Not to be enlightened, the judges turned it down on the spot. Robespierre, hired as a lawyer, spent the next two years submitting the question to one academy after the other until he was able, finally, to deliver to the council of the province of Artois the *plaidoyer*, of which he now carried a copy in his pocket. Another copy had gone to Franklin in its day, with the tribute that "the least of your virtues is to be the most illustrious scientist in the universe."[15]

"I wonder why," said Lavoisier, "it took France so long to accept the lightning rod, considering that it was our late colleague, Dalibard, who, in 1752 I believe, carried out not far from here the experiment that proved the validity of Franklin's hypothesis on the electrical nature of lightning. Had he known about that, back in Philadelphia, Franklin would not have risked his life in that key and kite venture."[16]

"It came to my attention," remarked Condorcet, "that as late as 1756 our *Encyclopédie* still recommended the sound of several large bells as the best method to repulse lightning, or the sound of cannon to provoke its fragmentation. Now listen to this: 'It is essential,' proclaimed the *Encyclopédie*, 'not to ring the bells while the clouds are directly over them, for it might cause them to tear apart, thus dropping the lightning, just as happened in Lower Brittany in 1718 when three churches whose bells were ringing were struck, whereas the neighboring churches were spared.'"[17]

They chuckled. "And a good thing, too," added Condorcet, "that the *Encyclopédie* mended its ways just in time for Franklin's arrival, when its *Supplement* of 1777 published such a vibrant tribute to his discovery. What a wonder, that Franklin! A foreigner, an elderly man, so often afflicted by gout or stone, and yet he was to be found in the vanguard of so many campaigns for new ideas. He spread the good word for smallpox inoculation when our medical corps was still resisting it with all its might. He helped Parmentier introduce the potato when our peasants were still convinced that it would cause leprosy. He went wild over the first balloons. Novelty did not frighten him at all—on the contrary, he plunged right into it."

Here was Condorcet pushing, as usual, for quicker reform but Robespierre wanted to keep talking about the lightning rod.

"What about all those translations of Turgot's epigram on Franklin?" he asked. "Those five Latin words, *Eripuit coelo fulmen sceptrumque tyrannis*, that all of Paris was trying to translate and that nobody seemed able to render in less than four lines?"

Yes, they remembered the countless ways in which the French had vied with each other in expressing the notion that

Franklin had snatched the lightning from the sky and the scepter from the tyrants. The hitch was the word *coelo*. Was it from the skies (*aux cieux*) that he had snatched lightning, making his victory one of man over nature, or was it from the gods (*aux dieux*), as some had suggested, implying a dangerous foray into theology?

Mme Helvétius spoke up: "Franklin told me that he had been very careful to attribute his discovery to God, knowing how unpalatable it would be in certain quarters of New England."[18]

"It was a victory over the irrational," proclaimed Robespierre. "Lightning has accepted its laws. Losing its powers of blind and irresistible destruction, it has learned to recognize the objects that it should spare!"

Lavoisier listened in awe. That man believes he knows everything, he thought. He has the eyes of a fanatic, but his voice is pure gold. No wonder he holds the Jacobin club under his sway. They are beginning to call him The Incorruptible. A frightening thought! I wish I knew what Mirabeau, so intelligent, so corruptible, thinks about him. . . . But Mirabeau's massive presence was silent, his eyes lowered. Lavoisier felt he should make one last contribution to the topic of the lightning rod:

"Franklin helped our Academy with its plans for rebuilding the spire of the Strasbourg cathedral when it was destroyed by lightning. Even though he did not attend our meetings very often, he served on many commissions. . . ."

"Your commissions! Your sacred academic commissions! That is where Condorcet should have studied his fossils!" Such rage, such a flow of rancor—it could only be Marat speaking. Eyes ablaze, skin blotched by the disease he had contracted while hiding in the sewers during his life-long rebellion, l'Ami du Peuple, as he liked to call both himself and his much-feared paper, exploded:

"When your precious academic bodies would hardly take my views into consideration, Franklin understood and appreciated them. My pioneering work on the nature of fire, for which I coined the term *igneous fluid*, had to be carried out practically in secret because I knew that you people would steal my ideas when they turned out to be valid. I did not even dare sign my name to the memoir that I left at Franklin's house in the closing days of 1778. But I knew he would read it because it was written in English. That was a great link I enjoyed with Franklin, my fluency in English. I spent ten years of my youth on the British Isles, studying medicine, observing politics, writing. And let me tell you something else. Franklin and I held our degrees from the same university: St. Andrews, in Scotland. His, an honorary one, in law; mine, a medical one. All through the spring of '79, as I beseeched him to witness the series of experiments I had prepared—120 of them—I hid behind a pseudonym. I had no choice."[19]

Condorcet shuddered. Persecution mania. That was what the doctors called this type of mental derangement. What sweet chances for revenge the Revolution was going to give this man!

Marat was working himself up to a state of exaltation. "He would have gladly accepted my invitation, that great man who was in our midst, but just as he was made minister plenipotentiary, that spring, and finally rid of his burdensome colleagues—Monsieur Adams and Monsieur Lee—he was hit by the gout, time after time. Yes, I guess that at this very moment you are telling yourselves that Franklin was making up excuses to spare himself the embarrassment of disagreeing with me, but you are wrong. As soon as he was able to move,

he *did* come to the rue de Bourgogne where the marquis—
I mean the former marquis—de l'Aubépine had set up a lab-
oratory for me." (At the name of the marquis de l'Aubépine,
every person around the table mentally added: "whose wife
was your mistress," but not a sound was heard and no expression changed.)[20]

"Not only did Franklin come," pursued Marat, "he showed
great interest in the instrument I had invented to prove my
point, the *microscope solaire*. Monsieur Sage, the mineralogist,
one of my few loyal friends, was there, and he published the
following account: 'M. Marat sets out to show us the igneous
fluid in a tangible manner. He exposes to the solar microscope
a metal ball that he then heats and around which one perceives
an undulating sphere of vapors. . . . M. Franklin, having exposed his bald head to the focus of the microscope, we see it
surrounded by undulating vapors that all end in spirals. They
look like those flames through which painters symbolize Genius.'[21] If, as I hope, we ever publish a calendar of lay saints, we
should consecrate a day to Franklin."[22]

Marat drew a deep breath: "The Academy's report, that
time, was so favorable that I used it as an introduction to my
essay, 'Découvertes sur le Feu.'"

Lavoisier and Condorcet exchanged a perplexed look. That
academy report, as they well remembered, had been more am-
biguous than enthusiastic. Written by Franklin's great friend,
the physicist Le Roy, who had persuaded him to witness
Marat's experiments, it reflected an uneasy mixture of admiration for the ingenuity of Marat's contrivances and lingering
doubts as to the validity of his theories.[23] But Marat had chosen to interpret it as a wholehearted endorsement. This em-
boldened him to try once again to enroll Franklin on his side,
this time to attack Newton's theory on optics. At this point the
academy had put down its collective foot and wanted nothing

more to do with him. What price would there be to pay now for such boldness?

At the sight of Condorcet turning red with fury, Lavoisier felt panicky. His old colleague, this man of science, always mild and diffident, had recently become a politician so given to unexpected, wildly imprudent outbursts that his friends had started nicknaming him *le mouton enragé* (the enraged sheep). It may have been the influence of that radical Englishman, Tom Paine, often to be seen in Mme Condorcet's salon. Anyway, this was not the moment to fly at Marat, just as the man was becoming powerful. Condorcet, luckily, controlled his temper and concentrated on his glazed pheasant.

With an almost imperceptible flick of the eyelids, the hostess signaled to the abbé Morellet that the moment had come for him to enter the conversation. While harboring no scientific or political ambitions, Morellet, an economist, had spent enough time in the Bastille to establish his credentials and had acquired intellectual fame by introducing into France the ideas of the great Italian jurist Cesare Beccaria.[24]

"If you'll excuse me, Monsieur Marat," said the abbé politely, "I believe Dr. Franklin was interested mostly in that wonderful invention of yours, the solar microscope. How he loved machines! Tinkering, you know, was the first basis of our friendship. And if *you*'ll excuse me, Monsieur Condorcet, you are not, of the people around this table, the first to make Franklin's acquaintance. You met him, you said, by correspondence, in '73. I met him face to face, in '72, in England, at one of those prolonged parties that the English—in this case Lord Shelburne—like to give at their country estates. The two stars on that occasion were the actor David Garrick and Benjamin Franklin, and it would be hard to tell which one outshone the other. What a joy for me to find in Franklin a simple, everyday kind of man, a fellow economist with whom it was easy to talk!

We discovered our shared love of music and drew up a list, in French and English, of the range of emotions it can convey. This was a prelude to the happy hours we would spend playing duets—he on his glass armonica, I on my cello. He also showed me the stove he had invented, and thinking of the good such a stove would do in France, I bought one and started little improvements of my own. Look at the tool box I brought: it was Franklin's own, he left it with me in memory of the pleasure we both found in hitting nails."[25]

"And look at the armchair over there," interrupted Mme Helvétius, "he also left that with the abbé who could not resist having something in Latin engraved on it."

"*Hic sedebat Franklin,* very simple Latin," the abbé tried to explain, but Madame continued: "Franklin may have lived in Passy, but his real home was here. His place was always set at this very table. He could come any time, and did. After Versailles in all its pomp and circumstance, he needed our disordered ways, the dogs and cats running all over the place, the house jokes, the bantering."

She looked up at the Franklin portrait hanging over the chimney, the Van Loo, all greys and blues, with its amused half-smile and twinkle.[26]

"How proud I felt the day I handed Franklin my husband's Masonic apron, which had also been Voltaire's! My husband had this dream of a truly intellectual and liberal lodge, but he did not live to see it come into being, his lodge of the Nine Sisters . . . though I must confess that I can never remember the names of those nine Muses."[27]

Worried perhaps that one of her guests might start listing them, Mme Helvétius changed topic abruptly, a habit of hers that the abbé Morellet had always found annoying.

"It was his streak of irreverence, I believe, that made Franklin so much one of us, one of what he loved to call the Academy of Auteuil—and me, impudent that he was, he dubbed Notre-Dame d'Auteuil. He really was much more French than he realized. He entered our society with such zest! How he liked to laugh, to sing us the songs of his youth, to play on his glass armonica, to try punning in our language, to have our help in translating those bagatelles of his that he would then rush to print on his own little press. Poor man, he must not have laughed often after he went back to Pennsylvania."

"Madame," said Condorcet a little sternly, "he had the privilege of working on his country's Constitution."

"Do you like their Constitution?" asked Robespierre, glad to get away from sentimental discourse and back to politics.

"Not very much," replied Condorcet. "I think that, despite all their efforts, it is still too aristocratic. As I wrote Franklin, when I thanked him for having made me a member of the Philosophical Society, I suppose it was the best they could do under the circumstances.[28] But I believe they will hold a new convention in a few years to change that Constitution. Strange, isn't it, that Franklin, who wrote the Constitution of Pennsylvania and had always stood so firmly for a single assembly, should accept this bicameral arrangement?"

"Things are different over there," said Lavoisier. "They pride themselves on their ability to compromise. They don't like to go on arguing forever, the way we do, to make a theoretical point."

"Why on earth," interjected Marat, "should one stop short of total victory? What is the matter with them?"

"I used to tease him," chuckled Mme Helvétius, "about the fact that he loved people only as long as he saw them. Do you think he forgot us, out there?"

"No," said Morellet, "but he changed. He became intensely patriotic and very touchy. You couldn't comment on any of the Americans' shortcomings without making him bristle. Take their economic policy, for instance, so far from the laissez-faire that Franklin had preached, as we all did, while he was here. When I pointed out to him how protectionist the Americans were becoming, he defended the system as the best possible under the circumstances. Or take the Order of Cincinnatus. He detested the idea of hereditary honors when he was here. In fact, he wrote such an attack against it that I felt obliged to advise him to tone it down, better yet not to publish it at all."[29]

At that point, Mirabeau motioned that he wanted to speak. He had sat quietly so far, breathing with difficulty, eating little, obviously at death's door. Mme Helvétius had stolen many a glance in his direction, fascinated by his pockmarked face, so devilishly repulsive, so roguishly attractive. A passionate face— powerful, worn out by past debauchery and current overwork. Rumors flew that he was on the king's payroll and using his immense prestige to save the monarchy. The only man who could dominate the assembly through his sheer eloquence, Mirabeau was also the only one capable of steering the Revolution on a somewhat stable course.

"I was in jail for most of the time that Franklin spent in France," he said. "Across town from him for years, he in Passy, myself locked up in the fortress of Vincennes, courtesy of my father, as usual. When I finally had the privilege of meeting that venerable man, he turned the conversation to the Order of Cincinnatus, having heard that I was about to publish a book on the subject. He told me how reluctant he was to see the principle of hereditary aristocracy introduced into America, but he also felt that the abbé Morellet was right to caution him against publication. As a result, many of his views found their way into my work, the first of my writings to appear under my own name."[30]

Mirabeau paused, visibly moved. Everybody knew about the hatred his father had borne him ever since he was an ugly little boy disfigured by smallpox; the vindictiveness with which his father had punished his every act of youthful rebellion, as if pushing him deliberately toward ever wilder behavior. Had he yearned, like the rest of France, to call Franklin "Papa"?

His face was solemn when he spoke. "Never," he said, "never did I feel as powerfully at one with the National Assembly and the people of France as that day, last June, when I told them of Franklin's death."

It had, in truth, been one of his great moments. In a brief statement of poignant intensity, Mirabeau had not only given the sad news, which he had just received from England, but suggested that the assembly go into mourning for three days, thus making it the first political body in the world to pay homage to a simple citizen of another land.

"Wouldn't it be worthy of you, gentlemen," he had asked, "to pay this tribute to the philosopher who has done the most to ensure the Rights of Man all over the globe? The ancients would have built altars to that genius whose thought encompassed heaven and earth. Enlightened and free Europe owes no less to the memory of one of the greatest men who ever served philosophy and liberty!" Seconded by the duc de La Rochefoucauld and by Lafayette, the motion had been carried by acclamation. Henceforth, it proclaimed, merit would replace privilege.[31]

Merit replacing privilege now became the topic of a conversation so animated that Franklin might have protested, as he supposedly was wont to do: "If you French would only speak four at a time, one might understand you!" The guests, none of whom had ever made a living with his hands, as Franklin had, were now vying with one another, each trying to position himself closest to the people, the fount of all that was good and true.

Listening to them, Lavoisier felt overwhelmed, once again,

by a wave of anguish. It was strange. All seemed to be going well in his life: he had been appointed to a commission meant to secure, at long last, the uniformity of weights and measures. The metric system, which he had proposed, was soon to be adopted. He was working on a new scheme of taxation. He had just been named commissary to the Treasury. And yet . . .

He had opened his heart to Franklin about this anxiety only a few months after the fall of the Bastille, but never knew whether Franklin was still alive to read his letter. "We look upon our revolution as accomplished," he had written, "and having reached a point of no return. . . . Moderate people who kept cool during this general effervescence believe that circumstances have carried us too far, that it was not a good idea to arm the whole citizenry, that it is politically unwise to place power in the hands of those who should obey, and finally that our new Constitution may run into trouble on the part of the very people for whose benefit it has been drafted. . . . How we regret your absence from France at this time! You would have been our guide and you would have shown us the limits we should not have transgressed."[32]

Lavoisier missed Franklin keenly. He remembered the many talks they had had while serving on the commission that investigated Mesmer's theory and practice of animal magnetism.[33] While daydreaming about their scientific discussions and warm friendship, he lost track of the conversation.

The abbé Morellet was describing Franklin's efforts to help two convicts who had been condemned to the galleys. The first, Marc-François Gauthier, had offered to serve on an American ship, where he could be of great use thanks to his knowledge of both the French and American coasts. Franklin forwarded his request, with a brief note, to the minister for foreign affairs, who forwarded it to the minister of the navy, who submitted it to the king. Within six weeks, the man was set free. There followed a deluge of applications, pathetic appeals from the very depths of human misery, but Franklin could not respond to them all. In the second case, however, that of Pierre-André Gargaz, obviously a cultivated man whose wrongdoing has never been revealed, Franklin felt moved enough to print on his own press the *Plan for Perpetual Peace* that Gargaz had conceived while serving his sentence. Eventually released, Gargaz walked all the way from Provence to Paris to thank his benefactor.[34]

The gathering was most impressed by the episode. What a pity, remarked Robespierre, that none of Franklin's eulogists had been informed of this. It would have been more telling than all the praise heaped on him for his magic squares and other intellectual achievements by the various orators speaking in the name of the academy, the Masonic lodge, the Commune of Paris, and other institutions.

"The best ceremony by far," declared Marat, "was the one that the Parisian printers organized. To show their respect for a colleague who had started out, like them, as a poor journeyman, they brought along the tools of their trade and, as one of them read his eulogy, the others set it in type and had the speech printed up within minutes of its delivery."[35]

Everybody nodded in agreement: it had been an amazing performance.

"And what about the eulogy of the abbé Fauchet?" asked Condorcet. "Didn't he hit exactly the right note when he said that Franklin had spread a catechism of happiness among the masses, that he had tried to open education to the lower classes, so that they would no longer be condemned to accept false ideas?"

Lavoisier agreed: "He knew how to speak to plain people, Franklin, and that is an art most of us still have to learn. I hear that *The Way to Wealth*, his condensation of many *Poor*

Richard's Almanacks, is going to be distributed in our schools. An excellent idea."

And then someone brought up the difficult, the inevitable question: "What is happening in America? Why isn't any official tribute being paid to his memory there?"

Silence. Nobody knew. They had heard a number of puzzling rumors but no explanation. They had believed at first that both houses in the United States had gone into mourning for Franklin, but discovered later that the Senate had categorically refused to do so. They learned that the president of the French National Assembly had sent Washington and the members of Congress a message of condolence, along with a bulky package containing copies of the eulogy delivered in the name of the Commune of Paris. But then President Washington had refused to open the package and had forwarded it, without a message, to the president of the Senate, John Adams. The next day, Adams returned both letter and package, still unopened, with a note to the effect that the Senate requested Washington to open it. Rather than do that, Washington sent it to Secretary of State Thomas Jefferson, who finally opened it and recommended to lay the French condolences before Congress. Washington, instead, sent it to the Senate once again, where John Adams, no friend of Franklin as the French knew only too well, supposedly made some sarcastic remarks about the letter and sent all twenty-six copies of the eulogy to the House. The House sent half of them back to the Senate.[36]

An explanation offered by subtle minds was that all this may have had to do with the separation between the executive and legislative branches. But then, as if the situation were not puzzling enough, there arrived in Paris a still more mystifying answer from Washington. Instead of the polite formulas of appreciation dictated by protocol, it contained advice as to the way France should conduct its internal affairs and the admonition that it give credit to Louis XVI for having broken the chains of the past.

What to make of this? Heads turned toward Mirabeau, whose political savvy was widely recognized.

"I may be wrong," he said, "but the way I understand it is that Monsieur Washington is deeply influenced by his minister of the Treasury, Monsieur Hamilton. And this Hamilton— unlike Monsieur Jefferson who understands us and likes us— loves England. What we are going to see, I believe, is America throwing itself into the arms of England and turning against us. Where is all that trade that Franklin kept promising us? It is going to England. Franklin's enemies are almost in power now. If he were still alive, he would do well to come back to us."

The dinner was drawing to a close. The snow in the center-piece had melted into rivulets that in turn formed little lakes on which floated tiny swans. Miniature spring flowers, violets and hyacinths, daffodils and tulips, had emerged, glistening, from the frost.[37]

And the gathering, for one brief, miraculous moment, felt mellow, as if Franklin had shaken over their souls the magic cane with which he used to still the waves with drops of oil. The guests glanced at each other without hatred, one might almost say with cordiality. They took leave of their hostess, under the cold moon, with the elaborate courtesy of bygone days, lingering for one last minute of nostalgia before they proceeded, each one in his own way, to their brutal and bloody destinies.

Franklin was a lucky man. His own star never stopped rising in the revolutionary firmament, even when France went on a rampage, destroying every day the idols of yesterday. More and more streets were named after him; statues were erected, parks dedicated, allegories drawn, and poems composed.[38]

In 1802, an officer fighting in Napoleon's army in Italy wrote back to his wife: "Be sure you buy Franklin's *Memoirs* and give them to our son to read. Franklin had a formula for happiness within·the common man's reach, and there is nobody I would rather have our son emulate than him." Who was this admirer? A writer who has recently burst into American consciousness through a play and a movie based on his diabolically erotic novel: *Les Liaisons Dangereuses, Dangerous Acquaintances.* Even Choderlos de Laclos was enraptured with Franklin. Yes, Franklin was a lucky man, even in the timing of his death. By dying when he did, he was spared much grief, and possibly some guilt: as we know now, the many loans he had procured from France and the expenses of the American war contributed to that country's financial collapse, with all of its political consequences.

He would never know that his first political collaborator in France, the gentle duc de La Rochefoucauld, who had translated the constitutions of the thirteen states, would be stoned to death by a frenzied mob. Or that Lavoisier would be sent to the scaffold, along with twenty-seven other tax collectors, including his father-in-law, Jacques Paulze, who had given the young American republic its first financial boost by importing quantities of Virginia tobacco.[39] Or that his good friend, the old jurist Malesherbes, who had shipped some of his choice lettuce seed to Philadelphia, would be condemned in his seventies for having offered to defend the king—an offer he made not because he admired Louis XVI but because he was a lawyer and *noblesse oblige*. Or that his neighbor in Passy, Monsieur Le Veillard, whose proudest possession was the manuscript of the *Autobiography* (then known as the *Memoirs*) would be guillotined, too, even though he had greeted the fall of the Bastille with exultation.[40]

Franklin did not have to shed tears for Rosalie Filleul, the pretty young woman who had painted a very unrealistic portrait of him looking romantic and frisky. Nor did he learn that the Noailles ladies, mother and sister of Mme de Lafayette, his courteous hostesses, had been put to death.

He never found out that the obsequious Marat he had known would turn into the sanguinary Marat of history. Nor that the Robespierre who had fawned on him would become synonymous with terror and death.[41]

And finally, Condorcet. Tracked down like an animal, he was obliged to run for his life, to go into hiding for nine months. Tortured with anguish over the fate of his wife and child, for whom he could do nothing, and agonizing with guilt for endangering the person who gave him shelter, Condorcet experienced what would be one day the agonies of the Jews whose fate had once moved him. During his long confinement in that little room, his thoughts turned to America and to Franklin. He wrote his will in the form of a letter to his hostess, Mme Vernet, who had not even known him previously but, out of sheer decency, was willing to risk her life in order to save his. In case his wife perished, he asked, could Mme Vernet see to it that their little girl be taught English and sent across the ocean to stay either with Jefferson or with Franklin Bache—meaning Benny, Franklin's grandson? Condorcet then ran away from Mme Vernet's safe house. He wandered for three days and two icy nights, aroused suspicion, was arrested, and was taken to jail while his papers—which were false—were verified. The next morning, the jailer found him dead, lying face down on the floor. Scholars are still debating whether he died by his own hand, swallowing the poison a friend had provided him, or whether he was felled by a heart attack.[42] One thing is certain, however: Condorcet believed to his very last breath, just as Franklin did, that given a chance, the human spirit would soar forever higher.

Abbreviations

Adams Correspondence
> Lyman H. Butterfield, Richard L. Ryerson, et al., eds., *Adams Family Correspondence* (6 vols. to date, Cambridge, Mass., 1963–).

Adams Papers
> Robert J. Taylor, Richard L. Ryerson, et al., eds., *Papers of John Adams* (10 vols. to date, Cambridge, Mass., 1977–).

Adams Papers Microfilms
> Massachusetts Historical Society, Boston, 1954–59, 608 reels.

John Adams Diary
> Lyman H. Butterfield et al., eds., *Diary and Autobiography of John Adams* (4 vols., Cambridge, Mass., 1961).

APS
> American Philosophical Society. It was founded by Franklin in 1743 with the title of "American Philosophical Society held in Philadelphia, for promoting useful knowledge." Philosophy, in the eighteenth century, generally meant the study of natural sciences.

Autobiog.

> Leonard W. Labaree, Ralph L. Ketcham, Helen C. Boatfield, and Helene H. Fineman, eds., *The Autobiography of Benjamin Franklin* (New Haven, 1964).

Bachaumont, *Mémoires secrets*

> Born from conversations in a Parisian salon, these memoirs fill thirty-six volumes published in London, 1784–89. Louis Petit de Bachaumont died in 1771, after writing the first six volumes. The later ones are the work of his successors.

Beinecke

> Beinecke Rare Book and Manuscript Library, Yale University

Dubourg, *Oeuvres*

> Jacques Barbeu-Dubourg, *Oeuvres de M. Franklin* . . . (2 vols., Paris, 1773).

Jefferson Papers

> Julian P. Boyd, Charles T. Cullen, John Catanzariti, et al., eds., *The Papers of Thomas Jefferson* (25 vols. to date, Princeton, 1950–).

LC

> Library of Congress

Lopez, *Mon Cher Papa*

> Claude-Anne Lopez, *Mon Cher Papa: Franklin and the Ladies of Paris* (rev. ed., New Haven, 1990).

Lopez, *Lafayette*

> Claude-Anne Lopez, "Benjamin Franklin, Lafayette, and the *Lafayette*," *Proceedings of the American Philosophical Society* 108 (1964): 181–223.

Lopez and Herbert, *Private Franklin*

> Claude-Anne Lopez and Eugenia W. Herbert, *The Private Franklin: The Man and his Family* (New York, 1975).

PBF

> Barbara Oberg et al., eds. *The Papers of Benjamin Franklin*

(34 vols. to date, New Haven, 1959–). The publication of a definitive edition of the *Papers of Benjamin Franklin* was launched in the mid-1950s at the initiative of President Truman under the joint sponsorship of Yale University and the APS. Since that date, the project has published 34 volumes (up to April 30, 1781) as well as Franklin's autobiography. Unlike previous editions, this undertaking includes all the extant letters written to Franklin as well as his own. A vast majority of the originals are located at the APS, but the work is done at Yale because the incomparable resource provided by the William Mason Collection of eighteenth-century background material on Philadelphia, London, and Paris is lodged there. As of the spring of 1999, Ellen Cohn has succeeded Barbara Oberg as editor. Barbara Oberg is now the editor of the Jefferson Papers.

PMHB

> *Pennsylvania Magazine of History and Biography*

Sellers, *Franklin in Portraiture*

> Charles G. Sellers, *Benjamin Franklin in Portraiture* (New Haven, 1962).

Smyth, *Writings*

> Albert H. Smyth, ed., *The Writings of Benjamin Franklin* . . . (10 vols., New York, 1905–7).

Stevens, *Facsimiles*

> Benjamin F. Stevens, ed., *Facsimiles of Manuscripts in European Archives Relating to America, 1773–1783* (25 vols., London, 1889–98).

Turgot, *Oeuvres*

> Gustave Schelle, ed., *Oeuvres de Turgot et documents le concernant* (5 vols., Paris, 1913–23).

Van Doren, *Franklin*

> Carl Van Doren, *Benjamin Franklin* (New York, 1938).

WTF, *Memoirs*

> William Temple Franklin, ed., *Memoirs of the Life and Writings of Benjamin Franklin, L.L.D., F.R.S.,* . . . (3 vols.,

London, 1817–18). Temple waited nearly thirty years to publish this edition of the papers that his grandfather bequeathed to him.

Walpole Correspondence

Wilmarth S. Lewis et al., eds., *The Yale Edition of Horace Walpole's Correspondence* (48 vols., New Haven, 1939–83).

Chronology

A more detailed and lavishly illustrated chronology was published in 1996 by Kendall/Hunt Publishing Company. It can be procured from the Friends of Franklin, Inc., P.O. Box 40048, Philadelphia, Pa., 19106.

Introduction

1. Franklin to John Jay, June 13, 1780, *PBF* 32:515–18.

2. William Temple Franklin, the illegitimate son of William Franklin, born in England around 1760 of an unknown mother, was brought back to America by his grandfather in 1775 and given the Franklin name at that time. He accompanied Franklin to France in late 1776 and remained at his side throughout Franklin's mission. After returning to Philadelphia in 1785, he lived in Rancocas, N.J., until six months after his grandfather's death. At this point, he sailed for England, lived for a while with his father there, and had a daughter, Ellen (born ca. 1791), by the governor's sister-in-law. He gave Ellen his name but left for France alone. After acquiring a fortune in Paris through real estate speculation, he lost it around 1809 and died in poverty in Paris in 1823, shortly after marrying Hannah Collier. He is buried at the Père Lachaise Cemetery.

1: Franklin, Hitler, Mussolini, and the Internet

1. The institute categorically denies that they have ever owned or exhibited either the original or a copy of this document.

2. See Frederic Cople Jaher, *A Scapegoat in the Wilderness* (Cambridge, Mass., 1994), 94–95, 100.

3. See Leonard Dinnerstein, *Antisemitism in America* (Oxford, 1994) for a thorough survey of this period. See also Léon Poliakov, *Histoire de l'Antisémitisme* (Paris, 1977), 219–54.

4. For his tribulations, see Milton M. Klein, "A Jew at Harvard in the 18th Century," *Proceedings of the Massachusetts Historical Society* 97 (1985): 135–45.

5. Quoted in Poliakov, *Histoire de l'Antisémitisme*, 228.

6. Franklin to Adams, November 26, 1781, LC, Adams manuscripts.

7. The other scholars were Charles A. Beard, Carl van Doren, Julian P. Boyd, Henry Butler Allen, Alfred Rigling, and John Clyde Oswald.

8. See NEXUS, U.S. Newswire, December 1990–January 1991, p. 11.

9. Max Hall has tracked down the Polly Baker saga in *Benjamin Franklin and Polly Baker: The History of a Literary Deception* (Pittsburgh, 1990).

10. See "Franklin and Slavery: A Sea Change."

2: The Only Founding Father in a Sports Hall of Fame

1. *Autobiog.*, 105–6.

2. Ibid., 53–54.

3. John Locke, *Some Thoughts Concerning Education* (London, 1745), 9, quoted in *PBF* 3:403.

4. *PBF* 20:133.

5. *Autobiog.*, 104.

6. *PBF* 15:295–98.

7. *Experiments and Observations on Electricity* . . . (London, 1769), 463–66.

8. *PBF* 20:46–55. The result of their correspondence appeared in his *Oeuvres de M. Franklin* . . . (2 vols., Paris, 1773), 2:246–57.

9. *PBF* 20:131–33.

10. Lopez, *Mon Cher Papa*, 281.

11. For more on Benny's diary, see "Franklin and Mesmer: A Confrontation."

12. From information kindly provided by Mr. Preston Levi, director of the Henning Library at the International Swimming Hall of Fame, Fort Lauderdale, Fla., May 13, 1998.

3: Three Women, Three Styles

1. Franklin's relationships with French women have been described in Lopez, *Mon Cher Papa*. Some passages in this essay have been reproduced from Lopez and Herbert, *Private Franklin*, which is no longer in print.

2. See William G. Roelker, ed., *Benjamin Franklin and Catharine Ray Greene: Their Correspondence, 1755–1790* (Philadelphia, 1949). See also the biographical notice in *PBF* 5:502n.

3. *PBF* 5:502–4; 535–37.

4. *PBF* 6:182–86.

5. *PBF* 6:96–97.

6. *PBF* 5:537.

7. *PBF* 6:225.

8. William Franklin, Franklin's only surviving son, was born out of wedlock to an unknown mother but was promptly recognized and given the Franklin name. He followed first in his father's footsteps, then took a law degree in London and was appointed royal governor of New Jersey. He sided with the Loyalists during the Revolution, went to London in exile in 1781, and died there in 1813.   ·

9. *PBF* 22:350; 23:292. Emma Thompson is a tantalizing figure. All we know about her comes from the spirited letter she wrote Franklin on February 6, 1777, from St. Omer in northern France. Her sympathies lay, no doubt, with the Tories. She called Franklin "you arch Rebel" but admitted humorously that her two most welcome visitors were women with whom she played whist, "tho friends to your Cause." After asking Franklin's advice as to where she should settle, given her slender means (Brussels? Lille?), she confessed ruefully that she still admired him: "For tho I know you a Rebel and myself a right Loyal, tho you deserve hanging and I deserve pensioning, still I feel you my Superior, feel a return of the great Respect I ever held you in, and feel, alas, unhappy, thinking I have been too bold" (*PBF* 23:291–92). His answer, two days later, was roguish: "You are too early, Hussy (as well as too saucy) in calling me Rebel; you should wait for the Event which will determine whether it is a Rebellion or only a Revolution. Here the Ladies are more civil; they call us *Les Insurgens,* a Character that usually pleases them. And methinks you, with all other Women who smart or have smarted under the Tyranny of a bad Husband, ought to be fix'd in *Revolution* Principles, and act accordingly" (*PBF* 23:296–99). Their one exchange of letters implies that they had many friends in common and had enjoyed a teasing kind of relationship, but Emma Thompson herself eludes us completely.

10. *PBF* 9:216–17. Their scientific exchanges appear mostly in this volume of the papers.

11. *PBF* 10:142–43.

12. *PBF* 9:121.

13. Although written in 1782, this passage is quoted in *PBF* 8:122n. See Whitfield J. Bell, Jr., " 'All Clear Sunshine': New Letters of Franklin and Mary

Stevenson Hewson," *American Philosophical Society Proceedings* 100 (1956): 521–36.

14. *PBF* 18:136–37.

15. *PBF* 19:300–302.

16. The "Mungo Elegy" has been put to fittingly noble music by Martin Mangold.

17. *PBF* 21:396–97; 29:408. Deborah also sent a couple of squirrels to the Shipleys' great friends, the Spencer family, direct ancestors of the late Diana, Princess of Wales.

18. *PBF* 23:303–6.

19. *PBF* 29:407–9.

20. *PBF* 31:44–45. The gift to Georgiana serves as a frontispiece to that volume. Now in private possession in the United States, it was the work of François Dumont, *miniaturiste* to Marie-Antoinette. He was inspired by the Duplessis "Gray Coat" portrait, currently at the New York Public Library. For background on the snuff box, see Sellers, *Franklin in Portraiture*, 267–69 and plate 25.

21. *Mon Cher Papa*, 314.

4: Grandfathers, Fathers, and Sons

1. Lopez and Herbert, *Private Franklin*, 228–32.

2. Samuel Cooper (1725–83), a celebrated theologian, was the first vice president of the American Academy of Arts and Sciences. Elected president of Harvard in 1774, he declined to serve but became a fellow of that college. See Charles W. Akers, "Religion and the American Revolution: Samuel Cooper and the Brattle Street Church," *William and Mary Quarterly* 35 (1978): 477–98. See also Charles W. Akers, *The Divine Politician* (Boston, 1982).

3. *PBF* 31:85–86.

4. F. Tuckerman, "The Descendants of Thomas Cooper of Boston," *New England Historical and Genealogical Register* 7 (1853): 142.

5. Adams Papers Microfilms, reels 4, 5, 330.

6. *John Adams Diary*, 2:417.

7. *PBF* 32:117–18.

8. *Insurgent* was the French term for the Americans. Franklin to Cooper, December 2, 1780, Huntington Library, San Marino, Calif.; *PBF* 34:96–97.

9. Robert Morris to Matthew Ridley, October 14, 1781, APS.

10. Marc Friedlaender and Mary-Jo Kline, eds., *The Book of Abigail and John* (Cambridge, Mass., 1975), 316.

11. M. de Marignac to Franklin, Collection of Miss Anna Scott (New York City).

12. G. Jaume to Franklin, November 20, 1781, APS.

13. Franklin to G. Jaume, December 7, 1781, LC.

14. Sammy Johonnot to Franklin, January 1, 1782, APS; G. Jaume to Franklin, December 23, 1781, University of Pennsylvania Library; Franklin to Sammy Johonnot, January 25, 1782, Boston Public Library.

15. Lopez and Herbert, *Private Franklin*, ch. 18.

16. Benny to William Temple Franklin, January 1, 1782, APS.

17. Dorcas Montgomery to Franklin, September 13, 1781, APS.

18. Mrs. Wesselow-Cramer to Franklin, May 15, 1781, APS.

19. Dorcas Montgomery to Franklin, November 17, 1781, APS.

20. Robert Morris to Matthew Ridley, July 8, 1782, Massachusetts Historical Society, Boston.

21. Louis Le Veillard to Franklin, June 9, 1782, APS.

22. Diary of Benjamin Franklin ("Benny") Bache. This diary, started on August 1, 1782, was kept by Benny until the day of his return to Philadelphia, September 15, 1785. The original in French has recently been recovered and is in the Bache Papers–Castle Collection at the APS. An English translation, made by one of Benny's grandsons, is also at the APS.

23. Samuel Cooper to Sammy, December 26, 1782, Beinecke.

24. Mrs. Hixon to Sammy, May 9, 1783. Beinecke. She was born Abigail Cooper and married Joseph Sayer Hixon, a merchant, in 1777.

25. Johonnot to Sammy, n.d., Beinecke. Johonnot to Franklin, May 25, 1783, APS. Johonnot's power of attorney to Jonathan Williams, March 23, 1782, Historical Society of Pennsylvania, Philadelphia.

26. Samuel Cooper to Sammy, June 23, 1783, Beinecke. Cooper to Franklin, May 5 and July 9, 1783, APS.

27. The domaine de Penthes now houses the Fondation de l'Histoire des Suisses à l'Etranger. It was just beyond the territory of the Geneva Republic.

28. Pigott to Franklin, November 26, 1782, APS. See the article on Pigott in the *Dictionary of National Biography*.

29. Pigott to Franklin, June 27, 1783, APS.

30. For the story of Franklin's involvement with the first balloons, see Lopez, *Mon Cher Papa*, 215–24.

31. Lebègue de Presle to Benny, August 1783, Beinecke.

32. Benny to Sammy, August 10, 1783, Beinecke.

33. Jonathan Williams to Franklin, August 13, 1783, APS. Livres tournois (*l.t.*), named after the city of Tours where the coinage took place, was the

French currency until the Revolution of 1789. One livre was equivalent to five U.S. dollars. One pound sterling was worth twenty-three or twenty-four *l.t.* The smaller denominations were deniers *(d.)* and sols *(s.)*.

34. Sammy to Franklin, August 14, 1783, APS.

35. Franklin to Sammy, August 19, 1783, Beinecke.

36. Sammy to Franklin, August 27, 1783, APS.

37. The "journal" is one that Sammy kept on their way from Spain to Paris in 1779–80.

38. John Quincy Adams to Sammy, August 25, 1783, Beinecke. See D. F. Musto, "The Youth of John Quincy Adams," *Proceedings of the American Philosophical Society* 113, no. 4 (1969): 269–82.

39. John Quincy Adams to Sammy, August 31, 1783, Beinecke.

40. Sammy to Franklin, April 21, 1784, APS.

41. Samuel Cooper to Franklin, October 16 and November 20, 1783, APS; Franklin to Cooper, December 26, 1783, APS.

42. Judge James Sullivan to Sammy, December 17, 1783, Beinecke.

43. Sammy to Franklin, April 21, 1784, APS.

44. For Benny's later career and destiny, see "Was Franklin Too French?"

45. *Jefferson Papers* 13:164. To make matters worse—although this does not appear anywhere in Jefferson's papers—the Marianne Glegg-Pigott whom Robert married was not even a legitimate daughter by Pigott's respectable Swiss wife, but the product of one of his many extramarital forays. Pigott himself was to have a colorful career during the French Revolution, befriending Brissot de Warville and Mme Roland. Luckier than they, he died in his bed in Toulouse (July 7, 1794). Information provided by Walter Zurbuchen, archivist of Geneva.

46. Jane Mecom to Franklin, August 16, 1784, APS, Bache Collection.

5: The Man Who Frightened Franklin

1. Franklin to Juliana Ritchie, January 19, 1777, *PBF* 23:211–12.

2. Allaire's family history appears in R. Bolton, *History of Westchester County* (New York, 1848), 1:429, and *Collections of the Huguenot Society of America* (New York, 1886), 1:212. For a genealogy see Eugene Haag, *La France Protestante* (10 vols., Geneva, 1966). Additional data on Allaire's commercial activities may be obtained from his own depositions as reported in [Charpentier], *La Bastille dévoilée; ou, Recueil de Pièces authentiques pour servir à son histoire* (3 vols., Paris, 1790), 3:10–14.

3. For a summary of Allaire's first message, see *PBF* 24:470. The manuscript is at the Historical Society of Pennsylvania, Philadelphia.

4. *PBF* 29:459–60.

5. See W. Bennet, *Alphabetical Index of Patentees and Inventions* (London, 1969). The powder was supposed to cure a wide range of distempers. Still broader claims were made for Dr. James's other brainchild, a pill patented in 1775.

6. Allaire himself stated to the Bastille investigators that he had come to Paris with Swinton to "solliciter du ministre de la marine la poudre du sieur James" (*Bastille dévoilée*, 3:12). On Swinton's career see Hélène Maspero-Clerc, "Une Gazette anglo-française pendant la guerre d'Amérique," *Annales Historiques de la Révolution Française* (Reims, 1976): 572–94; and E. Hatin, *Histoire Politique et Littéraire de la Presse en France* (Paris, 1859).

7. *Metropolitan Magazine*, November 1907, 180–87. It was reprinted in George G. Wood, ed., *Now and Then*, vol. 8 (Muncy, Penn., 1948), 297–305.

8. Julien-Pierre Allaire (1742–1816) held administrative posts until the Revolution, when he retired to his estate in Champagne and made important contributions to agriculture and sheep breeding. From information to be found at the Bibliothèque du Jardin des Plantes, kindly forwarded by M. Maurice Déchery of Paris.

9. Those common friends were indeed renowned scholars: ornithologist Mathurin Brisson and physicist Thomas Dalibard. Boulogne was suggested on the ground that it was a convenient location for Peter Allaire to wait for the conclusion of an important lawsuit pending in England. Rochambeau had sailed from Brest on May 2.

10. F. Funck Brentano, *Les Lettres de Cachet à Paris* (Paris, 1903), 405; *Bastille dévoilée*, 3:10–14.

11. *PBF* 32:429.

12. Jonathan Williams to William Temple Franklin, December 26, 1781, APS.

13. *American Jest Book* (Philadelphia, 1789), 11–12, Beinecke. No detail given in Allaire's account of the investigation is reproduced in this version of the story, but a new one is added: Allaire is said to have been offered the spiritual assistance of a Catholic priest and to have refused it, stressing that he was a Protestant.

14. W. B. Willcox, *Portrait of a General* (New York, 1964), 331.

15. On Swinton see Maspero-Clerc, "Une Gazette anglo-française"; and Hatin, *Histoire Politique*; on Bancroft see *PBF* 16:224–25 and Y. Bizardel, *Bottin des Américains à Paris sous Louis XVI et pendant la Révolution* (Paris, 1976), 19–20, 202. See also Julian Boyd, "Silas Deane: Death by a Kindly Teacher of Treason?" *William and Mary Quarterly* 3d ser., vol. 16 (1959): 165–87, 319–42, 515–50.

16. Truffé to Benjamin Franklin, March 9, 1784, APS. This long letter supplies most of the information on the Rebecca Allaire story.

17. R. B. Morris, ed., *John Jay, the Winning of the Peace: Unpublished Papers, 1780–1784* (New York, 1980), 722.

18. F. Turner, "English Policy towards America in 1790–91," *American Historical Review* 7, no. 4 (July 1902): 717–19 and 723–26; *Jefferson Papers* 17:911n. Boyd expressed his intention of publishing "a more extended account of Allaire" but did not carry it out.

6: Franklin and the Unfortunate Divine

1. For background details and the basic bibliography, see G. Howson, *The Macaroni Parson* (London, 1973).

2. On Johnson's involvement with Dodd's defense, see C. McC. Weis and F. Pottle, eds., *Boswell in Extremes, 1776–1778* (New York, 1970), 164.

3. *Walpole Correspondence* 9:273–74.

4. *The Letters of Philip Dormer Stanhope, 4th Earl of Chesterfield*, edited with an introduction by Bonamy Dobrée (6 vols., London and New York, 1932), vol. 6, June 5, 1765.

5. *PBF* 23:254–55.

6. *PBF* 22:282–83. Franklin lived in the vicinity, at High Street (now Market Street) between Third and Fourth.

7. *PBF* 20:419–20. Franklin's friendship with Dr. Hawkesworth is attested as far back as 1760–62; see *PBF* 9, esp. p. 265.

8. On Dodd's school for the preparation of "female boarders . . . desirous of being introduced into polite life," grandly entitled National Female Seminary (but probably connected with his schemes for the redemption of lost sheep), and on the scandal that caused its closing, there is some information in F. Fitzgerald, *A Famous Forgery* (London, 1859), a storehouse of interesting material, unfortunately presented without proper reference to sources.

9. I am indebted to Dr. Charles Harris, editor of the *Papers of William Thornton*, for calling my attention to this obituary and to two other excerpts from the *National Intelligencer* that enabled me to identify Mrs. Brodeau.

10. Sally Franklin Bache to Franklin, June 1, 1783, APS.

11. *Universal Asylum and Columbian Magazine* 1, no. 2 (October 1786).

12. [John McPherson], Macpherson's *Directory for the City and Suburbs of Philadelphia* (1785), 14; C. Biddle, *The Philadelphia Directory* (1791), 14.

13. *Dictionary of American Biography* under Thornton; A. C. Clark, "Dr. and Mrs. William Thornton," *Records of the Columbia Historical Society* 18 (1915): 144–208.

14. *PBF* 27:348–49; 28:592–93; 29:104, 686; 31:373.

15. Turgot, *Oeuvres*, 5:546–47, 575, 588.

16. F. F. Monaghan, "A New Document on the Identity of 'Junius,'" *Journal of Modern History* 4, no. 1 (March 1932): 68–71; *Correspondence of King George III*, vol. 2 (London, 1927), 1281, 1285.

17. Stevens, *Facsimiles* 9:907.

18. Ibid., 14:1413.

19. Ibid., 2:192; 16:1587; 16:1594.

20. Ibid., 8:759, undated but probably December 1777.

21. Monaghan, "New Document," 69; Mante to Amelot (the ministre de la maison du roi, the equivalent of the secretary of the interior), APS, n.d., but probably written during the summer of 1778 because it is a petition to be freed from an arbitrary imprisonment that has lasted for some time.

22. *PBF* 27:348–49.

23. Turgot, *Oeuvres*, 5:546, 588. See also Franklin's cash book (Account 18, *PBF* 26:3). There were two counts de Boisgelin, and both were guillotined; whether the one who caused Mante to be imprisoned was Louis-Bruno, "Master of the Wardrobe," or his cousin Louis-Dominique, an army man, is not clear.

24. Turgot, *Oeuvres*, 5:606, 623; *PBF* 31:373. One year later, Turgot again wrote Du Pont that Mante's translation needed revision.

25. Mentioned but not published in *PBF* 31:373n.

7: Franklin's Most Baffling Correspondent

1. The bibliography on d'Eon is daunting. Because my focus is on his relationship with Franklin—a topic on which there is very little in print—I have used secondary sources for background information on his life. The most scholarly and reliable of those is Didier Ozanam and Michel Antoine, eds., *Correspondance secrète du comte de Broglie avec Louis XV (1756–1774)* (2 vols., Paris, 1956–1961). I have also used the second volume (*L'Ombre de la Bastille*) of the three-volume series by Gilles Perrault, *Le Secret du Roi* (Paris, 1993). Two books dealing specifically with d'Eon are Michel de Decker, *Madame le chevalier d'Eon* (Paris, 1987); and Gary Kates, *Monsieur d'Eon Is a Woman: A Tale of Political Intrigue and Sexual Masquerade* (New York, 1995), which offers an interesting psychological interpretation of its subject. The primary sources are to be found at the University of Leeds (England), the Bibliothèque Municipale of Tonnerre, the Archives des Affaires étrangères, the Archives privées in Paris, and the APS in Philadelphia.

2. Ekaterina Romanovna Daschkova led a brilliant life as a traveler,

writer, and intellectual, president of the Academy of Sciences of St. Petersburg, founder of the Russian Academy, and member of the American Philosophical Society. See Pascal Pontremoli, ed., *Mémoires de la Princesse Dashkov* (Paris, 1989). Historians are now inclined to believe that the episodes of d'Eon's transvestitism at the Russian court are fabrications he made up later in order to give a professional origin to his change of sex.

3. Jean Drouet, a widely traveled businessman and philosopher, appears frequently in Ozanam and Antoine, eds., *Correspondance secrète*. He contacted Franklin during 1778 because he wanted to promote a plan that he had worked on for many years. It was no less than a vast opus on the proposed finances, constitution, legislation, and administration of the world power he prophesied that America would become. He met Franklin in August of that year to discuss it with him. See *PBF* 26:686–88.

4. See Gary Kates, *D'Eon's Books: The Library of an Eighteenth-Century Transsexual* (Binghamton, N.Y., 1992), 137–49.

5. See Jean-Claude David, "La Querelle de l'inoculation en 1763: Trois lettres inédites de Suard et du chevalier d'Eon," *Dix-huitième* 17 (1985): 271–84. See also Charles d'Eon, *Lettres sur l'utilité de la culture des mûriers et de l'éducation des vers à soie en France* (Paris, 1758).

6. The Grand Ohio, later known as the Walpole Company, dates back to the treaty of Fort Stanwix signed in 1768. It was meant to compensate the "suffering traders" for depredations at the hands of the Indians in 1763 and entailed a large cession of land south of the Ohio River. In spite of the inclusion among its founders of influential English politicians (led by the Hon. Thomas Walpole), the company never obtained the 20 million acres for which it had petitioned. Franklin, whose relations with the British government were deteriorating at that point, stayed in the background as of 1772 and agreed to an ostensible (but not real) withdrawal in 1774. For the vicissitudes of the enterprise, see under Walpole Company in *PBF*, vols. 16–22.

7. Franklin to Lord Howe, July 20, 1776, *PBF* 22:520.

8. *PBF* 23:49–50.

9. Du Coudray was so prickly that his death by drowning in Philadelphia's Schuylkill River was a source of unconcealed relief for many. *PBF* 24:266–67; 25:220–21.

10. Luckily, it had been photographed and can be found opposite p. 233 in the 1935 edition of H. Gaillardet, *Mémoires du Chevalier d'Eon* (Paris, 1935).

11. Franklin to the Emma Thompson mentioned in "Three Women, Three Styles," *PBF* 23:299.

12. Bachaumont, *Mémoires secrets*, 11:59.

13. *PBF* 25:515.

14. *PBF* 29:185–87.

15. For more detail, see A. O. Aldridge, *Franklin and His French Contemporaries* (New York, 1957), 113–17.

16. *PBF* 30:631.

17. Voltaire to Charles-Augustin Feriol, comte d'Argental, December 6, 1777; Theodore Besterman, ed., *The Complete Works of Voltaire* (Oxford Foundation, 1976), 129:126–27.

8: Franklin and the Mystery Turk

1. *PBF* 25:204; 218–19. For more details, see Lopez, *Mon Cher Papa*, 59.

2. An English translation of this poem appears in Lopez, *Mon Cher Papa*, pp. 77–78.

3. Vincent Le Ray de Chaumont, *Souvenirs des Etats-Unis* (Paris, 1859), 6–7.

4. Thomas Jefferson, *Writings* (20 vols., Washington, Jefferson Memorial Association, 1903–4), 18:168f.

5. Valltravers to Franklin, December 24, 1782, APS. On December 30, he gave Kempelen a personal letter of introduction to Franklin.

6. *An Introduction to the History and Study of Chess . . . by an Amateur* (n.p., 1804), 46–49.

7. See *Chess Monthly: An American Serial* 1 (July 1857): 199, where von Brühl's letter is mentioned. Franklin's involvement with chess is described on 193–200.

8. *The Speaking Figure and the Automaton Chess-Player, Exposed and Detected by Anonymous* (London, 1784).

9. Poe's exposé appeared in *Southern Literary Messenger* (Richmond, Va., April 1836).

10. *Chess Monthly* 1 (February 1857): 41–45.

11. Henry Ridgely Evans, *Edgar Allan Poe and Baron von Kempelen's Chess-Playing Automaton* (Kenton, Ohio, 1939), 23.

12. *PBF* 29:753. For background information on *The Morals of Chess* see ibid., 750–57. A photograph of Franklin's chess set, at the APS, is opposite p. 752. It may be the one that the duchesse de Deux-Ponts gave him. See "The Duchess, the Plenipotentiary, and the Golden Cap of Liberty."

13. Chaumont, *Souvenirs*, p. 7.

14. *PBF* 29:757.

9: Franklin and Mesmer

1. For general background see R. Darnton, *Mesmerism and the End of the Enlightenment in France* (Cambridge, Mass., 1968); Lopez, *Mon Cher Papa*, 163–73; J. Thuillier, *Franz-Anton Mesmer; ou, l'Extase Magnétique* (Paris, 1988); and Frank A. Pattie, *Mesmer and Animal Magnetism: A Chapter in the History of Medicine* (Hamilton, N.Y., 1994).

2. Darnton, *Mesmerism*, 165.

3. For more details on Robespierre and Marat's relationship with Franklin, see the Epilogue.

4. Darnton, *Mesmerism*, 36.

5. *PBF* 27:505.

6. Mme Brillon to Franklin, November 1, 1779, *PBF* 31:8–9.

7. La Condamine to Franklin, March 8, 1784; Franklin to La Condamine, March 19, 1784, APS.

8. Comtesse d'Houdetot to Franklin, March 10, 1784, APS.

9. Lafayette to Franklin, before June 12, 1784, APS.

10. Benny's diary (August 1, 1782–September 14, 1785) was written in French. The original is at the Bache-Castle Collection, and the APS has it on microfilm. An English translation was made by one of Benny's descendants.

11. This sounds like an echo of Franklin's letter to La Condamine.

12. Bailly's "Exposé des expériences" was read on September 4, 1784, and printed on September 24. The English text is my translation.

13. Smyth, *Writings*, 9:268.

14. Jefferson to the Rev. William Smith, February 19, 1791, *Jefferson Papers* 19:112.

10: Outfitting One's Country for War

1. *PBF* 28:153.

2. Franklin to Pierre-Samuel Dupont de Nemours, October 24, 1788, LC.

3. *PBF* 33:395–96.

4. On Chaumont's role in the American Revolution, see Th. Schaeper, *The Life of Jacques-Donatien Leray de Chaumont, 1725–1803* (Providence, R.I., 1995).

5. *PBF* 33:162.

6. *PBF* 32:547.

7. *PBF* 32:615.

8. Arthur Lee to James Bowdoin, December 25, 1780, Massachusetts Historical Society, Boston. See also Lee to Jonathan Trumbull, December 25, 1780, Trumbull Papers, Connecticut State Library, Hartford.

9. The journal covers only six weeks. See *PBF* 34:171–82.

10. *Panter and Co. Sale Catalogue of Prize Cargo of ship Marquis de Lafayette*, APS, vault 347.7.

11. *PBF* 34:274–75.

11: Franklin's Choice of a Dinner Set

1. Royal [crossed out] Manufactory of English pottery of Messrs. Clark and Company, established in Montereau-faut-Yonne, in virtue of the Council's decree of March 15, 1775, under the name of Queen's Ware, or Merchandise of the Queen.

2. See Guy Richard, *Noblesse d'affaires au XVIIIe siècle* (Paris, 1974), 97; *Annales de Normandie* (March 1961): 239–42.

3. See André Rémond, *John Holker: Manufacturier et grand fonctionnaire en France au XVIIIe siècle* (Paris, 1946).

4. See "Industrial Espionage in the Eighteenth Century" in John Harris, *Essays in Industry and Technology in the Eighteenth Century: England and France* (Hampshire, Eng., 1992), 168ff.

5. Trudaine, by the way, sold to Holker the land on which one of the manufactories was to be built. Holker *père* to Holker *fils*, October 20, 1779, Beinecke.

6. Archives nationales, Paris, F 12 1497 A.

7. Donald Towner, *Creamware* (London and Boston, 1978), 13.

8. Thomas Bentley, *Journal of a Visit to Paris, 1776*, ed. Peter France (Brighton, 1977), 71.

9. Printed by J. Smith in 1783, Newcastle, Staffordshire. The quotation is on pp. 11–12.

10. Franklin's London landlady, Mrs. Stevenson, bought two dozen plates from Wedgwood on February 24, 1772, APS. Sally's letter appears in *PBF* 20:452–54.

12: Franklin and the Nine Sisters

1. The term *accepted* applies to those who were not, properly speaking, masons and builders, but to the lawyers, clergymen, and men of property and good repute who had been allowed to join the movement in England during

the seventeenth century. While the symbolism remained that of the man who works with his hands, the content of discussions became abstract.

2. In 1742, Richard, viscount Ranelagh, opened to the public the mansion and gardens he had laid out on his estate near Chelsea, by the Thames. After a rotunda for concerts was built on the site, they became a resort for fashionable entertainment until 1803.

3. Bachaumont, *Mémoires secrets*, 12:43.

4. Niccolò Piccinni (1728–1800) was an Italian composer much in vogue among opponents of German music. The partisans of German music rallied around Glück.

5. Robert Palmer, *The Age of Democratic Revolution* (Princeton, 1959), 1:245.

13: The Duchess, the Plenipotentiary, and the Golden Cap of Liberty

1. *PBF* 29:710; Franklin to Duchess, *PBF* 29:748.

2. Franklin's mention of chess possibly alludes to the miniature traveling chess set now at the APS.

3. For more on that medal (Libertas Americana), see "Was Franklin Too French?"

4. July 13, 1787, LC.

14: Franklin Plays Cupid

1. *PBF* 31:170–71.

2. *PBF* 31:180–81.

3. *PBF* 28:74–75. In a subsequent appeal, dated October 28, 1779, Locke retraces his career in great detail but no longer mentions his marriage—he had met Mlle Desbois by then. *PBF* 30:606–7.

4. *Vital Records of Nantucket to the Year 1850* (Boston, 1925–28), 4:131, 192.

15: Was Franklin Too French?

1. For an exciting account of the Marly experiment, see *PBF* 4:302–10.

2. *PBF* 14:250–55.

3. Rochon's presentation is reported in *Procès-verbaux de l'académie des sciences* 99 (August 1780): 19.

4. Lopez, *Mon Cher Papa*, 215–22.

5. Franklin to Sir Joseph Banks, November 21, 1783, University of Pennsylvania Library.

6. *John Adams Diary*, 4, 118.

7. Lopez, *Mon Cher Papa*, 202–3.

8. Ibid., 19.

9. Ibid., 205.

10. Ibid., 92–95, 264–68.

11. John Adams to Robert Livington, May 25, 1783, Paris. Letterbook copy in John Thaxter's hand, marked by Adams "not sent." In Adams Papers Microfilms, reel 108.

12. Franklin to Robert Livingston, July 22, 1783, National Archives.

13. John Adams to Elbridge Gerry, September 3, 1783, in Francis Wharton, ed., *The Revolutionary Diplomatic Correspondence of the United States* (Washington, 1889), vol. 6, p. 670.

14. Franklin to Henry Laurens, April 29, 1784, Yale University Libraries.

15. John Adams to Robert Livingston, May 25, 1783.

16. Franklin to Samuel Huntington, *PBF* 33:160–66.

17. Lester C. Olson, "Benjamin Franklin's Commemorative Medal *Libertas Americana*: A Study in Rhetorical Iconology," *Quarterly Journal of Speech* 9 (1990): 23–45.

18. Franklin to Samuel Mather, May 12, 1784, in Smyth, *Writings*, 9:210.

19. Samuel Cooper to Franklin, May 5, 1783, ministère des affaires étrangères, Paris.

20. Franklin to John Adams and to John Jay, September 10, 1783, in Smyth, *Writings*, 9:91–93.

21. *Poor Richard*, September 1757.

22. Edmund C. Burnett, ed., *Letters of Members of the Continental Congress* (Washington, 1921–36) 3:554.

23. Franklin to Thomson, December 29, 1788, APS.

24. Benny's travails are vividly recounted in Jeffery A. Smith, *Franklin and Bache: Envisioning the Enlightened Republic* (New York, 1990). See also Richard N. Rosenfeld, *American Aurora: A Democratic-Republican Returns* (New York, 1997).

16: Innocents on the Ohio

1. See "Was Franklin Too French?"

2. The introduction is found in Guillotin to Franklin, June 18, 1787, APS. See also J. F. McDermott, "Guillotin Thinks of America," *Ohio Archaeological and Historical Quarterly* 47 (1938). The guillotine had come close to being

called, appropriately, the *louisette* after its real inventor, Dr. Louis. For information on Guillotin's being chosen commissioner, see "Franklin and Mesmer: A Confrontation."

3. Louis-Guillaume Le Veillard to Franklin, June 13, 1787; Le Veillard to William Temple Franklin, same date; Jean d'Arcet to Franklin, June 19, 1787. All three at the APS.

4. See especially H. M. Fouré Selter, *L'Odyssée américaine d'une famille française* (Baltimore, 1936), and S. E. Dicks, *Antoine Saugrain: A French Scientist on the American Frontier*, Emporia State Research Studies 25, no. 1 (Emporia, Kansas, 1976), with their bibliographies.

5. Lucas des Peintraux to Brissot de Warville, July 28, 1788, quoted in J. P. Brissot de Warville, *New Travels in the United States of America*, ed. M. S. Vance and D. Echeverria (Cambridge, Mass., 1964), 213.

6. Ibid.

7. Thomas Jefferson to G. R. Clark, June 21, 1787, *Jefferson Papers*, 11:487.

8. Picque to Franklin, October 18, 1787; February 10, 1788, and March 2, 1788. All three at the APS. A good number of letters must have been lost: Picque and Saugrain did not receive those they had expected from France in America, Picque's brother in France complained that his brother had not written to him, and Guillotin grumbled that he had not heard from Saugrain.

9. Autobiography of Major Samuel S. Forman, *Historical Magazine* (Boston) 2d ser., vol. 6 (December 1869): 325.

10. Mrs. Mary Dewees, "Mrs. Mary Dewees's Journal from Philadelphia to Kentucky, 1787–1788," *PMHB* 28, no. 2 (1904): 182–98.

11. Picque to Franklin, February 10, 1788, APS.

12. Guillotin to Franklin, March 19, 1788, APS.

13. Saugrain to De Lassize, April 16, 1788. A copy of this letter is at the APS.

14. "Dr. Saugrain's Relation of his Voyage down the Ohio River," E. F. Bliss, tr. *Proceedings of the American Antiquarian Society* 2 (1897).

15. General background and bibliography are in J. Finley, *Autobiography; or, Pioneer Life in the West* (Cincinnati, 1853); B. W. Bond, *The Civilization of the Old Northwest* (New York, 1934); and J. D. Barnhart, *Valley of Democracy* (Bloomington, 1953).

16. *Kentucky Gazette*, April 4, 1788; Franklin to Guillotin, May 4 and June 8, 1788, LC.

17. Franklin to Guillotin, October 23, 1788. Chicago Historical Society.

18. Le Veillard to Franklin, February 21, 1789, APS.

19. T. Ridout, "An Account of My Capture by the Shawnee Indians," *Western Pennsylvania Historical Mazagine* (Pittsburgh) 12 (1929): 31.

20. Delaunay des Blardières to Franklin, August 1, 1789, APS.

21. Benjamin Franklin, *The Bagatelles from Passy* (New York, 1967), 3. The essay is entitled "Remarks on the Politeness of the Savages."

17: Franklin and Slavery

1. *PBF* 1:345. For an account of slavery in Pennsylvania, see Lopez and Herbert, *Private Franklin*, 291–302.

2. *Observations Concerning the Increase of Mankind, Peopling of Countries* (1751), as quoted in John C. Van Horne's chapter, "Collective Benevolence and the Common Good," in J. A. Leo Lemay, ed., *Reappraising Benjamin Franklin: A Bicentennial Perspective* (Newark, Del., 1993), 433–38.

3. *PBF* 3:474.

4. *PBF* 6:425n.

5. Both quotations are from *PBF* 9:174–75.

6. *PBF* 7:356, 357.

7. *PBF* 10:396.

8. *PBF* 9:38.

9. *PBF* 19:192.

10. For more on this salon, see Lopez, *Mon Cher Papa*, 243–301.

11. An enormous amount has been written about Antoine Nicolas Caritat, marquis de Condorcet (1743–94). See especially K. M. Baker, *Condorcet: From Natural Philosophy to Social Mathematics* (Chicago, 1975).

12. Condorcet, *Oeuvres complètes* (21 vols., Paris, 1804), 11:85–198.

13. My translation.

14. "Excerpts from the papers of Dr. Benjamin Rush," *PMHB* 29:26.

15. Anthony Benezet (1713–84) was born in France into a Huguenot family that emigrated to Holland, then to England, and eventually to Philadelphia where he became a Quaker. He devoted his life to teaching and writing in favor of black and native Americans.

16. Smyth, *Writings* 10:67.

17. Jean-Pierre Brissot de Warville (1754–93) visited Franklin in Philadelphia in 1788. A brilliant man who was particularly dynamic in defending the rights of the blacks, he perished along with the other members of the Girondist party during the Reign of Terror.

18. *Federal Gazette*, February 17, 1790.

Epilogue

1. On the relationship between Franklin and Mme Helvétius, see Lopez, *Mon Cher Papa*, 243 to end.

2. Franklin stayed in France from December 3, 1776, to July 23, 1785.

3. Marie Jean Antoine Nicolas Caritat, marquis de Condorcet (1743–94); Antoine Laurent Lavoisier (1743–94); Jean Paul Marat (1743–93); Honoré Gabriel Riqueti, comte de Mirabeau (1749–91); André Morellet (1727–1819); and Maximilien François Marie de Robespierre (1758–94).

4. Franklin to Mme Helvétius, October 25, 1788, manuscripts at LC and the Bibliothèque Nationale. His French reads: "Je ne peux pas laisser partir cette Occasion, my chère Amie, sans vous dire que je vous aime toujours, et que je me porte bien. Je pense continuellement des Plaisirs que j'ai joui dans la douce Société d'Auteuil. Et souvent dans mes Songes, je dejeune avec vous, je me place au côté de vous sur une de votre mille sofas, ou je promène avec vous dans votre belle jardin" (quoted in Lopez, *Mon Cher Papa*, 334).

5. Jacques Brillon to Franklin, December 30, 1785, APS.

6. See E. Badinter et R. Badinter, *Condorcet: Un intellectuel en politique* (Paris, 1988).

7. *PBF* 20:489.

8. *PBF* 21:151.

9. For more on this biting essay, see "Franklin and Slavery."

10. She was the sister of Emmanuel, marquis de Grouchy, who gained fame as one of Napoleon's marshals.

11. Condorcet to Franklin, July 8, [1788], APS.

12. Franklin to Lavoisier, October 23, 1788, APS.

13. Phlogiston, a notion that flourished for a century before being put to rest by Lavoisier, posited that inflammability was a material substance.

14. Lavoisier to Franklin, August 9, 1778, *PBF* 27:236. The relationship between Franklin and Lavoisier is discussed in Denis I. Duveen and Herbert S. Klickstein, "Benjamin Franklin and Antoine Laurent Lavoisier," *Annals of Science* 11 (1955): 103–28, 271–302; 13 (1957): 30–46. See also Claude-Anne Lopez, "Saltpetre, Tin and Gunpowder: Addenda to the Correspondence of Lavoisier and Franklin," *Annals of Science* 16 (1960): 83–94.

15. Robespierre to Franklin, October 1, 1783, APS.

16. For a thrilling account of Thomas François Dalibard's experiment, see *PBF* 4:302–10.

17. See Marie-Hélène Huet, "Thunder and Revolution: Franklin, Robespierre, Sade" in Sandy Petrey, ed., *The French Revolution, 1789–1989: Two Hundred Years of Rethinking* (Lubbock, Tex., 1989), 13–32.

18. "It has pleased God in his Goodness to Mankind, at length to discover to them the Means of securing their Habitations and other Buildings from Mischief by Thunder and Lightning. The Method is this . . ." See *PBF* 4:408–9.

19. See *PBF* 29:105–7, 112, 147, 208, 213, 228–29, 311–12, 626–27. Marat's early letters were signed "L'Auteur."

20. Victor Hugo evokes the liaison between Marat and the marquise de l'Aubépine in *Les Misérables*.

21. Balthazar G. Sage, *Analyse chimique et concordance des trois règnes* (3 vols., Paris, 1786), 1:117. That was exactly what Sage had written about the occasion, and Franklin did indeed look like a saint with that halo of steam. See also Ch. Vellay, "Lettres inédites de Marat à Benjamin Franklin (1779–83)," *Revue historique de la Révolution française et de l'Empire* 11 (1912): 353–61; Charles C. Gillispie, *Science and Polity in France at the End of the Old Regime* (Princeton, 1980); and Sidney L. Phipson, *Jean-Paul Marat: His Career in England and France before the Revolution* (London, 1924), 39–47. As of August 1779, Marat felt confident enough to sign his letters to Franklin.

22. They did, eventually, publish such a calendar. Franklin's day was June 12. See H. Blanc and P. F. X. Bouchard, *Almanach républicain, dans lequel on a substitué le nom des hommes célèbres à celui des ci- devant martyrs, vierges, etc.* . . . *Paris, an III [1795]*, Bibliothèque Nationale, Paris.

23. The friendship between Franklin and Jean-Baptiste Le Roy lasted for almost forty years. During this time, they wrote frequently on such diverse topics as electricity, the nature of water, free trade, comets, the ventilation of hospitals, expeditions to the North Pole, and optical glass.

24. Cesare Bonesana, marchese di Beccaria (1738–94), had published anonymously, in 1764, his *Dei delitti e delle pene*, still considered the basis of modern criminology. Voltaire wrote the preface to the French translation.

25. Edited by Dorothy Medlin, Jean-Claude David, and Paul Leclerc, the entire correspondence of the abbé Morellet has been published by Oxford University Press in three volumes (1991, 1994, 1996). For the "list of emotions," see Ellen Cohn, "Benjamin Franklin and Traditional Music," in J. A. Leo Lemay, ed., *Reappraising Benjamin Franklin* (Newark, Del., 1993), 312–13.

26. The portrait is now at the APS, having been purchased from the descendants of Mme Helvétius. See Sellers, *Franklin in Portraiture*, 391–96.

27. See "Franklin and the Nine Sisters."

28. Condorcet to Franklin, July 8, [1788], APS.

29. See Lopez, *Mon Cher Papa*, 288–300.

30. Mirabeau's *Considérations sur l'Ordre de Cincinnatus* was published in London in September 1784 and in Philadelphia two years later.

31. See A. O. Aldridge, *Franklin and His French Contemporaries* (New York, 1957), 209–12.

32. Lavoisier to Franklin, February 2, 1790, APS.

33. See "Franklin and Mesmer: A Confrontation."

34. For Gargaz see *PBF* 28:540 and *Jefferson Papers* 9:99–100, 175.

35. The best account of the many eulogies delivered in Paris is in Aldridge, *Franklin and His French Contemporaries*, 209–29.

36. The section on the American reaction to Franklin's death is based on Julian Boyd's essay, "The Politics of Mourning," *Jefferson Papers* 19:78–106.

37. C. Kunstler, *La Vie quotidienne sous Louis XVI* (Paris, 1950), 238–40.

38. The French navy was never without a *Franklin*. The warship by that name was the last to surrender to Horatio Nelson at the 1807 Battle of Aboukir.

39. More precisely, the men, "farmers general," were tax collectors who also handled the royal monopolies. Some made huge fortunes in the process; others were honest. They were all condemned to death.

40. The manuscript, eventually sold by a Le Veillard descendant to American ambassador John Bigelow, is now one of the glories of the Huntington Library, San Marino, Calif.

41. Mirabeau died of natural causes on April 2, 1791. On July 13, 1793, Charlotte Corday stabbed Marat in his bathtub. In 1794, Condorcet died on March 29, Lavoisier on May 8, and Robespierre on July 27. As for the abbé Morellet, he survived the Revolution (d. 1819) but experienced the sorrow of expulsion from the Auteuil home after his views were deemed too reactionary by the other members of the Helvétius circle.

42. If Condorcet used poison, he had probably received it from his brother-in-law, Pierre-Georges Cabanis, a young doctor who resided with Mme Helvétius and eventually inherited the residence. Cabanis's writings contain many memories of Franklin.

Index